THE LOEB CLASSICAL LIBRARY

FOUNDED BY JAMES LOEB 1911

EDITED BY

JEFFREY HENDERSON

EDITOR EMERITUS

G. P. GOOLD

TERENCE

II

LCL 23

TERENCE

PHORMIO
THE MOTHER-IN-LAW
THE BROTHERS

EDITED AND TRANSLATED BY

JOHN BARSBY

HARVARD UNIVERSITY PRESS
CAMBRIDGE, MASSACHUSETTS
LONDON, ENGLAND
2001

Library of Congress Catalog Card Number 2001016919
CIP data available from the Library of Congress

ISBN 0-674-99598-8

CONTENTS

PHORMIO

INTRODUCTORY NOTE

Phormio, one of two of Terence's plays based on a Greek original by Apollodorus, is essentially a lighthearted play of intrigue, in which an engaging trickster outwits two fathers in order to further the love affairs of their two sons. It depends for its effect on the neatness of its construction, the delineation of the major antagonists, the comic justice of the ending, and, for connoisseurs of the genre, the skilful way in which the conventions are exploited and varied.

During the absence of Demipho and Chremes on separate trips overseas, their sons Antipho and Phaedria have both fallen in love. Phaedria has fallen for a music girl owned by a pimp, Antipho for a poor orphan named Phanium. Antipho has moreover actually married his beloved, thanks to the machinations of the hanger-on Phormio, who, posing as a friend of the young woman's family and alleging that Antipho was her nearest male relative, had obtained a court judgment compelling him to do so. Demipho, who is the first of the fathers to return, is predictably furious at Antipho's marriage; he summons Phormio, and a spirited confrontation ends with Demipho threatening to expel the girl and Phormio threatening to take Demipho to court if he does. Phaedria then appears arguing with the pimp, who is about to sell his girl to a soldier if Phaedria cannot himself produce the purchase price. Next Chremes returns from his overseas trip. It transpires that he has been to Lemnos to trace an illegitimate daughter there, and that the two fathers have agreed to marry this daughter to Antipho to cover up the situation; it is imperative therefore that they undo Antipho's marriage to Phanium. Phormio now offers, through Demipho's slave Geta, to marry Phanium himself if they will provide him with a large dowry. Demipho refuses, but Chremes eagerly accepts the offer, and the money is duly handed over. At this stage Phanium's nurse recognises Chremes as Phanium's father, which means that the marriage planned by the two fathers has actually taken place, and they hasten to cancel their agreement with Phormio. But Phormio refuses to give back the dowry money, which he has used to buy Phaedria's girl fom the pimp, and moreover reveals Chremes' guilty secret to his wife Nausistrata. The play ends with Nausistrata brushing aside Chremes' objections to Phaedria's affair, and refusing to forgive her husband until she has consulted her son.

This summary will serve to make clear the neatness of the plot and its morally satisfying dénouement. As with most of Terence's plays, the plot is double, involving two fathers and two sons; the two halves are united by the close associations of all of the characters (Demipho and Chremes are in fact brothers as well as neighbours) and by the figure of Phormio, who confronts both fathers and solves the problems of both sons. The characterisation of Phormio is unusual and impressive. He is not the standard parasite of Roman comedy, who is typically either a flatterer accompanying a soldier (like Gnatho in Terence's *The Eunuch*) or a wit earning free meals from a patron by his conversational skills (like Peniculus in Plautus' *The*

Menaechmus Twins); he is a master schemer and plotter, and his two confrontations with the old men give a vivid picture of his audacity and his argumentative skills. The third confrontation, in which Phormio offers to marry Phanium in return for a dowry, is carried out for Phormio by proxy through the slave Geta, who might otherwise have played the tricky slave role in the play but is reduced to being Phormio's right-hand man. It was a bold move on Terence's part to split the trickery in this way, and it is interesting that Molière in his imitation *Les Fourberies de Scapin* recombined the two into a single role. The two fathers are well contrasted and individualised. Demipho is by no means the typical gullible angry father, but proves a good match for Phormio, showing both determination and a detailed awareness of the legal situation. Chremes, though terrified that his wife may find out his secret, is also concerned to do the best for his daughter, and, though humiliated in the end, is treated rather more gently than the typical old lecher of Plautus. Nausistrata too is an interesting character, not the usual unpleasant dowried wife, but a much more sympathetically drawn figure.

One interesting aspect of the play is the element of surprise. The audience does not find out the reason for Chremes' trip to Lemnos until the play is almost half over; and the true identity of Phanium is not confirmed until three quarters of the way through. This means that much of the irony of the first half is lost, or at least enjoyable only in retrospect. The audience will begin by assuming (wrongly) that Demipho's opposition to the marriage is based on the common rich father's aversion to a poor daughter-in-law; they will not appreciate at the time that Phormio's fiction is actually very close to the truth

(Antipho and Phanium are in fact cousins) or that Demipho is opposing a marriage which he has already agreed to promote. It is often claimed that it was Terence who created the surprise element by omitting an expository divine prologue from the Greek original, but this must remain a matter of conjecture. The suggestion that Terence expanded the part of Antipho in the middle of the play is rather more plausible; if so, he was filling out the double plot by giving more prominence to the sons, and at the same time (since Antipho among other things takes Phaedria's side against the pimp) emphasising the ideal of mutual helpfulness which is part of the general humanity of his plays.

SELECT BIBLIOGRAPHY

Editions and Commentaries

Barsby, J. (Bristol, 1991) (with *The Eunuch* and *The Brothers*).

Dziatzko, K., rev. by E. Hauler (Leipzig, 1913).

Martin, R. H. (London, 1959).

Criticism

Arnott, W. G. *"Phormio Parasitus:* A Study in Dramatic Methods of Characterisation." *Greece and Rome* 17 (1970): 32–57.

Barsby, J. "The Stage Action of Terence, *Phormio* 979–989." *Classical Quarterly* 43 (1993): 329–335.

Konstan, D. *"Phormio:* Citizen Disorder," in *Roman Comedy.* Ithaca, 1983: 115–129.

PHORMIO

Lefèvre, E. *Der Phormio des Terenz und der Epidikazomenos des Apollodor von Karystos*. Munich, 1978.

Lowe, J. C. B. "Terentian Originality in the *Phormio* and *Hecyra*." *Hermes* 111 (1983): 433–452.

DIDASCALIA

INCIPIT TERENTI PHORMIO
ACTA LVDIS ROMANIS
L. POSTVMIO ALBINO L. CORNELIO MERVLA AEDILIBVS
CVRVLIBVS
EGERE L. AMBIVIVS TVRPIO L. ATILIVS PRAENESTINVS
MODOS FECIT FLACCVS CLAVDI
TIBIIS IMPARIBVS TOTA
GRAECA APOLLODORV EPIDICAZOMENOS
FACTA IIII C. FANNIO M. VALERIO COS.

C. SULPICI APOLLINARIS PERIOCHA

Chremetis frater aberat peregre Demipho
relicto Athenis Antiphone filio.
Chremes clam habebat Lemni uxorem et filiam,
Athenis aliam coniugem et amantem unice
fidicinam gnatum. mater e Lemno advenit
Athenas; moritur; virgo sola (aberat Chremes)
funus procurat. ibi eam visam Antipho
cum amaret, opera parasiti uxorem accipit.
pater et Chemes reversi fremere. dein minas
triginta dant parasito, ut illam coniugem
haberet ipse. argento hoc emitur fidicina.
uxorem retinet Antipho a patruo agnitam.

---

[1] This festival was by far the oldest of the Roman festivals, going back probably to the 6th century B.C., and took place annually in September.

[2] For Ambivius Turpio see Introduction. Atilius was probably the

8

PRODUCTION NOTICE

Here begins the Phormio of Terence, acted at the Ludi Romani[1] in the curule aedileship of L. Postumius Albinus and L. Cornelius Merula. The producers were L. Ambivius Turpio and L. Atilius of Praeneste.[2] Music composed by Flaccus, slave of Claudius, for unequal pipes throughout. Greek original The Claimant of Apollodorus.[3] The author's fourth play, performed in the consulship of C. Fannius and M. Valerius.[4]

SYNOPSIS BY C. SULPICIUS APOLLINARIS

Chremes' brother Demipho was absent overseas, having left his son Antipho at Athens. Chremes secretly had a wife and daughter on Lemnos; at Athens he had another wife and a son who was devotedly in love with a music girl. The girl's mother comes from Lemnos to Athens and dies; in Chremes' absence the girl takes care of the funeral by herself. Antipho sees her there, falls in love, and with the help of a parasite takes her as his wife. On their return his father and Chremes are furious. Presently they give thirty minas to the parasite to take the girl as his wife himself. This money is used to purchase the music girl, and Antipho retains his wife, who has now been recognised by his uncle.

coproducer, or second actor of Ambivius' troupe, though some have seen him as the producer of later revivals.

[3] Apollodorus is generally supposed to have been a pupil of Menander's, though few fragments of his plays survive. He provided the model also for Terence's *The Mother-in-Law,* as Donatus makes clear.

[4] That is, in 161 B.C., which was the same year as the performance of *The Eunuch.*

PERSONAE

DAVOS servos
GETA servos
ANTIPHO adulescens
PHAEDRIA adulescens
DEMIPHO senex
PHORMIO parasitus
HEGIO advocatus
CRATINUS advocatus
CRITO advocatus
DORIO leno
CHREMES senex
SOPHRONA nutrix
NAUSISTRATA matrona

Scaena: Athenis

CHARACTERS

DAVUS, a slave
GETA, slave of Demipho
ANTIPHO, a young man, son of Demipho, lover of Phanium
PHAEDRIA, a young man, son of Chremes, lover of a music
   girl
DEMIPHO, an old man, brother of Chremes, father of
   Antipho
PHORMIO, a parasite and trickster
HEGIO, CRATINUS, CRITO, friends and advisers of
   Demipho
DORIO, a pimp
CHREMES, an old man, brother of Demipho, father of
   Phaedria and (as it turns out) of Phanium
SOPHRONA, a nurse of Chremes' family
NAUSISTRATA, a matron, wife of Chremes, mother of
   Phaedria

Staging

The stage represents a street in Athens. On it are three houses,
belonging to Demipho, Chremes, and the pimp Dorio. The exit
on the audience's right leads to the forum and to the house of
Phormio;[5] that on their left leads to the harbour.

---

[5] The location of Phormio's house is conjectural.

PHORMIO

postquam poeta vetus poetam non potest
retrahere a studio et transdere hominem in otium,
maledictis deterrere ne scribat parat.
qui ita dictitat, quas ante hic fecit fabulas
5   tenui esse oratione et scriptura levi,
quia nusquam insanum scripsit adulescentulum
cervam videre fugere et sectari canes
et eam plorare, orare ut subveniat sibi.
quod si intellegeret, quom stetit olim nova,
10   actoris opera magis stetisse quam sua,
minus multo audacter quam nunc laedit laederet.
nunc si quis est qui hoc dicat aut sic cogitet,
"vetus si poeta non lacessisset prior,
nullum invenire prologum potuisset novos
15   quem diceret, nisi haberet cui male diceret,"
is sibi responsum hoc habeat, in medio omnibus
palmam esse positam qui artem tractent musicam.
ille ad famem hunc a studio studuit reicere;

14 potuisset *codd.*, posset *Bentley edd.* '*prologum' anapaestum scan-
dere contra Terenti normam nolentes*

---

6 The reference is to Luscius of Lanuvium (see Introduction).

12

PHORMIO

Since the old playwright[6] cannot drive our playwright from his
calling and force him into retirement, he is trying to deter him
from writing by the use of slander. He keeps on saying that the
plays our author has previously written are thin in style and light
in content, just because he has nowhere portrayed a lovesick
youth who sees a hind in flight with hounds in pursuit, begging
and beseeching him to come to its aid.[7] But if he realised that,
when one of his own new plays once succeeded, its success was
more due to the producer than to himself, he would be much
less brazen in his attacks than he is now.

Now if there is anyone who is saying or thinking that, if the
old playwright had not provoked him first, the young one would
not have had the material for a prologue, not having anyone to
abuse, let him take this as an answer, that the prize is freely
available to everybody who practises the dramatic art.

He set himself to drive our author from his calling and force

---

[7] This must be a reference to a recent play by Luscius, which Ter-
ence is criticising for an overblown tragic style inappropriate to com-
edy; the details of the plot can only be conjectured, but it may have in-
volved a delirious young man who had mistaken his beloved for a hind
and pursued her with his own hounds (as in the Cephalus and Procris
story).

hic respondere voluit, non lacessere.
20   benedictis si certasset, audisset bene;
quod ab illo allatumst, sibi esse rellatum putet.
de illo iam finem faciam dicundi mihi,
peccandi quom ipse de se finem non facit.
nunc quid velim animum attendite: apporto novam
25   Epidicazomenon quam vocant comoediam
Graeci, Latini Phormionem nominant
quia primas partis qui aget is erit Phormio
parasitus, per quem res geretur maxume,
voluntas vostra si ad poetam accesserit.
30   date operam, adeste aequo animo per silentium,
ne simili utamur fortuna atque usi sumus
quom per tumultum noster grex motus locost;
quem actoris virtus nobis restituit locum
bonitasque vostra adiutans atque aequanimitas.

ACTUS I

I. I: DAVOS.

35 **DAV** amicus summus meus et popularis Geta
heri ad me venit. erat ei de ratiuncula
iampridem apud me relicuom pauxillulum
nummorum. id ut conficerem. confeci: affero.

---

[8] This is the only play for which Terence has changed the Greek ti-
tle; the effect is to put the focus on the character of Phormio rather than
on a point of Greek law which would have been unfamiliar to the
Romans.

[9] Literally, "parasite"; but Phormio is a very different character
from Gnatho in *The Eunuch*, who is the traditional sponger.

[10] This is a reference to the failure of the first performance of

him to starve; all *he* wanted was to respond, not to provoke. If he had set up a competition in compliments, he would have received compliments himself; he must realise that he has been repaid in kind for what he himself started. I will now refrain from talking about him, though he himself does not refrain from doing wrong.

Now listen carefully to what I want to say. I bring you a new comedy which is called in Greek "The Claimant"; its Latin name is "Phormio,"[8] since the man who plays the leading part will be the trickster[9] Phormio, through whom most of the action will be carried out, if the playwright has the benefit of your good will.

Pay attention, and listen in silence with open minds, so that we do not suffer the same fate as we suffered when our company was driven from the stage by an uproar.[10] Now we are restored to the stage by the courage of our producer, supported by your goodness and your sense of fair play.

ACT ONE

Enter DAVUS *from the right, carrying a small bag of money.*

DAV   My great friend and fellow countryman[11] Geta came to
see me yesterday. There was a tiny bit of money outstanding on a debt I owed him from some time ago, and he
wanted me to find it. I've done so, and I've got it here (*in-*

Terence's *The Mother-in-Law* (in 165 B.C.), which is described in the Prologue to the second performance of that play. The subsequent successes of *The Self-Tormentor* (163) and *The Eunuch* (161) had restored Terence's place in the theatre.   11 The common slave names Davus and Geta may both indicate Thracian origin.

nam erilem filium eius duxisse audio
40 uxorem. ei credo munus hoc corraditur.
quam inique comparatumst, ii qui minus habent
ut semper aliquid addant ditioribus!
quod ille unciatim vix de demenso suo
suom defrudans genium compersit miser,
45 id illa univorsum abripiet, haud existumans
quanto labore partum. porro autem Geta
ferietur alio munere ubi era pepererit;
porro autem alio ubi erit puero natalis dies;
ubi initiabunt. omne hoc mater auferet:
50 puer causa erit mittundi. sed videon Getam?

I. II: GETA. DAVOS.

GET si quis me quaeret rufus—
DAV praestost: desine.
GET oh!
at ego obviam conabar tibi, Dave.
DAV accipe, em.
lectumst; conveniet numerus quantum debui.
GET amo te et non neglexisse habeo gratiam.
55 DAV praesertim ut nunc sunt mores. adeo res redit:
si quis quid reddit, magna habendast gratia.
sed quid tu's tristis?
GET egone? nescis quo in metu et
quanto in periclo simus.
DAV quid istuc est?

---

12 According to Donatus slaves received a certain amount of grain a
month as their allowance; it is likely that this could be commuted into
cash.   13 Donatus implies that in Apollodorus' play there was a spe-
cific reference to initiation in the Samothracian mysteries; the Roman
audience did not need to know the details.

16

dicating the bag). I hear his master's son has got himself a wife, and I suppose he's scraping together a present for her. How unfair life is, when the have-nots are expected to contribute all the time to the haves! He's struggled to save this up bit by bit from his allowance,[12] poor fellow, denying his own pleasures, and she'll take the lot, without a thought of the hard work it took to acquire it. On top of that Geta will be stung for another present when his mistress gives birth, and then for another when the child's birthday comes round, and when it's initiated.[13] The mother will take it all; the child will just be the excuse for the gifts. (*as Demipho's door opens*) But is that Geta?

Enter GETA *from Demipho's house.*

GET   (*speaking back inside the house*) If a redheaded fellow[14] comes looking for me—

DAV   He's here. Forget it.

GET   Oh! I was on my way to find you, Davus.

DAV   (*offering him the bag of money*) Here you are: take it. It's good money. and you'll find it's exactly what I owed you.

GET   It's very good of you. I'm grateful that you didn't ignore my request.

DAV   So you should be, the way things are today. We've reached a state where, if anyone repays a debt, it's an occasion for immense gratitude. But why are you so gloomy?

GET   Me? You don't realise the worry and the danger we face.

DAV   What do you mean?

[14] Red was a common hair colour for slaves in comedy (compare Plautus, *Pseudolus* 1218).

GET   scies,
         modo ut tacere possis.

DAV   abi sis, insciens!

60   quoius tu fidem in pecunia perspexeris,
         verere verba ei credere, ubi quid mihi lucrist
         te fallere?

GET   ergo ausculta.

DAV   hanc operam tibi dico.

GET   senis nostri, Dave, fratrem maiorem Chremem
         nostin?

DAV   quidni?

GET   quid? eius gnatum Phaedriam?

65 DAV   tam quam te.

GET   evenit senibus ambobus simul
         iter illi in Lemnum ut esset, nostro in Ciliciam
         ad hospitem antiquom. is senem per epistulas
         pellexit modo non montis auri pollicens.

DAV   quoi tanta erat res et supererat?

GET   desinas:

70   sic est ingenium.

DAV   oh! regem me esse oportuit.

GET   abeuntes ambo hic tum senes me filiis
         relinquont quasi magistrum.

DAV   o Geta, provinciam
         cepisti duram.

GET   mi usu venit, hoc scio.
         memini relinqui me deo irato meo.

75   coepi adversari primo. quid verbis opust?
         seni fidelis dum sum, scapulas perdidi.

DAV   venere in mentem mi istaec: namque inscitiast
         advorsus stimulum calces.

18

GET   I'll tell you, provided you can keep a secret.

DAV   Come off it, you idiot! When you've found a man honest over money, are you afraid to trust him with words? What would I gain by betraying you?

GET   Listen, then.

DAV   I'm at your service.

GET   Davos, you know our old man's older brother Chremes?

DAV   Of course.

GET   And his son Phaedria?

DAV   As well as I know you.

GET   It so happened that both the old men went overseas at the same time, Chremes to Lemnos, and our old man to a longstanding friend in Cilicia,[15] who enticed him there by letters promising him practically a mountain of gold.

DAV   When he had wealth enough and to spare?

GET   Never mind! That's his nature.

DAV   Oh! If only I'd been a rich man!

GET   When the two old men went away, they left me behind here as a sort of guardian for their sons.

DAV   That was a tough assignment, Geta.

GET   So I found out, I can tell you. I recall the gods were against me from the day the old men left. I stood up to the boys at first. Need I say more? Loyalty to the old man proved a disaster to my shoulder blades.

DAV   That's just what I was thinking. It's folly to kick against the pricks.[16]

[15] Lemnos is an island in the northeast of the Aegean sea; Cilicia is in the south of Turkey, facing the island of Cyprus.

[16] This is an old Greek proverb, first found in Aeschylus (compare *Acts of the Apostles* 26.14).

GET   coepi eis omnia
      facere, obsequi quae vellent.

DAV   scisti uti foro.

80 GET noster mali nil quicquam primo. hic Phaedria
      continuo quandam nactus est puellulam
      citharistriam; hanc ardere coepit perdite.
      ea serviebat lenoni impurissumo,
      neque quod daretur quicquam: id curarant patres.
85   restabat aliud nil nisi oculos pascere,
      sectari, in ludum ducere et redducere.
      nos otiosi operam dabamus Phaedriae.
      in quo haec discebat ludo, exadvorsum ilico
      tonstrina erat quaedam. hic solebamus fere
90   plerumque eam opperiri dum inde iret domum.
      interea dum sedemus illi, intervenit
      adulescens quidam lacrumans. nos mirarier.
      rogamus quid sit. "numquam aeque" inquit "ac modo
      paupertas mihi onus visumst et miserum et grave.
95   modo quandam vidi virginem hic viciniae
      miseram suam matrem lamentari mortuam.
      ea sita erat exadvorsum neque illi benivolus
      neque notus neque vicinus extra unam aniculam
      quisquam aderat qui adiutaret funus. miseritumst.
100   virgo ipsa facie egregia." quid verbis opust?
      commorat omnis nos. ibi continuo Antipho

82 ardere *Charisius edd.*, amare *codd.*
98 vicinus *D¹G Don.*, cognatus *cett.*

---

17 Literally "to use the market," a proverbial expression referring to
traders who adapted their prices to market conditions.
18 Evidently her music school (a feature of Greek education rather

GET So I began to do everything for them, and let them have what they wanted.

DAV You knew how to cut your cloth![17]

GET Our Antipho didn't get into any mischief at first. But Phaedria here (*pointing to Chremes' house*) immediately picked up some music girl, and fell desperately in love with her. She belonged to a filthy pimp, and there wasn't any money to pay for her: the fathers had seen to that. He hadn't much option but to feast his eyes on her, follow her around, escort her to school[18] and back. We hadn't much to do, so we kept an eye on Phaedria. Right opposite the school where she had her lessons was a barber's shop. We were generally in the habit of waiting here until it was time for her to go home. One day, while we were sitting there, a young man came up in tears.[19] We wondered at this and asked him what the matter was. "I've never realised until now" he said "what a wretched cruel burden poverty is. I've just seen a young girl round the corner miserably lamenting her dead mother. The body was laid out facing the door and there was no well-wisher or acquaintance or neighbour there to assist with the funeral apart from one old woman. It stirred me to pity. And the girl herself was exceedingly good looking." In short, we were all moved. Immediately Antipho said: "Shall we go

than Roman). Music was one of the services that such girls offered to their clients, and it was in the pimp's interest that they should improve their skills.   [19] As Donatus makes clear, the young man is Terence's invention. In Apollodorus' version the story is told by the barber, who has cut the girl's hair in mourning. This is a Greek custom (the Romans loosened their hair in mourning) which Terence has omitted in order not to confuse the Roman audience.

"voltisne eamus visere?" alius "censeo.
eamus, duc nos sodes." imus, venimus,
videmus. virgo pulchra, et quo magis diceres,
105   nil aderat adiumenti ad pulchritudinem.
capillus passus, nudus pes, ipsa horrida,
lacrumae, vestitus turpis, ut, ni vis boni
in ipsa inesset forma, haec formam exstinguerent.
ill' qui illam amabat fidicinam tantummodo
110   "satis" inquit "scitast." noster vero—

DAV   iam scio:
amare coepit.

GET   scin quam? quo evadat vide.
postridie ad anum recta pergit; obsecrat
ut sibi eius faciat copiam. illa enim se negat
neque eum aequom facere ait. illam civem esse Atticam,
115   bonam bonis prognatam. si uxorem velit,
lege id licere facere. sin aliter, negat.
noster quid ageret nescire; et illam ducere
cupiebat et metuebat absentem patrem.

DAV   non, si redisset, ei pater veniam daret?

120 GET   ille indotatam virginem atque ignobilem
daret illi? numquam faceret.

DAV   quid fit denique?

GET   quid fiat? est parasitus quidam Phormio,
homo confidens. qui illum di omnes perduint!

DAV   quid is fecit?

GET   hoc consilum quod dicam dedit.

125   "lex est ut orbae, qui sint genere proxumi,
eis nubat, et illos ducere eadem haec lex iubet.

22

and look?" Someone else said: "Good idea. Let's go. Lead the way, if you will." Off we went; we arrived; we took a look. The girl was lovely, and the more so because she had nothing to enhance her loveliness. She had loose hair and bare feet, she was dishevelled, weeping, and shabbily dressed. Had she not been endowed with true natural beauty, all of this would have destroyed it. Phaedria, who was in love with the music girl, merely said: "She's not bad." But our Antipho—

DAV Don't tell me; he fell in love with her.

GET And how! Hear the sequel. The next day he went straight to the old woman, and begged her to let him approach the girl. She said no, and told him he was behaving improperly. The girl was an Athenian citizen, a respectable girl from a respectable family. If he wanted to marry her, he could do so legally; otherwise, the answer was no. Antipho didn't know what to do; on the one hand he was eager to marry the girl, on the other he was afraid of his absent father.

DAV Wouldn't the father have given permission on his return?

GET Him? To marry a girl without a dowry from a humble family? Never!

DAV What happened in the end?

GET What happened? There's a trickster[20] called Phormio, an insolent fellow. (*with feeling*) May all the gods destroy him!

DAV What did he do?

GET He worked out a plan, which I'll explain. "There is a law" he said "that orphan girls shall marry their next-of-kin, and this same law compels the next-of-kin to marry

[20] See note 9.

ego te cognatum dicam et tibi scribam dicam.
paternum amicum me assimulabo virginis.
ad iudices veniemus. qui fuerit pater,
130 quae mater, qui cognata tibi sit, omnia haec
confingam, quod erit mihi bonum atque commodum.
quom tu horum nil refelles, vincam scilicet.
pater aderit, mihi paratae lites: quid mea?
illa quidem nostra erit."

DAV   iocularem audaciam!
135 GET persuasit homini. factumst, ventumst, vincimur,
duxit.

DAV   quid narras?

GET   hoc quod audis.

DAV   o Geta,
quid te futurumst?

GET   nescio hercle. unum hoc scio:
quod fors feret feremus aequo animo.

DAV   placet.
em istuc virist officium.

GET   in me omnis spes mihist.
140 DAV laudo.

GET   ad precatorem adeam, credo, qui mihi
sic oret: "nunc amitte, quaeso, hunc; ceterum
posthac si quicquam, nil precor." tantummodo
non addit: "ubi ego hinc abiero, vel occidito."

DAV quid paedagogus ille qui citharistriam,
145 quid rei gerit?

GET   sic, tenuiter.

DAV   non multum habet
quod det fortasse?

---

135 persuasit Σ, persuasumst A

24

them.[21] I'll say that you are related to her and bring a case against you, pretending that I'm a friend of the girl's father. We'll go to court. As for her father's identity and her mother's and her precise relationship to you, I'll invent the details to suit my interest and advantage. Since you won't deny any of it, I'll win the case, obviously. Your father will return and it's trouble for me, but I don't care: the girl will be ours."

DAV What a joke! What cheek!

GET He persuaded the boy. It was done, we went to court, we lost the case, he married her.

DAV What are you saying?

GET What you are hearing.

DAV Geta, what will become of you?

GET I don't know, for god's sake. But one thing I do know, (*heroically*) whatever fortune brings I will bear it with equanimity.

DAV Quite right. That's how a man should behave.

GET My only hope is in myself.

DAV Good for you.

GET I suppose I'll go and find someone to plead for me along these lines: "Let him off now, I beg you; but, if he does anything in future, I raise no objection," which is as good as adding: "The moment I've left, put him to death if you like."

DAV What about the other one who was escorting the music girl? How's he doing?

GET (*snapping his fingers*) Like this. Poorly.

DAV He hasn't much to offer, perhaps?

---

[21] This is an Athenian law, not Roman, and Terence has no doubt spelled it out for the sake of the Roman audience.

GET	immo nil nisi spem meram.
DAV	pater eius rediit an non?
GET	nondum.
DAV	quid? senem

quoad exspectatis vostrum?

GET non certum scio,
sed epistulam ab eo allatam esse audivi modo
150 et ad portitores esse delatam. hanc petam.

DAV numquid, Geta, aliud me vis?

GET ut bene sit tibi.
puer, heus! nemon hoc prodit? cape, da hoc Dorcio.

I. III: ANTIPHO. PHAEDRIA.

ANT adeon rem redisse ut qui mi consultum optume uelit
 esse,
 Phaedria, patrem ut extimescam ubi in mentem eius ad-
 venti venit!
155 quod ni fuissem incogitans, ita eum exspectarem ut par
 fuit.

PHAE quid istuc?

ANT rogitas, qui tam audacis facinoris mihi conscius sis?
 quod utinam ne Phormioni id suadere in mentem inci-
 disset
 neu me cupidum eo impulisset, quod mihi principiumst
 mali!
 non potitus essem: fuisset tum illos mi aegre aliquot dies,
160 at non cotidiana cura haec angeret animum—

PHAE audio.

---

[22] Dorcium is presumably Geta's concubine (not wife, since slaves
could not legally be married).

GET No, nothing but bare hope.

DAV Has his father returned or not?

GET Not yet.

DAV What about your old man? When are you expecting him?

GET I don't know for sure. But I've just heard that a letter has arrived from him and been delivered to the customs office. I'll go and look for it.

DAV (*making to leave*) Anything else I can do for you, Geta?

GET Just look after yourself. (*Davus exits right*) (*knocking at the door of Demipho's house*) Hello, boy! Is nobody coming? (*as a slave appears*) Take this and give it to Dorcium.[22] (*he gives the bag of money to the slave and exits left towards the harbour, leaving the stage empty*)

Enter ANTIPHO *and* PHAEDRIA *from Chremes' house.*

ANT To think that things have come to such a pass that I'm terrified at the thought of my father's return, when he's got my best interests at heart! If I hadn't been so thoughtless, I could be looking forward to seeing him as a son should.

PHAE What's the matter?

ANT How can you ask, when you were involved with me in that crazy scheme? If only it hadn't entered Phormio's head to propose it! If only he hadn't taken advantage of my eagerness and pushed me into it, which was the beginning of my troubles! I wouldn't have gained possession of the girl; I'd have been upset for those few days; but I wouldn't have this anxiety tormenting my mind day after day—

PHAE Quite.

ANT —dum exspecto quam mox veniat qui adimat hanc mi
consuetudinem.

PHAE aliis quia defit quod amant aegrest: tibi quia superest do-
let.

amore abundas, Antipho.

nam tua quidem hercle certo vita haec expetenda optan-
daquest.

165 ita me di bene ament, ut mihi liceat tam diu quod amo
frui,

iam depecisci morte cupio. tu conicito cetera,

quid ego ex hac inopia nunc capiam et quid tu ex ista co-
pia,

ut ne addam quod sine sumptu ingenuam ac liberalem
nactus es,

quod habes, ita ut voluisti, uxorem sine mala fama palam,

170 beatus, ni unum desit, animus qui modeste istaec ferat.

quod si tibi res sit cum eo lenone quo mihist, tum sentias.

ita plerique ingenio sumus omnes: nostri nosmet paeni-
tet.

ANT at tu mihi contra nunc videre fortunatus, Phaedria,

quoi de integrost potestas etiam consulendi quid velis,

175 retinere, amare, amittere. ego in eum incidi infelix locum

ut neque mihi sit amittendi nec retinendi copia.

sed quid hoc est? videon ego Getam currentem huc ad-
venire?

is est ipsus. ei! timeo miser quam hic mihi nunc nuntiet
rem.

I. IV: GETA. ANTIPHO. PHAEDRIA.

GET nullus es, Geta, nisi iam aliquod tibi consilium celere
reperis,

ANT —expecting him to come back at any moment and put an end to my relationship.

PHAE Others are upset because they have too little access to their beloveds; you're complaining because you have too much. You're spoiled for love, Antipho. You have a life which god knows is to be desired and envied. Heaven help me, I'd be ready to bargain away my life right now to be allowed to enjoy my love (*snapping his fingers*) this long. As for the rest, you just add up what I get now from my lack and what you get from your plenty, to say nothing of the fact that without any expense you've got yourself a respectable freeborn woman and have married her, just as you wanted, all in the open and without any harm to your reputation. You're blessed in all but one thing, that you lack the sense to appreciate what you've got. But if you had to deal with a pimp as I do, then you'd see. (*shrugging his shoulders*) In general this is what we human beings are like: we're dissatisfied with our own lot.

ANT On the contrary, I regard you as the fortunate one, Phaedria. You're still free to decide from the beginning what you want, whether to keep her and love her or let her go, whereas I'm in the unhappy position where the choice to let her go or keep her isn't mine. (*looking down the street*) But what's this? Is that Geta running this way? It's the very man. Oh dear! I'm afraid he's bringing me bad news.

Enter GETA *left from the direction of the harbour in some agitation.*

GET (*not seeing Antipho and Phaedria*) You're done for, Geta, if you don't find yourself a plan, and quickly. All of a sud-

180		ita nunc imparatum subito tanta te impendent mala;
		quae neque uti devitem scio neque quo modo me inde extraham,
181a		quae si non astu providentur me aut erum pessum dabunt.
		nam non potest celari nostra diutius iam audacia.
	ANT	quid illic commotus venit?
	GET	tum temporis mihi punctum ad hanc remst: erus adest.
	ANT	quid illuc malist?
185	GET	quod quom audierit, quod eius remedium inveniam iracundiae?
		loquarne? incendam. taceam? instigem. purgem me? laterem lavem.
		heu me miserum! quod mihi paveo, tum Antipho me excruciat animi:
		eius me miseret, ei nunc timeo, is nunc me retinet. nam absque eo esset,
		recte ego me vidissem et senis essem ultus iracundiam;
190		aliquid convasassem atque hinc me conicerem protinam in pedes.
	ANT	quam hic fugam aut furtum parat?
	GET	sed ubi Antiphonem reperiam, aut qua quaerere insistam via?
	PHAE	te nominat.
	ANT	nescioquod magnum hoc nuntio exspecto malum.
	PHAE	ah!
		sanus es?
	GET	domum ire pergam;
195		ibi plurumumst.

181a (= *And.* 208) *hic habent* AD¹L¹P, *post* 182 *cett., omittunt edd. nonn.*

den you're threatened with a pile of troubles and you're quite unprepared. I don't know how to avoid them or rescue myself from them. If this business isn't managed with some skill, it'll be the ruin either of myself or of my master. Our crazy scheme can't be kept secret any longer.

ANT   (*aside*) What's he so excited about?

GET   And I don't have a moment to spare. The master's back.

ANT   (*not quite hearing*) What the hell's going on?

GET   How am I going to soothe his anger when he gets to hear of it? Tell him? It'll inflame him. Say nothing? It'll provoke him further. Defend myself? Water through a sieve.[23] Oh! What a misery! I'm scared enough for myself, but it's Antipho I'm in torments for. He's the one I'm sorry for; he's the one I'm worried about; he's the one who's keeping me here. If it weren't for him, I'd have looked out for myself and paid back the old man for his bad temper. I'd have picked up a few things and taken to my heels fast.

ANT   (*aside*) What's this about thieving and running away?

GET   But where shall I find Antipho? Where do I begin to look for him?

PHAE   (*to Antipho*) He mentioned your name.

ANT   (*to Phaedria*) I'm sure he's bringing terrible news.

PHAE   (*to Antipho*) Oh! Don't be silly.

GET   I'll go on home. That's where he usually is. (*he makes to leave*)

---

[23] Literally, "I'd be washing bricks," a Greek proverbial expression for wasting one's time.

---

189 protinam *Don. Fest. edd.*, protinus *contra metrum codd.*
194–195 *metro incerto varie dividunt edd.*

PHAE   revocemus hominem.

ANT   sta ilico.

GET   hem!

satis pro imperio, quisquis es.

ANT   Geta.

GET   ipsest quem volui obviam.

ANT cedo, quid portas, obsecro? atque id, si potes, verbo expedi.

GET faciam.

ANT   eloquere.

GET   modo apud portum—

ANT   meumne?

GET   intellexti.

ANT   occidi!

PHAE   hem!

ANT quid agam?

PHAE   quid ais?

GET   huius patrem vidisse me et patruom tuom.

200   ANT nam quod ego huic nunc subito exitio remedium inveniam miser?

quodsi eo meae fortunae redeunt, Phanium, abs te ut distrahar,

nullast mihi vita expetenda.

GET   ergo istaec quom ita sunt, Antipho,

tanto magis te advigilare aequomst. fortis fortuna adiuvat.

ANT non sum apud me.

GET   atqui opus est nunc quom maxume ut sis, Antipho.

205   nam si senserit te timidum pater esse, arbitrabitur

commeruisse culpam.

PHAE (*to Antipho*) Let's call him back.

ANT (*to Geta*) Stay where you are.

GET (*not turning round*) What! You're pretty good at issuing orders, whoever you are.

ANT Geta!

GET (*seeing Antipho*) It's the very man I wanted to see.

ANT Tell me, what's the news, for goodness' sake? Make it short, if you can.

GET All right.

ANT (*impatiently*) Go on.

GET At the harbour just now—

ANT My—?

GET (*nodding*) You've got it.

ANT Damnation!

PHAE What!

ANT What am I going to do?

PHAE (*to Geta*) What were you saying?

GET (*to Phaedria*) I saw his father, your uncle.

ANT Oh dear, how am I going to find a solution for this crisis at short notice? (*dramatically*) If my fate decrees that I'm to be torn away from you, Phanium,[24] I don't want to live any longer.

GET That being so, Antipho, it's all the more important to keep your wits about you. Fortune favours the brave.[25]

ANT I'm beside myself.

GET But you mustn't be, now of all times, Antipho. If your father sees that you're apprehensive, he'll think you've a guilty conscience.

---

[24] This is the first mention in the play of the name of Antipho's bride.   [25] Another common proverbial expression, found here for the first time in Latin.

33

PHAE	hoc verumst.
ANT	non possum immutarier.
GET	quid faceres si aliud quid gravius tibi nunc faciundum fo-
	ret?
ANT	quom hoc non possum, illud minus possem.
GET	hoc nil est, Phaedria: ilicet.
	quid hic conterimus operam frustra? quin abeo?
PHAE	et quidem ego?
ANT	obsecro,
210	quid si assimulo? satinest?
GET	garris.
ANT	voltum contemplamini. em,
	satine sic est?
GET	non.
ANT	quid si sic?
GET	propemodum.
ANT	quid sic?
GET	sat est:
	em, istuc serva. et verbum verbo par pari ut respondeas,
	ne te iratus suis saevidicis dictis protelet.
ANT	scio.
GET	vi coactum te esse invitum.
PHAE	lege, iudicio.
GET	tenes?
215	sed hic quis est senex quem video in ultima platea? ipsus
	est.
ANT	non possum adesse.
GET	ah! quid agis? quo abis, Antipho?
	mane, inquam.

---

26 If masks were worn in Roman comedy, as seems likely (see Intro-

PHAE That's true.

ANT I can't change myself.

GET What would you do now if you had to face some greater challenge?

ANT Since I can't cope with this, I'd be even less able to cope with that.

GET (*to Phaedria in mock despair*). It's no good, Phaedria; it's all over. Why are we wasting our efforts here? I'm off.

PHAE (*to Geta*) So am I.

ANT (*in alarm*) Please don't go. Suppose I pretend. Would that do?

GET (*scornfully*) You're joking!

ANT (*putting on a brave face*) Look at my expression.[26] There you are, is this all right?

GET No.

ANT (*trying again*) How about this?

GET Nearly.

ANT (*trying again*) Or this?

GET Very well, keep that one. And make sure you answer him word for word, tit for tat, or he'll rout you with raging words. He's in an angry mood.

ANT I know.

GET Say that you were compelled by force against your will.

PHAE And by a legal judgment.

GET Do you understand? (*looking down the street*) But who's this old man I see at the end of the street? It's him.

ANT (*in a panic*) I can't face him. (*he turns to run away*)

GET Oh! What are you doing? Where are you going, Antipho? Stop, I say.

duction), the audience would have had to imagine Antipho's attempts to put on a brave face.

35

ANT   egomet me novi et peccatum meum.
       vobis commendo Phanium et vitam meam.

PHAE Geta, quid nunc fiet?

GET   tu iam litis audies;

220   ego plectar pendens, nisi quid me fefellerit.
       sed quod modo hic nos Antiphonem monuimus,
       id nosmet ipsos facere oportet, Phaedria.

PHAE aufer mi "oportet." quin tu quid faciam impera.

GET   meministin olim ut fuerit vostra oratio

225   in re incipiunda ad defendendam noxiam,
       iustam illam causam, facilem, vincibilem, optumam?

PHAE memini.

GET   em, nunc ipsast opus ea aut, si quid potest,
       meliore et callidiore.

PHAE   fiet sedulo.

GET   nunc prior adito tu; ego in insidiis hic ero

230   succenturiatus, si quid deficias.

PHAE   age.

ACTUS II

II. I: DEMIPHO. PHAEDRIA. GETA.

DEM   itane tandem uxorem duxit Antipho iniussu meo?
       nec meum imperium—ac mitto imperium—non simul-
          tatem meam
       revereri saltem! non pudere! o facinus audax! o Geta
          monitor!

GET   vix tandem.

229 insidiis *codd. pl.*, subsidiis *DGpE*[2]

---

27 The language is military, as often with the tricky slave of comedy.

ANT   I know myself and I know what I've done wrong. I entrust Phanium and my life to you. (*he runs off right*)

PHAE Geta, what'll happen now?

GET   You'll be in for a reprimand, and I'll be strung up for a thrashing, unless I'm much mistaken. But the advice we've just given to Antipho we should carry out ourselves, Phaedria.

PHAE Not so much of the "should"; just you tell me what to do.

GET   Do you remember the argument you two used at the beginning of this business to justify your conduct, that your case was just, simple, incontrovertible, perfect?

PHAE Yes, I do.

GET   Very well, that's the argument we need now, or something better and cleverer, if we can find it.

PHAE I'll do my best.

GET   You attack him first; I'll be lying in wait here in reserve in case you need some support.[27]

PHAE Come on then. (*they both withdraw to the back of the stage*)

ACT TWO

Enter DEMIPHO *left from the direction of the harbour in travelling clothes.*

DEM   (*to himself*) Has Antipho actually married a wife just like that without my permission? Doesn't he respect my authority—never mind my authority, doesn't he even fear my anger? Doesn't he feel any shame? What outrageous behaviour! So much for Geta as a guardian!

GET   (*aside, with a wry grin*) A mention at last!

DEM   quid mihi dicent aut quam causam reperient?
235   demiror.

GET   atqui reperiam. aliud cura.

DEM   an hoc dicet mihi:
"invitus feci. lex coegit"? audio, fateor.

GET   places.

DEM   verum scientem, tacitum causam tradere advorsariis,
etiamne id lex coegit?

PHAE   illud durum.

GET   ego expediam. sine!

DEM   incertumst quid agam, quia praeter spem atque incredi-
      bile hoc mi optigit.

240   ita sum irritatus animum ut nequeam ad cogitandum
      instituere.

      quam ob rem omnis, quom secundae res sunt maxume,
      tum maxume

      meditari secum oportet quo pacto advorsam aerumnam
      ferant,

      pericla, damna, exsilia. peregre rediens semper cogitet

      aut fili peccatum aut uxoris mortem aut morbum filiae

245   communia esse haec, fieri posse, ut ne quid animo sit
      novom;

      quidquid praeter spem eveniat, omne id deputare esse in
      lucro.

GET   o Phaedria, incredibile quantum erum ante eo sapientia:

      meditata mihi sunt omnia mea incommoda erus si re-
      dierit:

      molendum esse in pistrino, vapulandum, habendae com-
      pedes,

249 esse *AD¹GL¹ Don.*, usque *cett. Don. in comm. edd. nonn.*

38

DEM What are they going to say to me? What justification will they offer? I can't imagine.

GET *(aside)* Well, I'll find one. Don't worry.

DEM Will he say: "I did it against my will. The law compelled me"? All right. Granted.

GET *(aside)* That's good of you.

DEM But to let the case go by default deliberately and without saying a word. Did the law compel that too?

PHAE *(to Geta)* That's a hard one.

GET *(to Phaedria)* I'll solve it. Leave it to me.

DEM I just don't know what to do. What's happened to me is so unexpected, so incredible. I'm so angry I can't get any thoughts together. *(calming himself)* The moral is that, when people are at their most prosperous, they should be pondering most carefully how they're going to endure adversity—dangers, losses, exile. A man returning from overseas should always reflect that certain things are universal and can occur to anybody—a son's misdeeds, a wife's death, a daughter's sickness—so that nothing can take him by surprise. Then everything better than what he anticipated he can count as pure gain.

GET *(to Phaedria)* Phaedria, you wouldn't believe how much I surpass my master in wisdom. I've pondered all the problems which could arise for me if my master returns: grinding in the mill,[28] beatings, fetters, working on the

---

[28] Being sent to the mill is one of the more extreme punishments with which slaves are threatened in comedy. Slaves were evidently chained to mills, which were simple hand-driven affairs, to prevent escape, and flogged if they slackened.

250   opus ruri faciundum. horum nil quicquam accidet animo
           novom.
       quidquid praeter spem eveniet, omne id deputabo esse
           in lucro.
       sed quid cessas hominem adire et blande in principio al-
           loqui?
DEM   Phaedriam mei fratris video filium mi ire obviam.

PHAE   mi patrue, salve.
DEM   salve. sed ubist Antipho?
255 PHAE   salvom venire—
DEM   credo. hoc responde mihi.
PHAE   valet, hic est. sed satin omnia ex sententia?
DEM   vellem quidem.
PHAE   quid istuc est?
DEM   rogitas, Phaedria?
       bonas me absente hic confecistis nuptias.
PHAE   eho, an id suscenses nunc illi?
GET   artificem probum!
260 DEM   egon illi non suscenseam? ipsum gestio
       dari mi in conspectum, nunc sua culpa ut sciat
       lenem patrem illum factum me esse acerrumum.
PHAE   atqui nil fecit, patrue, quod suscenseas.
DEM   ecce autem similia omnia! omnes congruont:
265   unum quom noris omnis noris.
PHAE   haud itast.
DEM   hic in noxast, ille ad defendundam causam adest.
       quom illest, hic praestost. tradunt operas mutuas.
GET   probe horum facta imprudens depinxit senex.

   266 noxa *codd. pl. Don.*, noxia *AG¹P¹E¹*

farm, none of these will take me by surprise. Everything better than my expectations I'll count as pure gain. But why don't you go up to him and say something soothing to start with?

DEM *(as Phaedria approaches)* That's my brother's son Phaedria coming over.

PHAE Good day, uncle.

DEM Good day. But where's Antipho?

PHAE Your safe return—

DEM *(impatiently)* I'm sure. But answer my question.

PHAE He's fine; he's here. But is everything to your liking?

DEM I wish it were.

PHAE What's the matter?

DEM As if you didn't know, Phaedria. You people have contrived a fine marriage here in my absence.

PHAE *(with feigned astonishment)* Hey, is that why you're angry with him?

GET *(aside)* What a fine act he's putting on!

DEM Should I *not* be angry with him? I can't wait for him to show his face, so I can tell him that his easygoing father has become an extremely harsh one and it's all his fault.

PHAE And yet, uncle, he hasn't done anything to make you angry.

DEM Listen to that! It's all the same. They're all alike: know one, you know them all.

PHAE It's not like that.

DEM One's on a charge, the other's there to defend the case. The second's accused, up pops the first. It's a mutual aid society.

GET *(aside)* The old man's got the picture exactly right, though he doesn't realise it.

41

DEM nam ni haec ita essent, cum illo haud stares, Phaedria.

270 PHAE sist, patrue, culpam ut Antipho in se admiserit,
ex qua minus rei foret aut famae temperans,
non causam dico quin quod meritus sit ferat.
sed si quis forte malitia fretus sua
insidias nostrae fecit adulescentiae

275 ac vicit, nostran culpa east an iudicum,
qui saepe propter invidiam adimunt diviti
aut propter misericordiam addunt pauperi?

GET ni nossem causam, crederem vera hunc loqui.

DEM an quisquam iudex est qui possit noscere

280 tua iusta, ubi tute verbum non respondeas,
ita ut ille fecit?

PHAE   functus adulescentulist
officium liberalis. postquam ad iudices
ventumst, non potuit cogitata proloqui;
ita eum tum timidum ibi obstupefecit pudor.

285 GET laudo hunc, sed cesso adire quam primum senem?
ere, salve. salvom te advenisse gaudeo.

DEM   oh!
bone custos, salve, columen vero familiae,
quoi commendavi filium hinc abiens meum.

GET iamdudum te omnis nos accusare audio

290 immerito et me omnium horunc immeritissumo.
nam quid me in hac re facere voluisti tibi?
servom hominem causam orare leges non sinunt
neque testimoni dictiost.

DEM   mitto omnia.
do istuc "imprudens timuit adulescens"; sino

295 "tu servo's." verum si cognata est maxume,

294 do *Fleckeisen*, addo *A*, adde Σ *Don*.

42

DEM If it wasn't so, Phaedria, you wouldn't be standing up for him.

PHAE If it is the case that Antipho has committed a crime as a result of which he is endangering his property or his reputation, I raise no objection to his suffering what he deserves. But if perhaps someone out of pure malice has laid a trap for us young men and won, is that our fault or the fault of the jury, who often take away from the rich through envy or give to the poor through pity?

GET (*aside*) If I didn't know the case, I'd believe he was speaking the truth.

DEM But there isn't a juryman in the world who could know your side of the case, if you utter not a word in defence, as he did.

PHAE He behaved like the well bred young man he is. When it came to the trial, he couldn't bring himself to deliver his prepared speech. He was so apprehensive, and he was overcome with embarrassment.

GET He's done well, but it's high time I confronted the old man. (*going up to Demipho*) Good day, master. I'm glad to see you safely back.

DEM (*with bitter irony*) Oh! Good day, faithful guardian, mainstay of my household, the man to whom I entrusted my son when I went away.

GET I've been listening to you just now while you were accusing us all unjustly and myself most unjustly of all. What did you expect me to do in this situation? The laws don't allow a slave to argue a case in court or to give evidence.

DEM Never mind all that. I grant you that the young lad was apprehensive through inexperience; I accept that you are a slave. But however closely related the girl was, it

43

non fuit necessum habere, sed is quod lex iubet,
dotem daretis, quaereret alium virum.
qua ratione inopem potius ducebat domum?

GET   non ratio, verum argentum deerat.

DEM   sumeret

300   alicunde.

GET   alicunde? nil est dictu facilius.

DEM   postremo, si nullo alio pacto, fenore.

GET   hui! dixti pulchre. siquidem quisquam crederet
te vivo.

DEM   non, non sic futurumst: non potest.
egon illam cum illo ut patiar nuptam unum diem?

305   nil suave meritumst. hominem commonstrarier
mihi istum volo aut ubi habitet demonstrarier.

GET   nemp' Phormionem?

DEM   istum patronum mulieris.

GET   iam faxo hic aderit.

DEM   Antipho ubi nunc est?

GET   foris.

DEM   abi, Phaedria, eum require atque huc adduce.

PHAE   eo

310   recta via quidem illuc.

GET   nempe ad Pamphilam.

DEM   ego deos penatis hinc salutatum domum
devortar. inde ibo ad forum atque aliquos mihi

---

29 Since the son remained in his father's *potestas* until the father's
death, any contract entered into by the son without the father's permis-
sion would be invalid.

30 This is the first mention in the play of the name of Phaedria's girl.

31 The reference to the Roman *penates* must be due to Terence; it
necessitates Demipho entering his house and then reemerging to go to

wasn't necessary to marry her. You could have given her a dowry, as the law provides, and he could have found her another husband. What was he thinking of when he chose to marry a pauper?

GET   There was no shortage of thought, just money.

DEM   He could have got some from somewhere.

GET   Somewhere? That's easily said.

DEM   As a last resort, if there was no other way, by taking out a loan.

GET   (*ironically*) Wow! A brilliant suggestion. As if anyone would lend him money while you were alive![29]

DEM   No, no, it won't do. It can't proceed. How can I allow this marriage to continue for a single day? Stern measures are called for. I want you to point the fellow out to me or show me where he lives.

GET   You mean Phormio?

DEM   The fellow who championed the girl.

GET   I'll have him here in no time.

DEM   Where is Antipho now?

GET   He's gone out.

DEM   Go and find him, Phaedria, and bring him here.

PHAE   I'll go straight there. (*he exits right as if to the forum but slips into Dorio's house*)

GET   (*aside*) To Pamphila,[30] that is. (*he exits right in the direction of Phormio's house*)

DEM   I'll call in home and pay my respects to the household gods.[31] Then I'll go to the forum and call on some friends

---

the forum. In the Greek context Demipho would have paid his respects to an altar of Apollo outside the house and could then have left directly for the forum.

amicos advocabo ad hanc rem qui adsient,
ut ne imparatus sim si veniat Phormio.

II. II: PHORMIO. GETA.

315 PHO itane patris ais conspectum veritum hinc abiisse?
GET   admodum.
PHO Phanium relictam solam?
GET   sic.
PHO   et iratum senem?
GET oppido.
PHO   ad te summa solum, Phormio, rerum redit.
tute hoc intristi, tibi omnest exedendum: accingere.
GET obsecro te—
PHO   si rogabit—
GET   in te spes est.
PHO   eccere,
320   quid si reddet—?
GET   tu impulisti.
PHO   sic opinor.
GET   subveni.
PHO cedo senem. iam instructa sunt mi in corde consilia om-
nia.
GET quid ages?
PHO   quid vis, nisi uti maneat Phanium atque ex crimine hoc
Antiphonem eripiam atque in me omnem iram derivem
senis?
GET o vir fortis atque amicus! verum hoc saepe, Phormio,
325 vereor, ne istaec fortitudo in nervom erumpat denique.

---

315 conspectum *ADG Don.*, adventum *cett.*

---

32 Literally, "you cooked this, you must eat it up," a proverbial ex-
pression that, as Donatus points out, is especially suitable for parasites.

to support me in this business, so that Phormio doesn't catch me unprepared. (*he goes into his house, emerges again almost immediately, and departs right in the direction of the forum, leaving the stage empty*)

Enter PHORMIO *and* GETA *right.*

PHO Do you say he ran away in fear of facing his father?
GET Exactly.
PHO Leaving Phanium alone?
GET Yes.
PHO And the old man furious?
GET Absolutely.
PHO (*to himself*) The whole thing's back in your hands, Phormio. You got them into this mess, you must get them out of it.[32] Gird yourself for action.
GET I implore you—
PHO (*to himself*) If he asks—-
GET Our hopes lie in you.
PHO (*to himself*) Look, what if he replies—?
GET It was you who pushed him into it.
PHO (*to himself*) That's it, I think.
GET Help us.
PHO Bring on the old man. All my plans are now drawn up in my mind.
GET What are you going to do?
PHO What do you want, other than that Phanium stays, I rescue Antipho from the charges against him, and I divert all the old man's anger on to myself?
GET What a brave man you are and a true friend! But I often worry, Phormio, that this bravery of yours will land you in jail.

47

PHO   ah!

non itast; factumst periclum, iam pedum visast via.

quot me censes homines iam deverberasse usque ad ne-
cem,

hospites, tum civis? quo magis novi, tanto saepius.

cedo dum, enumquam iniuriarum audisti mihi scriptam
dicam?

330 GET   qui istuc?

PHO   quia non rete accipitri tennitur neque miluo,

qui male faciunt nobis: illis qui nil faciunt tennitur.

quia enim in illis fructus est, in illis opera luditur.

aliis aliundest periclum unde aliquid abradi potest:

mihi sciunt nil esse. dices: "ducent damnatum domum";

335   alere nolunt hominem edacem et sapiunt mea sententia,

pro maleficio si beneficium summum nolunt reddere.

GET non potest satis pro merito ab illo tibi referri gratia.

PHO immo enim nemo satis pro merito gratiam regi refert.

ten asymbolum venire unctum atque lautum e balineis,

340   otiosum ab animo, quom ille et cura et sumptu absumi-
tur!

dum tibi fit quod placeat, ille ringitur. tu rideas,

prior bibas, prior decumbas; cena dubia apponitur.

GET quid istuc verbist?

330, 331 tennitur *Don. in comm. edd.*, tenditur *codd.*

---

33 At Athens enslavement for debt was forbidden by a law of Solon's; the reference here is to the Roman practice whereby a debtor could be made over to his creditor as a bondsman until the debt was paid.

34 There is a reference here to the Greek practice of clubbing together for dinner with each person paying a contribution (συμβολή).

48

PHO   Ah! Not so. I've tested the ground, and I can see where to put my feet. How many men do you think I've beaten to the point of death, foreigners and citizens? The more practice I get, the more often I do it. Tell me, now, have you ever heard of a case being brought against me for assault?

GET   But why's that?

PHO   Because nobody sets nets for harmful birds like hawks or kites. They set them for harmless birds, because there's profit in them, whereas with the others you're wasting your time. People who offer some sort of plucking are at risk from various quarters, but they know I've got nothing. You'll say: "They'll get you convicted and haul you off home."[33] But they don't want to feed a man with an appetite like mine, and they're wise in my opinion if they refuse to do me a good turn in return for a bad one.

GET   My master can't thank you enough for your services.

PHO   On the contrary, it's the patron who can't be thanked enough for his services. You come oiled and washed from the baths, without contributing a thing[34] and without a care in the world, while he's consumed with worry and expense. Everything's done to satisfy your desires, while he can only gnash his teeth.[35] You laugh, you take the first drink and the first place at table, and then this problematical meal is laid before you.

GET   What sort of an expression's that?

---

[35] Donatus tells us that this whole passage did not come from the Greek original by Apollodorus but from a Roman poet whom he does not name.

49

PHO   ubi tu dubites quid sumas potissumum.
haec quom rationem ineas quam sint suavia et quam cara
    sint,

345   ea qui praebet, non tu hunc habeas plane praesentem
    deum?

GET   senex adest: vide quid agas. prima coitiost acerruma:
si eam sustinueris, postilla iam ut lubet ludas licet.

II. III: DEMIPHO. HEGIO. CRATINUS. CRITO.
PHORMIO. GETA.

DEM   enumquam quoiquam contumeliosius
audistis factam iniuriam quam haec est mhi?

350   adeste, quaeso.

GET   iratus est.

PHO   quin tu hoc age:
iam ego hunc agitabo. pro deum immortalium,
negat Phanium esse hanc sibi cognatam Demipho?
hanc Demipho negat esse cognatam?

GET   negat.

PHO   neque eius patrem se scire qui fuerit?

GET   negat.

355 DEM   ipsum esse opinor de quo agebam. sequimini.

PHO   nec Stilponem ipsum scire qui fuerit?

GET   negat.

PHO   quia egens relictast misera, ignoratur parens,
neglegitur ipsa. vide avaritia quid facit!

PHO   The problem is what to take to eat first. When you con-
       sider how pleasant this all is and how expensive, don't you
       regard the man who provides it as a manifest god on
       earth?

GET   (*looking down the street*) Here's the old man. Be careful
       what you do. The first onslaught's the worst; once you've
       resisted that, you can play with him as you like. (*they
       stand aside*)

Enter DEMIPHO *right from the forum with three advisers,*
HEGIO, CRATINUS, *and* CRITO.

DEM   (*to his advisers*) Have you ever heard of anyone insulted
       as outrageously as I have been here? Please give me your
       support.

GET   (*aside to Phormio*) He's furious.

PHO   (*aside to Geta*) Just concentrate on this. I'm now going to
       stir him up. (*aloud, for Demipho to hear*) By the immor-
       tal gods, does Demipho deny that Phanium here is re-
       lated to him? Does Demipho deny that she's a relative of
       his?

GET   He does.

PHO   He denies any knowledge of her father's identity?

GET   He does.

DEM   (*to his advisers*) I think that's the man I was talking about.
       Follow me. (*they move centre stage*)

PHO   (*still pretending not to see them*) He denies any knowl-
       edge of Stilpo?

GET   He does.

PHO   Because the poor girl's left penniless, her father's un-
       known, and she herself is disowned. See what greed can
       do!

51

GET   si erum insimulabis malitiae, male audies.

360   DEM   o audaciam! etiam me ultro accusatum advenit?

PHO   nam iam adulescenti nil est quod suscenseam,
     si illum minus norat. quippe homo iam grandior,
     pauper, quoi opera vita erat, ruri fere
     se continebat. ibi agrum de nostro patre

365   colendum habebat. saepe interea mihi senex
     narrabat se hunc neglegere cognatum suom.
     at quem virum! quem ego viderim in vita optumum.

GET   videas te atque illum ut narras.

PHO   in' malam crucem?
     nam ni ita eum existumassem, numquam tam gravis

370   ob hanc inimicitias caperem in vostram familiam,
     quam is aspernatur nunc tam illiberaliter.

GET   pergin ero absenti male loqui, impurissume?

PHO   dignum autem hoc illost.

GET   ain tandem, carcer?

DEM   Geta!

GET   bonorum extortor, legum contortor!

DEM   Geta!

375   PHO   responde.

GET   quis homost? ehem!

DEM   tace!

GET   absenti tibi
     te indignas seque dignas contumelias
     numquam cessavit dicere hodie.

DEM   desine.
     adulescens, primum abs te hoc bona venia peto,

GET   (*with pretended anger*) If you accuse my master of be-
having badly, you won't hear the last of it.

DEM   (*to his advisers*) The impudence! Does *he* actually come
here and make accusations against *me*?

PHO   There's no reason why I should be cross with the young
man for not knowing who her father was. He was a poor
man of advancing years, whose whole life was his work,
and he kept himself to the country most of the time,
where he had some land to farm from my father. The old
man used to tell me in those days how this relative of his
neglected him. But what a man! The best I've seen in my
whole life!

GET   You could try being like him yourself, if he's what you say
he is.

PHO   You go to hell! If I hadn't thought so highly of him, I'd
never have got into this quarrel with your family over the
girl, whom *he* now spurns in this ungentlemanly manner.

GET   Are you going to keep abusing my master behind his
back, you filthy scoundrel?

PHO   It's what he deserves.

GET   Do you say so, you jailbird?

DEM   (*trying to attract his attention*) Geta!

GET   You extortioner of property, you contortioner of the laws!

DEM   Geta!

PHO   (*to Geta*) Answer him.

GET   Who is it? (*as if seeing Demipho for the first time*) Oh
hello!

DEM   Stop this!

GET   This fellow has never ceased insulting you behind your
back today, in terms which fit him rather than you.

DEM   That's enough. (*to Phormio*) Young man, first I request
you, with your kind permission, if it pleases you, to an-

		si tibi placere potis est, mi ut respondeas.
380		quem amicum tuom ais fuisse istum, explana mihi,
		et qui cognatum me sibi esse diceret.
	PHO	proinde expiscare quasi non nosses.
	DEM	nossem?
	PHO	ita.
	DEM	ego me nego; tu qui ais redige in memoriam.
	PHO	eho tu, sobrinum tuom non noras?
	DEM	enicas.
385		dic nomen.
	PHO	nomen? maxume.
	DEM	quid nunc taces?
	PHO	perii hercle! nomen perdidi.
	DEM	quid ais?
	PHO	Geta,
		si meministi id quod olim dictumst, subice. hem!
		non dico. quasi non noris, temptatum advenis.
	DEM	ego autem tempto?
	GET	Stilpo.
	PHO	atque adeo quid mea?
390		Stilpost.
	DEM	quem dixti?
	PHO	Stilponem, inquam, noveras.
	DEM	neque ego illum noram nec mihi cognatus fuit
		quisquam istoc nomine.
	PHO	itane? non te horum pudet?
		at si talentum rem reliquisset decem—
	DEM	di tibi malefaciant!
	PHO	—primus esses memoriter
395		progeniem vostram usque ab avo atque atavo proferens.

388 noris Σ *Don.*, nosses A *edd.*

54

swer this question: explain to me who you say this friend
of yours was and how he claimed he was related to me.

PHO You're just fishing, as if you didn't know him.

DEM Know him?

PHO Yes.

DEM I say I don't. If you say I do, jog my memory.

PHO Hey, don't you know your own cousin?

DEM You're annoying me. Tell me the name.

PHO The name? Certainly. (*he hesitates*)

DEM Why the silence?

PHO (*aside*) God damn it, I've forgotten the name.

DEM What did you say?

PHO (*aside to Geta*) Geta, if you remember what we just said,
whisper it. (*to Demipho*) Hey, I'm not telling you. You're
trying to trap me, as if you didn't know.

DEM Me? Trap you?

GET (*whispering*) It's Stilpo.

PHO (*to Demipho, changing tactics*) But after all what do I
care? It's Stilpo.

DEM Who did you say?

PHO I'm saying you knew Stilpo.

DEM I did *not* know him, nor did I have any relative of that
name.

PHO Really? Aren't you ashamed? In front of these gentle-
men? (*pointing to Demipho's advisers*). But if he'd left an
estate worth ten talents—

DEM (*aside*) May the gods do you mischief!

PHO —you'd have recited your lineage right from your grand-
father and your grandfather's grandfather, and remem-
bered it perfectly.

DEM ita ut dicis. ego tum quom advenissem qui mihi
cognata ea esset dicerem: itidem tu face.
cedo, qui est cognata?

GET   eu, noster, recte! heus tu, cave!

PHO dilucide expedivi quibus me oportuit
iudicibus. tum id si falsum fuerat, filius
400 quor non fefellit?

DEM   filium narras mihi,
quoius de stultitia dici ut dignumst non potest?

PHO at tu qui sapiens es magistratus adi
iudicium de eadem causa iterum ut reddant tibi,
405 quandoquidem solus regnas et soli licet
hic de eadem causa bis iudicium adipiscier.

DEM etsi mihi facta iniuriast, verum tamen
potius quam litis secter aut quam te audiam,
itidem ut cognata si sit, id quod lex iubet
410 dotis dare, abduc hanc, minas quinque accipe.

PHO hahahae! homo suavis!

DEM   quid est? num iniquom postulo?
an ne hoc quidem ego adipiscar quod ius publicumst?

PHO itan tandem, quaeso, itidem ut meretricem ubi abusu'
sis,
mercedem dare lex iubet ei atque amittere?

415 an, ut ne quid turpe civis in se admitteret
propter egestatem, proxumo iussast dari,

---

36 Athenian law specifically forbade the retrial of a case once it had
been decided. Roman law did allow for retrial but only in special cir-
cumstances.

37 Five minas (or one twelfth of a talent) was in fact the sum laid
down by Athenian law for cases of this kind. This is a paltry sum com-

DEM (*controlling his anger*) As you say. But I'd have stated right from the beginning how the girl was related to me. You do the same. Come on, how *is* she related?

GET (*to Demipho*) Well done, master, good point! (*to Phormio*) Hey you, look out!

PHO I explained perfectly clearly to the proper authority, namely the court. If I'd made it up, why didn't your son refute me at the time?

DEM Don't talk to me about my son! I can't find words to describe his stupidity.

PHO Well, since you're the clever one, go to the magistrates and get them to grant you a retrial. (*with heavy irony*) You're the dictator here and the only person who can have the same case tried twice.[36]

DEM (*slowly and deliberately*) Even though I'm the injured party, nonetheless, rather than take you to court or listen to your pleading, exactly as if she were a relative, accept the amount of dowry prescribed by the law, and take her away. Here are five minas.[37]

PHO (*refusing the proffered money*) Hahahahaha! What a smooth fellow!

DEM What's the matter? Is that an unreasonable demand? Am I not even to be allowed common justice?

PHO Tell me, if I may ask, do you really mean to say that the law bids you pay her fee and send her away, just as if you'd used the services of a prostitute? Doesn't it rather bid you marry her to her nearest relative, so that a citizen woman doesn't fall into disgrace through poverty but

pared with the dowries offered by wealthy fathers in comedy, for example, two talents in *The Self-Tormentor* (line 838) and ten talents in *The Woman of Andros* (line 951).

	ut cum uno aetatem degeret? quod tu vetas.
DEM	ita, proxumo quidem. at nos unde? aut quam ob rem—?
PHO	ohe!
	"actum" aiunt "ne agas."
DEM	non agam? immo haud desinam
420	donec perfecero hoc.
PHO	ineptis.
DEM	sine modo!
PHO	postremo tecum nil rei nobis, Demipho, est.
	tuos est damnatus gnatus, non tu. nam tua
	praeterierat iam ducendi aetas.
DEM	omnia haec
	illum putato quae ego nunc dico dicere.
425	aut quidem cum uxore hac ipsum prohibebo domo.
GET	iratus est.
PHO	tu te idem melius feceris.
DEM	itan es paratus facere me advorsum omnia,
	infelix?
PHO	metuit hic nos, tam etsi sedulo
	dissimulat.
GET	bene habent tibi principia.
PHO	quin quod est
430	ferundum fers? tuis dignum factis feceris,
	ut amici inter nos simus?
DEM	egon tuam expetam
	amicitiam? aut te visum aut auditum velim?
PHO	si concordabis cum illa, habebis quae tuam
	senectutem oblectet. respice aetatem tuam.
435 DEM	te oblectet, tibi habe.

---

[38] This was the Roman ideal: the word *univira* is common on tombstones of Roman wives.

lives her life with a single husband?[38] And this is what you're preventing.

DEM To her nearest relative, that's right. But where do we come in? Why—?

PHO Hold on now! "What's done can't be undone," as the saying goes.

DEM Can't be undone? On the contrary I won't give up until I've seen this business through.

PHO You're being absurd.

DEM You just wait and see!

PHO At the end of the day, we've no business with you, Demipho. It was your son who lost the case, not you. (*mockingly*) You were a bit too old for marriage.

DEM Regard everything I'm now saying as said by him. If he doesn't agree, I'll shut him out of the house, wife and all.

GET (*aside to Phormio*) He's furious.

PHO (*to Demipho*) Better do the same to yourself.

DEM Are you determined to oppose me on everything, you wretch?

PHO (*aside to Geta*) He's afraid of us, though he's doing his best to hide it.

GET (*aside to Phormio*) So far, so good.

PHO (*to Demipho*) Why don't you accept what you have to accept, behave in a manner worthy of you, and let us be friends?

DEM Me? Look for friendship with you? I don't want to set eyes on you or hear your voice again.

PHO If you make it up with her, you'll have someone to amuse you in your old age. Think of your years.

DEM She can amuse *you*; have her yourself.

PHO   minue vero iram.

DEM   hoc age:
satis iam verborumst. nisi tu properas mulierem
abducere, ego illam eiciam. dixi, Phormio.

PHO si tu illam attigeris secus quam dignumst liberam,
dicam tibi impingam grandem. dixi, Demipho.
si quid opus fuerit, heus, domo me.

440   GET   intellego.

     II. IV: DEMIPHO. GETA. HEGIO. CRATINUS. CRITO.

DEM quanta me cura et sollicitudine afficit
gnatus, qui me et se hisce impedivit nuptiis!
neque mi in conspectum prodit, ut saltem sciam
quid de hac re dicat quidve sit sententiae.

445   abi, vise redieritne iam an nondum domum.

GET eo.

DEM   videtis quo in loco res haec siet.
quid ago? dic, Hegio.

HEG   ego? Cratinum censeo,
si tibi videtur.

DEM   dic, Cratine.

CRA   mene vis?

DEM te.

CRA   ego quae in rem tuam sint, ea velim facias. mihi

450   sic hoc videtur: quod te absente hic filius
egit, restitui in integrum aequomst et bonum,
et id impetrabis. dixi.

DEM   dic nunc, Hegio.

HEG ego sedulo hunc dixisse credo. verum itast:
quot homines tot sententiae, suos cuique mos.

PHO   Don't be so angry.

DEM   Let's come to the point; we've wasted enough words. If you don't take the woman away and quickly, I'll throw her out. That's my last word, Phormio.

PHO   If you lay a hand on her, against what is proper for a free woman, I'll bring a massive lawsuit against you. That's *my* last word, Demipho. (*to Geta*) Listen, if I'm needed for anything, I'll be at home.

GET   I understand. (*Phormio exits right in the direction of his house*)

DEM   (*to himself*) How much worry and anxiety my son is causing me by getting me and him entangled in this marriage! And he doesn't even show his face so that at least I could find out what he has to say about it and what his feelings are. (*to Geta*) Go and see if he's returned home yet or not.

GET   I'm going. (*he exits into Demipho's house*)

DEM   (*turning to his advisers, who have been lurking in the background*) You see the situation. What do I do? Speak, Hegio.

HEG   Me? I suggest Cratinus, if that's all right with you.

DEM   Speak, Cratinus.

CRA   You mean me?

DEM   Yes, you.

CRA   I would want you to do what is to your advantage. In my opinion it is right and proper for what your son did in your absence to be rendered null and void. And you'll win your case. That is my advice.

DEM   Now you, Hegio.

HEG   I'm sure that he (*pointing to Cratinus*) has given you excellent advice. But the truth is, there are as many opinions as there are people; everyone has his own way of

61

455	mihi non videtur quod sit factum legibus
	rescindi posse; et turpe inceptust.
DEM	dic, Crito.
CRI	ago amplius deliberandum censeo.
	res magnast.
HEG	numquid nos vis?
DEM	fecistis probe.
	incertior sum multo quam dudum.
GET	negant
460	redisse.
DEM	frater est exspectandus mihi.
	is quod mihi dederit de hac re consilium, id sequar.
	percontatum ibo ad portum, quoad se recipiat.
GET	at ego Antiphonem quaeram, ut quae acta hic sint sciat.
	sed eccum ipsum video in tempore huc se recipere.

ACTUS III

III. I: ANTIPHO. GETA.

465 ANT	enimvero, Antipho, multimodis cum istoc animo's vitu-perandus.
	itane te hinc abisse et vitam tuam tutandam aliis dedisse!
	alios tuam rem credidisti magis quam tete animum ad-vorsuros?
	nam, utut erant alia, illi certe quae nunc tibi domist consuleres,
	ne quid propter tuam fidem decepta poteretur mali.
470	quoi nunc miserae spes opesque sunt in te uno omnes sitae.

469 poteretur A^1 *Don.*, pateretur $A^2\Sigma$

62

looking at things. My own view is that what has been
done in accordance with the law cannot be rescinded,
and it is dishonorable to try.

DEM   Now you, Crito.

CRI   I suggest that this needs further deliberation. It's a
weighty matter.

HEG   (*to Demipho*) Is that all?

DEM   (*ironically*) You've been very helpful. (*aside*) I'm even
more uncertain than I was before. (*the advisers exit right
in the direction of the forum*)

GET   (*emerging from Demipho's house*) They say he's not back.

DEM   I'll have to wait for my brother. Whatever advice he gives
on this, I'll follow it. I'll go to the harbour and ask how
soon he's due back. (*he exits left in the direction of the
harbour*)

GET   (*to himself*) I'll go and find Antipho and tell him what has
happened here. (*looking down the street*) But there he is
coming this way, just at the right moment.

ACT THREE

Enter ANTIPHO right.

ANT   (*to himself*) Well, Antipho, you deserve to be roundly
censured, you and your cowardly attitude! Fancy going
off like that and leaving your life in other people's hands.
Did you really believe others would look after your inter-
ests better than you could yourself? If nothing else, you
should surely have taken some thought for the girl you
have at home, to save her from coming to some harm
through her misplaced trust in you. Poor girl, her hopes
and prospects depend entirely on you.

GET et quidem, ere, nos iamdudum hic te absentem incusa-
mus qui abieris.

ANT te ipsum quaerebam.

GET   sed ea causa nihilo magis defecimus.

ANT loquere, obsecro, quonam in loco sunt res et fortunae
meae?

numquid patri subolet?

GET   nil etiam.

ANT   ecquid spei porrost?

GET   nescio.

ANT   ah!

475 GET nisi Phaedria haud cessavit pro te eniti.

ANT   nil fecit novi.

GET tum Phormio itidem in hac re ut in aliis strenuom homi-
nem praebuit.

ANT quid is fecit?

GET   confutavit verbis admodum iratum senem.

ANT eu, Phormio!

GET   ego quod potui porro.

ANT   mi Geta, omnis vos amo.

GET sic habent principia sese ut dixi. adhuc tranquilla res est,

480 mansurusque patruom pater est dum hic adveniat.

ANT   quid eum?

GET   ut aibat,

de eius consilio sese velle facere quod ad hanc rem atti-
net.

ANT quantum metus est mihi videre huc salvom nunc pa-
truom, Geta!

nam per eius unam, ut audio, aut vivam aut moriar sen-
tentiam.

GET Phaedria tibi adest.

ANT   ubinam?

GET   (*coming forward*) To tell you the truth, master, we've spent all our time criticising you behind your back for going off.

ANT   (*seeing Geta*) I was looking for you.

GET   (*ignoring this*) But that didn't cause us to let you down at all.

ANT   Tell me, for goodness' sake, where do I stand? What are my chances? Does my father suspect anything?

GET   Not so far.

ANT   Is there any hope for the future?

GET   I don't know.

ANT   Oh dear!

GET   Though Phaedria hasn't stopped working away on your behalf.

ANT   That's just like him.

GET   And Phormio too has proved a staunch ally, as always.

ANT   What's he done?

GET   He quieted the old man down when he was pretty furious.

ANT   Good for you, Phormio!

GET   (*modestly*) And I've done what I could.

ANT   Dear Geta, I love you all.

GET   It started off as I've described. Things are quiet at the moment: your father's waiting for your uncle to return.

ANT   Why him?

GET   According to what he said, he wants to follow his advice in the matter.

ANT   How I'm dreading my uncle's safe return, Geta! From what you're saying, it's his decision alone whether I live or die.

GET   (*as the door of Dorio's house opens*) Here's Phaedria.

ANT   Where?

GET   eccum ab sua palaestra exit foras.

III. II: PHAEDRIA. DORIO. ANTIPHO. GETA.

485 PHAE Dorio,
      audi, obsecro.

DOR   non audio.

PHAE   parumper.

DOR   quin omitte me.

PHAE audi quod dicam.

DOR   at enim taedet audire eadem miliens.

PHAE at nunc dicam quod lubenter audias.

DOR   loquere, audio.

PHAE non queo te exorare ut maneas triduom hoc? quo nunc
      abis?

490 DOR mirabar si tu mihi quicquam afferres novi.

ANT ei! metuo lenonem ne quid suo suat capiti.

GET   idem ego vereor.

PHAE non mihi credis?

DOR   hariolare.

PHAE   sin fidem do?

DOR   fabulae!

PHAE feneratum istuc beneficium pulchre tibi dices.

DOR   logi!

PHAE crede mi, gaudebis facto. verum hercle hoc est.

DOR   somnium!

---

491 suo suat capiti *Antiphoni continuant codd., Getae dant Bentley edd.*

---

39 Literally, "wrestling ground," meaning the pimp's house.

40 Literally, "is sewing something for his own head," a colourful phrase which combines the metaphorical "stitch together trouble for someone" and the proverbial "bring something on one's own head."

PHORMIO

GET There, coming out of his private gymnasium.[39] (*they stand aside*)

Enter PHAEDRIA *and* DORIO *from Dorio's house.*

PHAE Dorio, listen to me, for goodness' sake.
DOR I'm not listening.
PHAE Just for a moment.
DOR Can't you leave me alone?
PHAE Hear what I have to say.
DOR I'm tired of hearing the same thing a thousand times.
PHAE But I'm about to say something you'll be glad to hear.
DOR Speak. I'm listening.
PHAE Can't I persuade you to wait these next three days? (*Dorio makes to depart*) Where are you off to?
DOR I thought it was strange if you had anything new to offer.
ANT (*aside to Geta, ironically*) Oh dear! I'm afraid the pimp is asking for trouble.[40]
GET (*aside to Antipho*) I fear so too.
PHAE You still don't believe me?
DOR (*sarcastically*) How did you guess?
PHAE What if I give my word?
DOR Nonsense!
PHAE You'll find your kindness was a splendid investment.
DOR Fairy tales!
PHAE Believe me, you'll be glad you did it. It's true, for god's sake.
DOR Dreams!

Some editors give these words to Geta, as a completion of the sentence begun by Antipho, though the MSS give the whole sentence to Antipho.

495	PHAE	experire. non est longum.
	DOR	cantilenam eandem canis.
	PHAE	tu mihi cognatus, tu parens, tu amicus, tu—
	DOR	garri modo!

PHAE adeon ingenio esse duro te atque inexorabili
      ut neque misericordia neque precibus molliri queas!

DOR adeon te esse incogitantem atque impudentem, Phae-
      dria,

500   ut phaleratis ducas dictis me et meam ductes gratiis!

ANT miseritumst.

PHAE   ei! veris vincor.

GET   quam uterquest similis sui!

PHAE neque Antipho alia quom occupatus esset sollicitudine,
      tum hoc esse mihi obiectum malum!

ANT   ah! quid istuc est autem, Phaedria?

PHAE o fortunatissume Antipho.

ANT   egone?

PHAE   quoi quod amas domist,

505   neque umquam cum huius modi usus venit ut conflicta-
      res malo.

ANT mihin domist? immo, id quod aiunt, auribus teneo lu-
      pum.

      nam neque quo pacto a me amittam neque uti retineam
      scio.

DOR ipsum istuc mihi in hoc est.

---

505 *sic Tyrrell metro consulens*, neque cum huius modi umquam tibi
usus venit *codd. edd.*

PHAE Try it. It's not for long.

DOR You're singing the same old song.

PHAE I see you as my relative, my father, my friend, my—

DOR Talk away!

PHAE To think that you can be so cruel and hardhearted that you can't be softened by prayers or pity!

DOR To think that you can be so ignorant and shameless, Phaedria, that you try to fool me with fancy[41] words and carry my girl off for nothing!

ANT (*aside to Geta, ironically*) There's pity for you!

PHAE (*to himself*) Oh dear! I can't fight the truth.

GET (*aside to Antipho*) How true to type they both are!

PHAE (*to himself*) If only this trouble of mine had arisen when Antipho was occupied with a different concern![42]

ANT (*going up to Phaedria*) Oh! What's the matter, Phaedria?

PHAE (*seeing him at last*) Antipho, you lucky, lucky fellow!

ANT Me?

PHAE Because you have your beloved at home, and you've never had the experience of grappling with this sort of problem.

ANT Mine at home? On the contrary, I'm holding the proverbial wolf by the ears. I don't know how to let go or how to hold on to her.

DOR (*wrily*) I have the same problem with him (*pointing to Phaedria*).

41 Literally "decorated"; the word *phaleratus* is elsewhere applied to the adornments of horses and to military medals.

42 This is an obscure remark; the required sense seems to be "I wish this had happened when Antipho was able to support me, but he is too preoccupied with the problems of his marriage."

ANT   heia! ne parum leno sies.
       numquid hic confecit?

PHAE   hicin? quod homo inhumanissumus,

510   Pamphilam meam vendidit.

ANT   quid? vendidit?

GET   ain? vendidit?

PHAE vendidit.

DOR   quam indignum facinus, ancillam aere emptam suo!

PHAE nequeo exorare ut me maneat et cum illo ut mutet fidem
       triduom hoc, dum id quod est promissum ab amicis ar-
       gentum aufero.
       si non tum dedero, unam praeterea horam ne oppertus
       sies.

515 DOR   obtunde.

ANT   haud longumst id quod orat, Dorio. exoret sine.
       idem hoc tibi, quod boni promeritus fueris, conduplica-
       verit.

DOR   verba istaec sunt.

ANT   Pamphilamne hac urbe privari sines?
       tum praeterea horunc amorem distrahi poterin pati?

DOR   neque ego neque tu.

PHAE   di tibi omnes id quod es dignus duint!

520 DOR   ego te compluris advorsum ingenium meum mensis tuli
       pollicitantem et nil ferentem, flentem. nunc contra om-
       nia haec
       repperi qui det neque lacrumet. da locum melioribus.

ANT   certe hercle, ego si satis commemini, tibi quidemst olim
       dies,
       quam ad dares huic, praestituta.

PHAE   factum.

DOR   num ego istuc nego?

525 ANT   iam ea praeteriit?

ANT   (*to Dorio*) Go on! Be like a true pimp. (*to Phaedria*) Has he done something?

PHAE Him? He's absolutely inhuman: he's sold my girl.

ANT   (*taken aback*) What? Sold her?

GET   (*equally startled*) Did you say, sold her?

PHAE Sold her.

DOR   (*ironically*) Quite outrageous, to sell a girl he's bought with his own money!

PHAE And I can't persuade him to break his agreement with the other man and give me three days, while I collect the money promised by my friends. (*to Dorio*) If I don't pay it then, don't wait a single hour longer.

DOR   Batter my ears!

ANT   It's not a long time he's asking for, Dorio. Let him persuade you. He'll pay you back your good turn in double measure.

DOR   These are empty words.

ANT   Will you let Pamphila be expelled from Athens? Aside from that, can you bear to see these two lovers torn apart?

DOR   No, I can't. Nor can you.

PHAE May all the gods destroy you as you deserve!

DOR   (*to Phaedria*) For several months against my better judgment I've put up with you promising and bringing nothing but tears. Now I've found just the opposite, a man who brings the money and doesn't weep. Make way for your betters.

ANT   (*to Phaedria*) Surely, if I remember rightly, you originally agreed to a day on which you would bring him the money.

PHAE Yes, I did.

DOR   I'm not denying it, am I?

ANT   Has it now passed?

DOR   non, verum haec ei antecessit.

ANT   non pudet
vanitatis?

DOR   minume, dum ob rem.

GET   sterculinum!

PHAE   Dorio,
itane tandem facere oportet?

DOR   sic sum. si placeo, utere.

ANT   sicin hunc decipis?

DOR   immo enimvero, Antipho, hic me decipit.
nam hic me huius modi scibat esse, ego hunc esse aliter
     credidi.

530   iste me fefellit, ego isti nihilo sum aliter ac fui.
sed utut haec sunt, tamen hoc faciam. cras mane argen-
     tum mihi
miles dare se dixit. si mi prior tu attuleris, Phaedria,
mea lege utar, ut potior sit qui prior ad dandumst. vale.

III. II: PHAEDRIA. ANTIPHO. GETA.

PHAE quid faciam? unde ego nunc tam subito huic argentum
     inveniam miser?

535   quoi minus nihilost? quod, hic si pote fuisset exorarier
triduom hoc, promissum fuerat.

ANT   itane hunc patiemur, Geta,
fieri miserum, qui me dudum, ut dixti, adiuverit comiter?
quin, quom opust, beneficium rursum ei experiemur
     reddere?

GET   scio equidem hoc esse aequom.

ANT   age ergo, solus servare hunc potes.

540 GET quid faciam?

ANT   invenias argentum.

GET   cupio. sed id unde edoce.

ANT   pater adest hic.

DOR   No, but this one has arrived first.

ANT   (*to Dorio*) Aren't you ashamed to be so unscrupulous?

DOR   Not at all, if I profit by it.

GET   You shit!

PHAE Dorio, should you really behave like this?

DOR   That's how I am. If you like me, do business with me.

ANT   Are you going to cheat him just like that?

DOR   On the contrary, Antipho, he's cheating *me*. He knew the
      sort of person I am, whereas I thought he was different.
      He's misled me, whereas I'm exactly the same as I was.
      But, however that may be, this is what I'll do. The soldier
      said he'd bring the money tomorrow morning. If you
      bring it before him, Phaedria, I'll follow my rule of first
      pay, first served. Goodbye. (*he goes back into his house*)

PHAEDRIA, ANTIPHO, and GETA remain on stage.

PHAE What am I to do? Poor me, where can I find him the
      money at such short notice, when I haven't a penny to my
      name? If only he could have been persuaded to give me
      three days, it was all promised.

ANT   (*to Geta*) Are we going to let him suffer like this, Geta,
      when, according to what you said, he generously stood by
      me just now? Why don't we try to return the favour, now
      he needs it?

GET   (*to Antipho, doubtfully*) I know that's the right thing to
      do.

ANT   Come on then, you're the only one who can save him.

GET   By doing what?

ANT   Finding the money.

GET   I'd like to. But explain where?

ANT   My father's back home.

GET   scio. sed quid tum?

ANT   ah! dictum sapienti sat est.

GET itane?

ANT   ita.

GET   sane hercle pulchre suades. etiam tu hinc abis?

non triumpho, ex nuptiis tuis si nil nanciscor mali,

ni etiamnunc me huius causa quaerere in malo iubeas
    crucem?

545 ANT verum hic dicit.

PHAE   quid? ego vobis, Geta, alienus sum?

GET   haud puto.

sed parumnest quod omnibus nunc nobis suscenset se-
    nex,

ni instigemus etiam ut nullus locus relinquatur preci?

PHAE alius ab oculis meis illam in ignotum abducet locum?
    hem!

tum igitur dum licet dumque adsum, loquimini mecum,
    Antipho,

550 contemplamini me.

ANT   quam ob rem? aut quidnam facturu's? cedo.

PHAE quoquo hinc asportabitur terrarum, certumst persequi
aut perire.

GET   di bene vortant quod agas! pedetemptim tamen.

ANT vide si quid opis potes afferre huic.

GET   "si quid"? quid?

ANT   quaere, obsecro,

ne quid plus minusve faxit quod nos post pigeat, Geta.

555 GET quaero. salvos est, ut opinor. verum etiam metuo malum.

ANT noli metuere: una tecum bona mala tolerabimus.

---

43 Literally, "a word's enough for the wise," a proverbial expression.

GET   I know. But what follows?

ANT   Oh! Can't you take a hint?[43]

GET   (*seeing the implication*) Really?

ANT   Really.

GET   That *is* fine advice, for god's sake! Get away with you! Isn't it a triumph enough for me if I avoid trouble over *your* marriage, without you telling me to get myself crucified on *his* behalf as well?

ANT   (*to Phaedria*) He has a point.

PHAE What? I'm one of the family, aren't I, Geta?

GET   I reckon so. But isn't it enough that the old man is furious with the lot of us, without us goading him to the point where there's no room left for mercy?

PHAE (*dramatically*) Shall another man take her out of my sight to an unknown land? Hey! While you can, Antipho, while I'm here, talk to me, look at me.

ANT   Why? What are you going to do? Tell us.

PHAE Wherever in the world she's taken, I am resolved to follow her or die.

GET   (*ironically*) May the gods grant you success in your enterprise! But don't rush it!

ANT   (*to Geta*) See if there's any way you can give him some help.

GET   Some help? What?

ANT   Try, for goodness' sake, or he'll do something dreadful which we'll regret afterwards, Geta.

GET   I'm trying. (*he ponders*) He's saved, I think. But I'm worried about the consequences.

ANT   Don't worry. We'll stand by you through thick and thin.

Antipho is implying that Geta should get the money out of his older master, as happens not infrequently in Roman comedy.

GET   quantum opus est tibi argenti, loquere.

PHAE   solae triginta minae.

GET   triginta? hui! percarast, Phaedria.

PHAE   istaec vero vilis est.

GET   age age, inventas reddam.

PHAE   o lepidum!

GET   aufer te hinc.

PHAE   iam opus est.

GET   iam feres.

560   sed opus est mihi Phormionem ad hanc rem adiutorem
dari.

PHAE praestost. audacissume oneris quidvis impone et feret.
solus est homo amico amicus.

GET   eamus ergo ad eum ocius.

ANT   numquid est quod opera mea vobis opus sit?

GET   nil. verum abi domum
et illam miseram, quam ego nunc intus scio esse exani-
matam metu,

565   consolare. cessas?

ANT   nil est aeque quod faciam lubens.

PHAE qua via istuc facies?

GET   dicam in itinere. modo te hinc amove.

ACTUS IV

IV. I: DEMIPHO. CHREMES.

DEM   quid? qua profectus causa hinc es Lemnum, Chreme,
adduxtin tecum filiam?

---

44 Thirty minas is in fact an average sum in comedy for the purchase
of a girl from a pimp; the range extends from twenty (*The Brothers* 191)

GET   (*to Phaedria*) Tell me how much money you want.

PHAE   Only thirty minas.

GET   Thirty? Wow! She's very expensive, Phaedria.

PHAE   She's cheap at the price.[44]

GET   All right, all right, I'll find you them.

PHAE   (*embracing him*) You splendid fellow!

GET   (*disentangling himself*) Get away with you!

PHAE   I need them now.

GET   You shall have them now. But I need to have Phormio to help me in this.

PHAE   He's at your service. You can confidently lay on him any burden you like and he'll be equal to it. He's a friend to his friends, if anybody is.

GET   Quickly, then, let's go and find him.

ANT   (*to Geta*) Do you need my services for anything?

GET   No. But go home and console the poor girl who I'm sure is fainting with fear inside. What are you waiting for?

ANT   There's nothing I'd rather do. (*he exits into his house*)

PHAE   (*to Geta*) How will you do it?

GET   I'll tell you on the way. Just come along. (*they exit right in the direction of Phormio's house, leaving the stage empty*)

ACT FOUR

Enter DEMIPHO *and* CHREMES *left from the harbour.* CHREMES *is in travelling clothes.*

DEM   Well, Chremes, what about the reason why you travelled to Lemnos? Have you brought your daughter back with you?

to forty (Plautus, *Epidicus* 51–52). Prices of twenty and thirty minas are attested for the purchase of expensive courtesans in real-life Athens.

CHR   non.

DEM   quid ita non?

CHR postquam videt me eius mater esse hic diutius,

570   simul autem non manebat aetas virginis

meam neglegentiam, ipsam cum omni familia

ad me profectam esse aibant.

DEM   quid illi tam diu,

quaeso, igitur commorabare, ubi id audiveras?

CHR pol me detinuit morbus.

DEM   unde? aut qui?

CHR   rogas?

575   senectus ipsast morbus. sed venisse eas

salvas audivi ex nauta qui illas vexerat.

DEM quid gnato obtigerit me absente audisti, Chreme?

CHR quod quidem me factum consili incertum facit.

nam hanc condicionem si quoi tulero extrario,

580   quo pacto aut unde mihi sit dicundum ordinest.

te mihi fidelem esse aeque atque egomet sum mihi

scibam. ille, si me alienus affinem volet,

tacebit dum intercedet familiaritas.

sin spreverit me, plus quam opus est scito sciet.

585   vereorque ne uxor aliqua hoc resciscat mea.

quod si fit, ut me excutiam atque egrediar domo

id restat. nam ego meorum solus sum meus.

DEM scio ita esse, et istaec mihi res sollicitudinist,

neque defetiscar usque adeo experirier,

590   donec tibi id quod pollicitus sum effecero.

589 usque *Prisc. Eugr.*, umquam *codd. pl.*, usquam *Lp.* adeo *codd. pl.*, ego γ

78

CHR No.

DEM Why not?

CHR I was told that her mother felt I was staying here too long, and the girl was of an age where she couldn't wait for me to act; so she set out with her whole household to come and find me.

DEM Why then, if I may ask, did you stay there so long, once you'd heard the news?

CHR I fell ill, for heaven's sake, and that kept me there.

DEM What illness? How did you catch it?

CHR You don't need to ask. Old age is an illness in itself. But I heard from the sailor who brought them over that they arrived safely.

DEM Have you heard what's happened to my son in my absence, Chremes?

CHR Yes, and it's left me uncertain what to do. If I offer the match to an outsider, I shall have to explain from beginning to end how she comes to be my daughter. In your case I knew I could depend on your loyalty as on my own. But, if an outsider wants to ally with our family, he'll keep the secret only so long as he and I are on good terms; if we fall out, he'll know more than he ought to know. And I'm afraid my wife may find out by some means. If that happens, I've no option but to clear out and leave home. I'm the only one of my possessions I can call my own.

DEM I know your situation and it worries me, and I won't slacken in my efforts until I've achieved what I promised you.

IV. II: GETA. DEMIPHO. CHREMES.

GET   ego hominem callidiorem vidi neminem
      quam Phormionem. venio ad hominem ut dicerem
      argentum opus esse, et id quo pacto fieret.
      vixdum dimidium dixeram, intellexerat.
595   gaudebat, me laudabat, quaerebat senem,
      dis gratias agebat tempus sibi dari
      ubi Phaedriae esse ostenderet nihilo minus
      amicum sese quam Antiphoni. hominem ad forum
      iussi opperiri: eo me esse adducturum senem.
600   sed eccum ipsum. quis est ulterior? attat! Phaedriae
      pater venit. sed quid pertimui autem belua?
      an quia quos fallam pro uno duo sunt mihi dati?
      commodius esse opinor duplici spe utier.
      petam hinc unde a primo institi. is si dat, sat est;
605   si ab eo nil fiet, tum hunc adoriar hospitem.

IV. III: ANTIPHO. GETA. CHREMES. DEMIPHO.

ANT   exspecto quam mox recipiat sese Geta.
      sed patruom video cum patre astantem. ei mihi!
      quam timeo adventus huius quo impellat patrem!
GET   adibo hosce. o noster Chreme!
CHR   salve, Geta.
610 GET   venire salvom volup est.
CHR   credo.
GET   quid agitur?
      multa advenienti, ut fit, nova hic?

597–598 esse . . . sese *Lachmann edd. pl.*, se(se) . . . esse *codd. Eugr.*

Enter GETA *right from the direction of Phormio's house. He pauses at the side of the stage.*

GET (*to himself*) I've never set eyes on a craftier man than Phormio. I went to see him to say that we needed money and ask how it could be found. I was scarcely halfway through and he'd grasped the situation. He was delighted, he congratulated me, he asked where the old man was, and he thanked the gods that he was being granted the opportunity to show himself as good a friend to Phaedria as he'd been to Antipho. I told him to wait for me in the forum, and I'd bring the old man there. (*suddenly noticing Demipho*) But there he is in person. Who's that beside him? Oh no! Phaedria's father's back. (*composing himself with difficulty*) But why did I get into a panic, dumb creature? Just because I'm presented with two people to trick instead of one? In my opinion it's better to have two strings to my bow. I'll try the one I targeted in the first place. If he pays up, that's fine. If I get nothing from him, then I'll tackle the new arrival.

Enter ANTIPHO *from his house.*

ANT (*to himself*) I'm expecting Geta to return any moment. (*seeing Chremes and Demipho*) But there's my uncle standing there with my father. Oh dear! I dread to think how my father will be influenced by his return. (*he stands back, unseen by the others*)

GET (*aside*) I'll go up to them. (*to Chremes*) Chremes!

CHR Good day, Geta.

GET I'm glad you're safely back.

CHR Quite so.

GET How are you doing? See many changes on your return, as usual?

CHR	compluria.
GET	ita. de Antiphone audistin quae facta?
CHR	omnia.
GET	tun dixeras huic? facinus indignum, Chreme,
	sic circumiri.
CHR	id cum hoc agebam commodum.
615 GET	nam hercle ego quoque id quidem agitans mecum sedulo
	inveni, opinor, remedium huic rei.
CHR	quid, Geta?
DEM	quod remedium?
GET	ut abii abs te, fit forte obviam
	mihi Phormio.
CHR	qui Phormio?
DEM	is qui istanc—
CHR	scio.
GET	visumst mihi ut eius temptarem sententiam.
620	prendo hominem solum: "quor non" inquam "Phormio,
	vides inter nos sic haec potius cum bona
	ut componamus gratia quam cum mala?
	erus liberalis est et fugitans litium.
	nam ceteri quidem hercle amici omnes modo
	uno ore auctores fuere ut praecipitem hanc daret."
625 ANT	quid hic coeptat aut quo evadet hodie?
GET	"an legibus
	daturum poenas dices, si illam eiecerit?
	iam id exploratumst. heia! sudabis satis
	si cum illo inceptas homine: ea eloquentiast.
630	verum pone esse victum eum. at tandem tamen
	non capitis eius res agitur sed pecuniae."
	postquam hominem his verbis sentio mollirier,

630 pone *codd. pl. Eugr.*, pono A

82

CHR Quite a lot.

GET Indeed. Have you heard what's happened to Antipho?

CHR The whole story.

GET (*to Demipho*) Did you tell him? (*to Chremes*) What a shocking business, Chremes, to have this going on behind your back!

CHR I was discussing it with him just now.

GET God knows, I've been giving it a lot of thought as well, and I think I've found a solution to the problem.

CHR What, Geta?

DEM What solution?

GET When I left you, I happened to run into Phormio.

CHR Who's Phormio?

DEM The fellow who got the girl—

CHR I know.

GET I thought I should test his view of the situation. I took him on one side. "Phormio," I said "why don't you see if we can settle this dispute amicably rather than with ill feeling? My master's a gentleman, and he's not keen on going to law. All the rest of his friends were unanimously urging him just now to throw the girl out on her ear."

ANT (*aside*) What's he up to? Where on earth is this leading?

GET "You may say that you'll have the force of the law on him if he turns her out. They've taken care of that. Come on now, you'll be in a fine sweat if you start anything with a man of his eloquence. And suppose he loses the case: at the end of the day it's not a matter of life and death for him, but only a fine."[45] Once I saw that he was being weakened by my argument, I went on: "We're alone

---

[45] Phormio, on the other hand, having no money to pay a fine, would be handed over to his creditor and lose his liberty (see note 33).

83

"soli sumus nunc hic," inquam "eho, quid vis dari
tibi in manum, ut erus his desistat litibus,

635   haec hinc facessat, tu molestus ne sies?"

ANT   satin illi di sunt propitii?

GET   "nam sat scio,
si tu aliquam partem aequi bonique dixeris,
ut est ille bonus vir, tria non commutabitis
verba hodie inter vos."

DEM   quis te istaec iussit loqui?

640 CHR   immo non potuit melius pervenirier
eo quo nos volumus.

ANT   occidi!

DEM   perge eloqui.

GET   a primo homo insanibat.

CHR   cedo, quid postulat?

GET   quid? nimium; quantum lubuit.

CHR   dic.

GET   si quis daret
talentum magnum—

DEM   immo malum hercle! ut nil pudet!

645 GET   quod dixi adeo ei: "quaeso, quid si filiam
suam unicam locaret? parvi retulit
non suscepisse. inventast quae dotem petat."
ut ad pauca redeam ac mittam illius ineptias,
haec denique eius fuit postrema oratio:

650   "ego" inquit "iam a principio amici filiam,
ita ut aequom fuerat, volui uxorem ducere.
nam mihi veniebat in mentem eius incommodum,
in servitutem pauperem ad ditem dari.
sed mi opus erat, ut aperte tibi nunc fabuler,

---

[46] The phrase *talentum magnum* ("large talent") refers to the Attic

84

here. Hey, how much do you want, cash in hand, for my master to forget about the lawsuit, the girl to take herself away from here, and you to stop causing any trouble?"

ANT   (*aside, aghast*) Have the gods deprived him of his wits?

GET   "For I'm quite sure that, if what you suggest is at all fair and reasonable, good man as he is, you won't need three words to complete the deal."

DEM   (*coldly*) Who gave you the authority to talk like that?

CHR   (*aside to Demipho*) No, there couldn't be a better way of getting what we want.

ANT   (*aside*) This is the end of me!

DEM   (*to Geta*) Go on, tell us the rest.

GET   At first the fellow was totally unreasonable.

CHR   Come on, what is he asking?

GET   What? Too much. He picked a sum out of the air.

CHR   Tell us.

GET   Suppose he was offered a talent—[46]

DEM   (*bridling*) A thrashing, more like, by god! Does he have no shame?

GET   Exactly what I said to him: "For heaven's sake, do you think he's marrying off his one and only daughter? It hasn't done him much good not to have raised a daughter of his own, if he's presented with another girl who needs a dowry." To cut the story short and to pass over his nonsense, this was his final argument: "Right from the beginning" he said "I intended to do the proper thing and marry my friend's daughter. I was conscious of the disadvantage to her of being married as a poor wife into slavery with a rich husband. But, to be quite frank with you, I

---

silver talent (of sixty minas), which had a wide currency in Hellenistic times. Unlike local currencies its weight was guaranteed.

655	aliquantulum quae afferret qui dissolverem
	quae debeo. et etiamnunc, si volt Demipho
	dare quantum ab hac accipio quae sponsast mihi,
	nullam mihi malim quam istanc uxorem dari."
ANT	utrum stultitia facere ego hunc an malitia
660	dicam, scientem an imprudentem, incertu' sum.
DEM	quid si animam debet?
GET	"ager oppositus pignori
	ob decem minas est."
DEM	age age, iam ducat: dabo.
GET	"aediculae etiam sunt ob decem alias."
DEM	oiei!
	nimiumst.
CHR	ne clama: repetito hasce a me decem.
665 GET	"uxori emunda ancillulast, tum pluscula
	supellectile opus est; opus est sumptu ad nuptias.
	his rebus pone sane" inquit "decem minas."
DEM	sescentas proinde scribito iam mihi dicas:
	nil do. impuratus me ille ut etiam irrideat?
670 CHR	quaeso, ego dabo, quiesce. tu modo filium
	fac ut illam ducat nos quam volumus.
ANT	ei mihi!
	Geta, occidisti me tuis fallaciis.
CHR	mea causa eicitur: me hoc est aequom amittere.
GET	"quantum potest me certiorem" inquit "face,
675	si illam dant, hanc ut mittam, ne incertus siem.
	nam illi mihi dotem iam constituerunt dare."

---

47 Literally, "owes his soul."   48 The total of thirty minas is exactly the sum required to buy Pamphila from the pimp (see line 557).

49 Literally, "six hundred," which is the Latin idiom for a large number.

86

needed a wife who could bring with her a bit of money to pay off my debts. And even now, if Demipho's willing to offer me as much as I'm getting from the girl I'm engaged to, there's no one I'd rather marry than your girl." (*nodding towards Demipho's house*)

ANT   (*aside*) I've no idea whether I should put this down to stupidity on his part or malice, whether it's deliberate or just thoughtless.

DEM   What if he's up to his ears in debt?[47]

GET   "There's a bit of land mortgaged for ten minas" he said.

DEM   All right, all right. Let him marry her straightaway. I'll pay up.

GET   "And there's a small cottage for another ten."

DEM   (*raising his voice*) Oh no! It's too much.

CHR   Don't shout. I'll refund you those ten.

GET   "I have to buy a little maid for my wife. And then I need a bit more furniture. And there are the expenses of the wedding. Say, if you will, another ten minas for the lot."[48]

DEM   He can bring hundreds[49] of lawsuits against me if he likes: I'm paying nothing. Is the filthy scoundrel to laugh at me as well?

CHR   Calm down, please. I'll pay it. You just make sure your son marries the girl we want him to.

ANT   (*aside*) Confound it! Geta, you've ruined me with your schemes.

CHR   (*to Demipho*) It's my fault she's being turned out: it's only fair that I should stand the loss.

GET   "Let me know as soon as possible if they're giving me the girl," he said, "so that I can break off with the other one and know where I stand. They've already agreed to hand over the dowry."

87

CHR   iam accipiat, illis repudium renuntiet,
      hanc ducat.
DEM   quae quidem illi res vortat male!
CHR   opportune adeo argentum nunc mecum attuli,
680   fructum quem Lemni uxoris reddunt praedia.
      ind' sumam; uxori tibi opus esse dixero.

IV. IV: ANTIPHO. GETA.

ANT   Geta!
GET   hem!
ANT   quid egisti?
GET   emunxi argento senes.
ANT   satin est id?
GET   nescio hercle. tantum iussu' sum.
ANT   eho, verbero, aliud mihi respondes ac rogo?
685 GET   quid ergo narras?
ANT   quid ego narrem? opera tua
      ad restim miquidem res redit planissume.
      ut tequidem omnes di deaeque, superi inferi,
      malis exemplis perdant! em, si quid velis,
      huic mandes, quod quidem recte curatum velis.
690   quid minus utibile fuit quam hoc ulcus tangere
      aut nominare uxorem? iniectast spes patri
      posse illam extrudi. cedo nunc porro: Phormio
      dotem si accipiet, uxor ducendast domum.
      quid fiet?
GET   non enim ducet.
ANT   novi. ceterum
695   quom argentum repetent, nostra causa scilicet
      in nervom potius ibit.

689 quod quidem recte curatum velis (= *Ad.* 372) *codd. pl.*, qui te ad
scopulum e tranquillo auferat *F²E*

88

CHR   (*to Demipho*) Let him have the money at once, tell them he's broken off the engagement, and marry this one.

DEM   And may it bring him nothing but misery!

CHR   As luck would have it, I've got the money with me now, the income from my wife's estates on Lemnos. I'll take it out of this, and tell my wife you needed it. (*they exit into Chremes' house*)

GETA *and* ANTIPHO *remain on stage.*

ANT   Geta!

GET   Yes?

ANT   What *have* you done?

GET   I've tricked the old men out of their money.

ANT   Is that all you've done?

GET   I don't know, for god's sake. It's all I was told to do.

ANT   Hey, you rogue, you're not answering my question!

GET   Well, what *are* you talking about?

ANT   What am I talking about? Without a shadow of doubt, thanks to you all that's left for me is the rope. May all the gods and goddesses in heaven and hell destroy you utterly! (*to the audience, ironically*) Look, if you want anything done, entrust it to him, that is, if you really want it seen to properly. (*to Geta*) What could have been more disastrous than to touch on that sore spot and mention my wife? You've encouraged my father to hope that she can be pushed out. And tell me the next step. If Phormio accepts the dowry, he has to marry her: what happens then?

GET   But he won't marry her.

ANT   (*with bitter irony*) Of course not. And, when they ask for the money back, I suppose he'll choose to go to jail for my sake.

89

GET   nil est, Antipho,
quin male narrando possit depravarier.
tu id quod bonist excerpis, dicis quod malist.
audi nunc contra. iam si argentum acceperit,
700   ducendast uxor, ut ais: concedo tibi.
spatium quidem tandem apparandi nuptias,
vocandi, sacruficandi dabitur paullulum.
interea amici quod polliciti sunt dabunt:
inde iste reddet.

ANT   quam ob rem? aut quid dicet?

GET   rogas?

705   "quot res postilla monstra evenerunt mihi!
introiit in aedis ater alienus canis;
anguis per impluvium decidit e tegulis;
gallina cecinit; interdixit hariolus;
haruspex vetuit; ante brumam autem novi
710   negoti incipere!" quae causast iustissuma.
haec fient.

ANT   ut modo fiant!

GET   fient: me vide.
pater exit. abi, dic esse argentum Phaedriae.

IV. V: DEMIPHO. CHREMES. GETA.

DEM   quietus esto, inquam. ego curabo ne quid verborum duit.
hoc temere numquam amittam ego a me quin mihi testis
      adhibeam.
715   quoi dem et quam ob rem dem commemorabo.

GET   ut cautus est ubi nil opust!

---

50 The *atrium* of a Roman house had a rectangular opening in the roof (*compluvium*) and a similarly shaped basin underneath to catch rainwater (*impluvium*). Here Terence is using *impluvium* to refer to the aperture (compare *The Eunuch* 589).

GET   There's nothing, Antipho, that can't be made worse in the telling. You're omitting the good things and mentioning only the bad. Now listen to the other side. Once he takes the money, he has to marry the girl, as you say: I grant you that. But there will after all be a breathing space while he prepares the wedding, invites the guests, and performs the sacrifices. Meanwhile Phaedria's friends will bring what they promised, and Phormio will pay back the money out of that.

ANT   But for what reason? What excuse will he give?

GET   What do you think? "The portents that have appeared to me since then! A strange black dog came into the house; a snake fell from the tiles through the skylight;[50] a hen crowed;[51] a soothsayer forbade the wedding; a diviner banned it. Fancy entering upon a new venture before the winter solstice!"—and that's a very good reason. It'll turn out all right.

ANT   If only it does!

GET   It will; trust me. (*as Chremes' door opens*) Your father's coming out. Go and tell Phaedria that we've got the money. (*Antipho exits right in the direction of the forum*)

Enter DEMIPHO *and* CHREMES *from Chremes' house.* DEMIPHO *is carrying a bag of money.*

DEM   Calm down, I tell you. I'll make sure he doesn't cheat us. I won't be so rash as to part with this money without having witnesses present. I shall make it clear who I am paying it to and for what purpose.

GET   (*aside*) How careful he is, when there's no need!

[51] According to Donatus this was an omen that the wife would outlive the husband.

CHR atque ita opus factost. et mature, dum lubido eadem haec
    manet.
    nam si altera illaec magis instabit, forsitan nos reiciat.
GET rem ipsam putasti.
DEM   duc me ad eum ergo.
GET   non moror.
CHR   ubi hoc egeris,
    transito ad uxorem meam, ut conveniat hanc prius quam
    hinc abit.
720 dicat eam dare nos Phormioni nuptum, ne suscenseat,
    et magis esse illum idoneum qui ipsi sit familiarior.
    nos nostro officio nil digressos esse; quantum is voluerit
    datum esse dotis.
DEM   quid tua, malum, id refert?
CHR   magni, Demipho.
    non sat est tuom te officium fecisse si non id fama appro-
    bat.
725 volo ipsius quoque voluntate haec fieri, ne se eiectam
    praedicet.
DEM idem ego istuc facere possum.
CHR   mulier mulieri magis convenit.
DEM rogabo.
CHR   ubi ego illas nunc reperire possim cogito.

ACTUS V

V. I: SOPHRONA. CHREMES.

SOPH quid agam? quem mi amicum inveniam misera? aut quoi
    consilia haec referam?
    aut unde auxilium petam?

726 convenit *A*, congruet Σ (*nisi* congruit *DG*)

CHR So you should. And hurry, while he's still in the mood. If the other girl puts more pressure on him, it's possible he may turn us down.

GET *(aside)* You've got it exactly!

DEM *(to Geta)* Take me to him, then.

GET I'm ready.

CHR When you've finished, come over to my wife and ask her to see the girl before she leaves. We don't want her to fly into a rage. Tell her to say we're giving her to Phormio to marry; he's a more suitable husband in that he's more one of the family. Also that we haven't neglected our duty, but have given him the dowry he asked for in full.

DEM What the hell does it matter to you?

CHR It matters a lot, Demipho. It's not enough to do your duty if popular opinion doesn't approve what you've done. I want this to be done with her own consent, so that she won't claim she was forced out.

DEM I can do that just as well myself.

CHR It's better woman to woman.

DEM I'll ask her. *(he exits right with Geta in the direction of the forum)*

CHR *(to himself)* I'm wondering where I can find the women now.[52]

ACT FIVE

Enter SOPHRONA from Demipho's house in an agitated state.

SOPH *(to herself)* What shall I do? Poor me, where can I find a friend? Who can I share my problems with? Who can I

[52] That is, his wife and daughter from Lemnos.

730   nam vereor era ne ob meum suasum indigne iniuria
           afficiatur.

      ita patrem adulescentis facta haec tolerare audio violen-
           ter.

CHR nam quae haec anus est exanimata a fratre quae egressast
           meo?

SOPH quod ut facerem egestas me impulit, quom scirem
           infirmas nuptias

      hasce esse, ut id consulerem, interea vita ut in tuto foret.

735 CHR certe edepol, nisi me animus fallit aut parum prospiciunt
           oculi,

      meae nutricem gnatae video.

SOPH   neque ille investigatur—

CHR   quid ago?

SOPH —quist pater eius.

CHR   adeo, maneo dum haec quae loquitur magis cognosco?

SOPH quodsi eum nunc reperire possim, nil est quod verear.

CHR   east ipsa.

      colloquar.

SOPH   quis hic loquitur?

CHR   Sophrona!

SOPH   et meum nomen nominat?

740 CHR respice ad me.

SOPH   di obsecro vos, estne hic Stilpo?

CHR   non.

SOPH   negas?

CHR concede hinc a foribus paullum istorsum sodes, Sophro-
           na.

      ne me istoc posthac nomine appellassis.

turn to for help? I'm afraid my mistress will get into terrible trouble from following my advice. From what I hear the young man's father is reacting very violently.

CHR *(aside)* Who's this old woman coming out of my brother's house in such a state?

SOPH It was poverty that drove me to it. I knew this wasn't a secure marriage, but I had to do something to protect her in the meantime.

CHR *(aside)* Good heavens, unless my memory is deceiving me or my eyes are failing, I'm sure it's my daughter's nurse.

SOPH And we can't track down—

CHR *(aside)* What do I do?

SOPH —that father of hers.

CHR *(aside)* Do I go up to her or wait until I get a clearer idea of what she's saying?

SOPH If only we could find him now, there would be nothing to worry about.

CHR *(aside)* It *is* her. I'll speak to her.

SOPH *(hearing him)* Who's that talking?

CHR Sophrona!

SOPH And calling me by name?

CHR Look at me.

SOPH *(turning round)* In the name of the gods, is it Stilpo?

CHR No.

SOPH *(going up to him)* Did you say no?

CHR Come away from the door a little, please, Sophrona, over there *(ushering her back from his own door towards Demipho's house)*. Don't you ever call me by that name again.

SOPH   quid? non, obsecro, es
        quem semper te esse dictitasti?

CHR   st!

SOPH   quid has metuis foras?

CHR   conclusam hic habeo uxorem saevam. verum istoc de no-
           mine,

745   eo perperam olim dixi ne vos forte imprudentes foris
          effutiretis atque id porro aliqua uxor mea resciceret.

SOPH   em, istoc pol nos te hic invenire miserae numquam po-
          tuimus.

CHR   eho, dic mihi quid rei tibist cum familia hac unde exis?
          ubi illae sunt?

SOPH   miseram me!

CHR   hem! quid est? vivontne?

SOPH   vivit gnata.

750   matrem ipsam ex aegritudine hac miseram mors conse-
          cutast.

CHR   male factum.

SOPH   ego autem, quae essem anus deserta, egens, ignota,
          ut potui, nuptum virginem locavi huic adulescenti
          harum quist dominus aedium.

CHR   Antiphonin?

SOPH   em istic ipsi.

CHR   quid? duasne uxores habet?

SOPH   au, obsecro, unam illequidem hanc solam.

755 CHR   quid illam alteram quae dicitur cognata?

SOPH   haec ergost.

CHR   quid ais?

SOPH Why? For goodness' sake, aren't you the person you always claimed to be?

CHR Shh!

SOPH Why *are* you afraid of that door?

CHR I have a fierce wife caged up in there. But about the name, I gave you a false one back then in case you should perhaps blurt it out inadvertently and my wife might somehow find out the truth.

SOS So that's why we poor things could never find you here, for heaven's sake!

CHR Hey, tell me, what's your connection with the house you've just come out of? Where are the others?[53]

SOS Oh dear!

CHR Oh, what's the matter? Are they still alive?

SOPH Your daughter is. Her poor mother passed away through all the anxiety you caused her.

CHR Bad news!

SOPH So I, being left on my own, a penniless old woman with no friends, did what I could and had the girl married to the young man who's master of this house here.

CHR (*incredulously*) To Antipho?

SOPH The very man.

CHR What? Does he have two wives?

SOPH Oh, for goodness' sake, *he* only has this one.

CHR What about the other girl, who's supposed to be a relative?

SOPH It's the same one.

CHR What are you saying?

---

[53] Another reference to his Lemnian wife and daughter.

SOPH composito factumst quo modo hanc amans habere posset
       sine dote.

CHR   di vostram fidem! quam saepe forte temere
       eveniunt quae non audeas optare! offendi adveniens
       quicum volebam et ut volebam collocatam gnatam.

760   quod nos ambo opere maxumo dabamus operam ut
         fieret,
       sine nostra cura, maxuma sua cura haec sola fecit.

SOPH nunc quid opus facto sit vide. pater adulescentis venit
       eumque animo iniquo hoc oppido ferre aiunt.

CHR   nil periclist.
       sed per deos atque homines meam esse hanc cave rescis-
         cat quisquam.

765 SOPH nemo ex me scibit.

CHR   sequere me. intus cetera audietis.

V. II: DEMIPHO. GETA.

DEM nostrapte culpa facimus ut malis expediat esse,
       dum nimium dici nos bonos studemus et benignos.
       ita fugias ne praeter casam, quod aiunt. nonne id sat erat
       accipere ab illo iniuriam? etiam argentumst ultro obiec-
         tum,

770   ut sit qui vivat dum aliud aliquid flagiti conficiat.

GET   planissume.

759 conlocatam gnatam *Faernus*, conlocatam filiam Σ *Prisc.*, con-
locatam amari *A*, filiam locatam *Bentley*   761 haec sola Σ *Don.*,
solus *A¹*, hic *Don. in comm.*   765 audietis *Weise*, audies *codd.*,
audiemus *Bentley*, *omittunt edd. nonn.*

---

[54] That is, without any fuss or scandal.

[55] Literally, "don't flee past the house," evidently a proverbial ex-

SOPH It was all arranged so that her lover could have her without a dowry.

CHR Heaven help us! How often things come to pass purely by chance which you wouldn't dare to hope for! I come home and find my daughter given in marriage to the man I wanted and in the way I wanted![54] What we two were working our hardest to bring about, she has achieved all by herself by her own effort without any help from us!

SOPH Now think what needs to be done. The young man's father has arrived, and they say he's very annoyed at the situation.

CHR There's nothing to worry about. But, in the name of gods and men, make sure that nobody discovers she's my daughter.

SOPH Nobody will find out from me.

CHR Come with me. I'll tell you the rest inside. (*they exit into Demipho's house, leaving the stage empty*)

Enter DEMIPHO *and* GETA *right from the direction of the forum.*

DEM We've only ourselves to blame if dishonesty pays, while we're so keen to maintain a reputation for honesty and kindness. When on the run, make for home, as the saying goes.[55] Wasn't it enough for us to be tricked by this fellow, without throwing him money as well to live on until his next outrageous scheme?

GET Undoubtedly.

pression, which Donatus interprets as meaning "don't run straight past your place of refuge." This does not seem particularly apt for Demipho's situation: something like "Don't jump from the frying pan into the fire" would be more appropriate.

DEM	eis nunc praemiumst qui recta prava faciunt.
GET	verissume.
DEM	ut stultissume quidem illi rem gesserimus.
GET	modo ut hoc consilio possiet discedi, ut istam ducat.
DEM	etiamne id dubiumst?
GET	haud scio hercle, ut homost, an mutet animum.
775 DEM	hem! mutet autem?
GET	nescio. verum, si forte, dico.
DEM	ita faciam, ut frater censuit, ut uxorem eius huc addu-
	cam,
	cum ista ut loquatur. tu, Geta, abi prae, nuntia hanc ven-
	turam.
GET	argentum inventumst Phaedriae, de iurgio siletur,
	provisumst ne in praesentia haec hinc abeat: quid nunc
	porro?
780	quid fiet? in eodem luto haesitas. vorsuram solves,
	Geta. praesens quod fuerat malum in diem abiit. plagae
	crescunt,
	nisi prospicis. nunc hinc domum ibo ac Phanium docebo
	ne quid vereatur Phormionem aut eius orationem.

V. III: DEMIPHO. NAUSISTRATA.

DEM	agedum, ut soles, Nausistrata, fac illa ut placetur nobis,
785	ut sua voluntate id quod est faciundum faciat.
NAU	faciam.

---

56 Literally, "you'll be paying off a borrowing," another proverbial
expression: the sense appears to be "you'll have to borrow to pay off
your previous loan," that is, "you'll be in even worse trouble than be-
fore."

DEM These days the prize goes to those who turn right into wrong.

GET Exactly.

DEM We've been absolute fools in the way we've handled this business.

GET Always supposing the end result of your scheme is that he marries her.

DEM Is that still in doubt?

GET I don't know, for god's sake. Being the man he is, he could well change his mind.

DEM Really! Change his mind?

GET I don't know. I'm just raising the possibility.

DEM I'll do as my brother suggested and fetch his wife over to talk to the girl. You go ahead, Geta, and warn them that she's coming. (*he exits into Chremes' house, leaving Geta on stage alone*)

GET (*to himself*) We've found the money for Phaedria, there's nothing about a lawsuit, and we've arranged things so that the girl can stay for the present. But what of the future? What's going to happen? You're stuck in the same mud, Geta. You're putting off the evil day.[56] The immediate trouble has been postponed, but the beatings are multiplying if you don't look out. Now I'll go home and explain to Phanium that she's not to be afraid of Phormio or anything he says. (*he exits into Demipho's house*)

Enter DEMIPHO *from Chremes' house with* NAUSISTRATA.

DEM Come now, Nausistrata, employ your usual tact and win her over to our point of view, so that she does what she has to do of her own free will.

NAU All right.

101

DEM	pariter nunc opera me adiuves ac re dudum opitulata's.
NAU	factum volo. ac pol minus queo viri culpa quam me dignumst.
DEM	quid autem?
NAU	quia pol mei patris bene parta indiligenter tutatur. nam ex eis praediis talenta argenti bina
790	statim capiebat. vir viro quid praestat!
DEM	bina, quaeso?
NAU	ac rebus vilioribus multo tamen duo talenta.
DEM	hui!
NAU	quid haec videntur?
DEM	scilicet—
NAU	virum me natam vellem. ego ostenderem—
DEM	certe scio.
NAU	—quo pacto—
DEM	parce, sodes, ut possis cum illa, ne te adulescens mulier defetiget.
795 NAU | faciam ut iubes. sed meum virum abs te abire video. |

NAUSISTRATA. CHREMES. DEMIPHO.

CHR	ehem, Demipho! iam illi datumst argentum?
DEM	curavi ilico.
CHR	nollem datum. ei! video uxorem. paene plus quam sat erat.
DEM	quor nolles, Chreme?
CHR	iam recte.

---

57 Apparently a back reference to line 681.
58 That is, the estates on Lemnos (see line 680).

DEM Do help me now with your good services as you sup-
ported me before with your money.[57]

NAU You're welcome. Heaven knows, it's my husband's fault
that I can't help you as much as I should.

DEM How so?

NAU Because he looks after my father's carefully acquired
property so carelessly, for heaven's sake. *He* used to get in
two talents of silver regularly from those estates.[58] How
one man differs from another!

DEM (*astounded*) Two talents, did you say?

NAU Two talents, even though things were much cheaper
then.

DEM Wow!

NAU What do you think about it?

DEM Evidently—

NAU (*angrily*) I wish I'd been born a man. I'd show him—

DEM I'm quite sure you would.

NAU —how—

DEM Please spare yourself, so that you can deal with her. She's
a young woman and she may tire you out.

NAU I'll take your advice. But there's my husband coming out
of your house.

Enter CHREMES *from Demipho's house.*

CHR (*to Demipho, excitedly*) Oh Demipho! Have you given
him the money yet?

DEM I saw to it at once.

CHR I wish you hadn't. (*aside, seeing Nausistrata*) Oh dear! It's
my wife. I nearly said too much.

DEM Why not, Chremes?

CHR It doesn't matter now.

103

DEM   quid tu? ecquid locutu's cum istac quam ob
      rem hanc ducimus?

CHR   transegi.

DEM   quid ait tandem?

CHR   abduci non potest.

DEM   qui non potest?

800   CHR   quia uterque utriquest cordi.

DEM   quid istuc nostra?

CHR   magni. praeterhac
      cognatam comperi esse nobis.

DEM   quid? deliras.

CHR   sic erit.
      non temere dico. redii mecum in memoriam.

DEM   satin sanus es?

NAU   au obsecro, vide ne in cognatam pecces.

DEM   non est.

CHR   ne nega.
      patris nomen aliud dictumst: hoc tu errasti.

DEM   non norat patrem?

805   CHR   norat.

DEM   quor aliud dixit?

CHR   numquamne hodie concedes mihi
      neque intelleges?

DEM   si tu nil narras?

CHR   perdis.

NAU   miror quid hoc siet.

DEM   equidem hercle nescio.

CHR   vin scire? at ita me servet Iuppiter,
      ut propior illi quam ego sum ac tu homo nemost.

DEM   di vostram fidem!

DEM What about you? Have you explained to the girl why we're bringing *her* over? (*indicating Nausistrata*)

CHR It's all arranged.

DEM What does she say, if I may ask?

CHR We can't send her away.

DEM Why not?

CHR Because they're very fond of each other.

DEM What's that matter to us?

CHR It matters a great deal. Anyway, I've discovered she's related to us.

DEM What! You're crazy.

CHR You'll see. I'm not just making it up. I've remembered.

DEM Are you in your right mind?

NAU (*butting in*) Oh for goodness' sake, don't go wronging a relative.

DEM She's not a relative.

CHR Don't you be so sure. They got her father's name wrong: that's what misled you.

DEM She didn't know her father?

CHR She did.

DEM So why did she get the name wrong?

CHR (*whispering*) Won't you ever leave off? Won't you try to understand?

DEM (*aside to Chremes*) Not if you talk nonsense.

CHR (*aside to Demipho*) You'll be the death of me.

NAU (*puzzled*) I wonder what this is all about.

DEM God knows, I haven't the slightest idea.

CHR (*to Demipho*) Do you want to know? As Jupiter is my witness, nobody's as closely related to her as you and me.

DEM Heaven help us! Let's go and see her. I want us all to find

eamus ad ipsam. una omnis nos aut scire aut nescire hoc
volo.

CHR   ah!

810 DEM quid est?

CHR   itan parvam mihi fidem esse apud te?

DEM   vin me credere?

vin satis quaesitum mi istuc esse? age, fiat. quid illa filia
amici nostri? quid futurumst?

CHR   recte.

DEM   hanc igitur mittimus?

CHR quidni?

DEM   illa maneat?

CHR   sic.

DEM   ire igitur tibi licet, Nausistrata.

NAU sic pol commodius esse in omnis arbitror quam ut coepe-
ras,

815 manere hanc. nam perliberalis visast, quom vidi, mihi.

DEM quid istuc negotist?

CHR   iamne operuit ostium?

DEM   iam.

CHR   o Iuppiter!

di nos respiciunt. gnatam inveni nuptam cum tuo filio.

DEM   hem!

quo pacto potuit?

CHR   non satis tutus est ad narrandum hic locus.

DEM at tu intro abi.

CHR   heus, ne filii quidem hoc nostri resciscant volo.

V. IV: ANTIPHO.

820 ANT laetus sum, utut meae res sese habent, fratri obtigisse
quod volt.

out together whether this is true or not. (*he moves to-wards his door*)

CHR (*checking him*) No!

DEM What's the matter?

CHR Do you have so little faith in me?

DEM You want me to take your word for it? You want me to re-gard the matter as closed? All right, so be it. What about our friend's daughter? What's to become of her?

CHR It's all right.

DEM So we let her go?

CHR Of course.

DEM And the other one stays?

CHR Yes.

DEM (*to Nausistrata*) You can go then, Nausistrata.

NAU Well, I think this is much better for all of us than what you started with, I mean letting her stay. I thought her a very ladylike girl, when I first saw her. (*she exits into Chremes' house*)

DEM (*to Chremes*) What's this all about?

CHR Has she shut the door yet?

DEM Yes, she has.

CHR By Jupiter, the gods are looking after us. I've found my daughter married to your son.

DEM (*in amazement*) What! How could she be?

CHR This isn't a very safe place to tell you.

DEM Well, go inside, then.

CHR Listen, I don't want even our sons to find out the truth. (*they exit into Demipho's house, leaving the stage empty*)

Enter ANTIPHO *right from the direction of the forum.*

ANT (*to himself*) Whatever my own situation, I'm delighted that my cousin has got what he wants. How wise it is to

quam scitumst eius modi in animo parare cupiditates
quas, quom res advorsae sient, paullo mederi possis!
hic simul argentum repperit, cura sese expedivit.
ego nullo possum remedio me evolvere ex his turbis

825 quin, si hoc celetur, in metu, sin patefit, in probro sim.
neque me domum nunc reciperem ni mi esset spes
    ostenta
huiusce habendae. sed ubinam Getam invenire possim,
    ut
rogem quod tempus conveniundi patris me capere iu-
    beat?

V. V: PHORMIO. ANTIPHO.

PHO argentum accepi, tradidi lenoni, abduxi mulierem,
830   curavi propria ut Phaedria poteretur. nam emissast
        manu.
        nunc una mihi res etiam restat quaest conficiunda, otium
        ab senibus ad potandum ut habeam. nam aliquot hos su-
        mam dies.
ANT sed Phormiost. quid ais?
PHO   quid?
ANT   quidnam nunc facturust Phaedria?
        quo pacto satietatem amoris ait se velle absumere?
835 PHO vicissim partis tuas acturus est.
ANT   quas?
PHO   ut fugitet patrem.
        te suas rogavit rursum ut ageres, causam ut pro se dice-
        res.
        nam potaturus est apud me. ego me ire senibus Sunium
        dicam ad mercatum, ancillulam emptum dudum quam
        dixit Geta,

entertain desires that can easily be cured when things go wrong! *He* escaped from *his* worries as soon as he acquired the money, whereas I have no way of extricating myself from my troubles: I'm in terror if my secret's kept, and in disgrace if it's revealed. I wouldn't be coming home now if I hadn't been led to hope that I could keep my wife. But where can I find Geta to ask him to suggest the best time to approach my father?

Enter PHORMIO *right from the direction of the forum.*

PHO (*to himself*) I got the money, paid the pimp, took the girl away,[59] and made sure that Phaedria can have her all to himself; she's now a free woman.[60] Now I've only one more thing to do, get away from the old men to do some drinking. I'm going to take a few days off.

ANT (*to himself*) It's Phormio. (*to Phormio*) Well then?

PHO What?

ANT What's Phaedria going to do now? How does he propose to take his fill of love?

PHO He's going to adopt your role.

ANT What role?

PHO Running away from his father. He asks you to play his role in turn, and plead his cause; he's coming to my place for some drinking. I'll tell the old men I'm going to Sunium[61] to the market to buy the maid Geta was talking of just

[59] This passage rather contradicts the impression given earlier (line 484) that Dorio's house is onstage: we have not seen Phormio paying him or collecting the girl. [60] The Latin *emissast manu* refers to the formal process of manumission by which slaves were granted their freedom. [61] This village at the southern tip of Attica, about 25 miles from Athens, was evidently known for its slave market.

		ne quom hic non videant me conficere credant argentum suom.

840   sed ostium concrepuit abs te.

ANT   vide quis egreditur.

PHO   Getast.

V. VI: GETA. PHORMIO. ANTIPHO.

GET   o Fortuna, o Fors Fortuna, quantis commoditatibus

quam subito meo ero Antiphoni ope vostra hunc onerastis diem—

ANT   quidnam hic sibi volt?

GET   —nosque amicos eius exonerastis metu!

sed ego nunc mihi cesso qui non umerum hunc onero pallio

845   atque hominem propero invenire, ut haec quae contigerint sciat?

ANT   num tu intellegis quid hic narret?

PHO   num tu?

ANT   nil.

PHO   tantundem ego.

GET   ad lenonem hinc ire pergam. ibi nunc sunt.

ANT   heus, Geta!

GET   em tibi!

num mirum aut novomst revocari, cursum quom institeris?

ANT   Geta!

---

[62] The emergence of a character from a stage house in comedy is regularly preceded by a reference to the noise made by the door opening, caused presumably by the rattling of the bolts or the creaking of the hinges.

[63] Fortuna and Fors Fortuna were worshipped at Rome as two dis-

110

now. I don't want them to think, if they don't see me around, that I'm just squandering their money. (*as the door of Demipho's house opens*) But I heard your door.[62]

ANT See who's coming out.

PHO It's Geta.

Enter GETA *from Demipho's house in an excited state.*

GET (*to himself*) O Fortune, O Lucky Fortune,[63] what a heap of unforeseen blessings you have bestowed with bounteous hand on my master Antipho today!

ANT (*to Phormio*) What on earth does he mean?

GET And what a heap of anxiety you have removed from us his friends! But why don't I throw my cloak over my shoulder,[64] and run and find him to tell him what has happened?

ANT (*to Phormio*) Do you understand what he's saying?

PHO (*to Antipho*) Do you?

ANT (*to Phormio*) Not a bit.

PHO (*to Antipho*) Me neither.

GET I'll go on to the pimp's; that's where they are. (*he turns to go*)

ANT (*calling him*) Hey, Geta!

GET (*not turning round*) Listen to that! Typical and predictable! As soon as you start to go, you're called back.

ANT Geta!

tinct divinities. Donatus explains that Fortuna was the goddess of uncertainty, Fors Fortuna the goddess of good luck.

[64] This was the typical practice of "running slaves" in comedy: compare Plautus, *The Captives* 778–779: "Now I've decided to imitate the slaves of comedy: I will throw my *pallium* around my neck, so that he shall hear this news from me first."

GET   pergit hercle! numquam tu odio tuo me vinces.

ANT   non manes?

850   GET   vapula.

ANT   id quidem tibi iam fiet nisi resistis, verbero!

GET   familiariorem oportet esse hunc; minitatur malum.

        sed isne est quem quaero an non? ipsust: congredere ac-
            tutum.

ANT   quid est?

GET   omnium quantumst qui vivont hominum homo ornatis-
            sume!

        nam sine controversia ab dis solus diligere, Antipho.

855   ANT   ita velim. sed qui istuc credam ita esse mihi dici velim.

GET   satine est si te delibutum gaudio reddo?

ANT   enicas.

PHO   quin tu hinc pollicitationes aufer et quod fers cedo.

GET   oh!

        tu quoque aderas, Phormio?

PHO   aderam. sed tu cessas.

GET   accipe: em!

        ut modo argentum tibi dedimus apud forum, recta do-
            mum

860   sumus profecti. interea mittit erus me ad uxorem tuam.

ANT   quam ob rem?

GET   omitto proloqui. nam nil ad hanc remst, Antipho.

        ubi in gynaeceum ire occipio, puer ad me accurrit Mida,

        pone reprendit pallio, resupinat. respicio, rogo

        quam ob rem retineat me. ait esse vetitum intro ad eram
            accedere.

---

[65] In a Greek house, the women's quarters were at the back, sepa-
rate from the men's.

GET There he goes again! (*aloud*) You'll never get your way by being unpleasant. (*he turns to go again*)

ANT Wait!

GET Get yourself thrashed!

ANT That's what you'll get if you don't stop, you scoundrel!

GET He must be someone I know; he's threatening to punish me. But is it the man I'm looking for or not? (*looking round*) It's the very man. (*to Antipho*) Quick, come here!

ANT What's this about?

GET You are the most blessed of all living men! Beyond all argument you are the one man who is loved by the gods, Antipho.

ANT I wish I were. But I'd like to be told why I should believe it.

GET Is it enough if I drown you in joy?

ANT You're trying my patience.

PHO (*stepping forward, to Geta*) Why don't you stop all this promising and tell us the news?

GET (*seeing Phormio*) Oh! You're here too, Phormio!

PHO Yes, I am. But you're wasting time.

GET All right, here you are. After we handed you the money in the forum, we set off straight home. (*to Antipho*) Presently my master sent me to fetch your wife.

ANT What for?

GET I'm dispensing with the preamble; it's not relevant to the matter in hand, Antipho. When I was just going into the women's quarters,[65] the slave boy Mida ran up to me, tugged at my cloak from behind, and pulled me back. I turned round and asked him why he was stopping me. He said that nobody was allowed in to see the mistress.

113

865 "Sophrona modo fratrem huc" inquit "senis introduxit
Chremem"

eumque nunc esse intus cum illis. hoc ubi ego audivi, ad
fores

suspenso gradu placide ire perrexi, accessi, astiti,

animam compressi, aurem admovi. ita animum coepi at-
tendere,

hoc modo sermonem captans.

PHO eu, Geta!

GET hic pulcherrumum

870 facinus audivi. itaque paene hercle exclamavi gaudio.

ANT quod?

GET quodnam arbitrare?

ANT nescio.

GET atqui mirificissumum.

patruos tuos est pater inventus Phanio uxori tuae.

ANT hem!

quid ais?

GET cum eius consuevit olim matre in Lemno clanculum.

PHO somnium! utine haec ignoraret suom patrem?

GET aliquid credito,

875 Phormio, esse causae. sed censen me potuisse omnia

intellegere extra ostium intus quae inter sese ipsi ege-
rint?

ANT atque ego quoque inaudivi hercle illam fabulam.

GET immo etiam dabo

quo magis credas. patruos interea inde huc egreditur
foras.

haud multo post cum patre idem recipit se intro denuo.

880 ait uterque tibi potestatem eius adhibendae dari.

denique ego sum missus te ut requirerem atque adduce-
rem.

114

"Sophrona has just brought in the old man's brother Chremes," he said "and he's now in there with them." When I heard that, I continued towards the doors on tip-toe without making a sound. I reached them, stood still, held my breath, and listened. I strained my ears like this (*cupping his ear*), trying to catch their conversation.

PHO Well done, Geta!

GET And then I heard the most glorious news. God knows, I nearly cried out for joy.

ANT What was it?

GET What do you think?

ANT I've no idea.

GET Well, it's the most marvellous news. Your uncle has been recognised as your wife's father.

ANT What! What are you saying?

GET He had a secret affair with her mother on Lemnos long ago.

PHO You're dreaming! So she didn't know her own father?

GET You can be sure there's an explanation, Phormio. You can't expect me to have picked up everything they were discussing inside from outside the door.

ANT (*aside*) For god's sake, I heard something about that story too.

GET And here's something else which will convince you. Presently your uncle came outside here, and soon after that he went back in again with your father. They both said you were given permission to have her as your wife. And lastly I was sent to find you and take you to them.

---

[877] *sic Fleckeisen*, hercle *om. A*, atque hercle ego illam audivi fabulam Σ

ANT   quin ergo rape me. quid cessas?

GET   fecero.

ANT   o mi Phormio,
vale.

PHO   vale, Antipho. bene, ita me di ament, factum. gaudeo.

V. VII: PHORMIO.

PHO   tantam fortunam de improviso esse his datam!

885   summa eludendi occasiost mihi nunc senes
et Phaedriae curam adimere argentariam,
ne quoiquam suorum aequalium supplex siet.
nam idem hoc argentum, ita ut datumst, ingratiis
ei datum erit. hoc qui cogam re ipsa repperi.

890   nunc gestus mihi voltusque est capiundus novos.
sed hinc concedam in angiportum hoc proxumum.
inde hisce ostendam me, ubi erunt egressi foras.
quo me assimularam ire ad mercatum, non eo.

V. VIII: DEMIPHO. CHREMES. PHORMIO.

DEM   dis magnas merito gratias habeo atque ago,

895   quando evenere haec nobis, frater, prospere.
quantum potest nunc conveniundust Phormio,
priusquam dilapidat nostras triginta minas,
ut auferamus.

PHO   Demiphonem si domist
visam ut quod—

DEM   at nos ad te ibamus, Phormio.

900 PHO   de eadem hac fortasse causa?

DEM   ita hercle.

PHO   credidi.
quid ad me ibatis?

882 o mi Σ, heus A

ANT   Well then, take me in quickly! What are you waiting for?

GET   At once.

ANT   Well, my dear Phormio, goodbye.

PHO   Goodbye, Antipho. Heaven help me, it's good news. I'm delighted. (*Geta escorts Antipho into Demipho's house*)

PHORMIO is left onstage alone.

PHO   (*to himself*) What an unexpected stroke of luck for them! Now I have the perfect opportunity to fool the old men and relieve Phaedria's financial worries, so he won't need to go begging to any of his friends. This sum of money, now that it's been handed over, will be his to keep, whether they like it or not. I've found a way to force their hand, given the situation. Now I must put on a new face and change my role. But I'll withdraw into this nearby alley, and appear to them from there when they come out. I'm cancelling my pretended trip to the market. (*he exits right*)

Enter DEMIPHO and CHREMES from Demipho's house.

DEM   I'm very grateful to the gods, brother, for the success of our venture, and I pay them the thanks that are due. Now we must meet Phormio as soon as possible, to get back our thirty minas before he squanders them.

PHO   (*entering right, as if from the forum, and pretending not to see them*) I'm coming to see if Demipho's at home, so that—

DEM   But we were coming to see you, Phormio.

PHO   About the same business, perhaps?

DEM   Yes indeed.

PHO   I thought so. Why were you coming to see me?

117

	DEM	ridiculum!
	PHO	verebamini

   ne non id facerem quod recepissem semel?
   heus, quanta quanta haec mea paupertas est, tamen
   adhuc curavi unum hoc quidem, ut mi esset fides.

905 CHR estne ita uti dixi liberalis?

   DEM   oppido.

   PHO idque ad vos venio nuntiatum, Demipho,
   paratum me esse. ubi voltis, uxorem date.
   nam omnis posthabui mihi res, ita uti par fuit,
   postquam id tanto opere vos velle animum advorteram.

910 DEM at hic dehortatus est me ne illam tibi darem.
   "nam qui erit rumor populi" inquit "si id feceris?
   olim quom honeste potuit, tum non est data.
   eam nunc extrudi turpest." ferme eadem omnia
   quae tute dudum coram me incusaveras.

915 PHO satis superbe illuditis me.

   DEM   qui?

   PHO   rogas?

   quia ne alteram quidem illam potero ducere.
   nam quo redibo ore ad eam quam contempserim?

   CHR "tum autem Antiphonem video ab sese amittere
   invitum eam" inque.

   DEM   tum autem video filium

920 invitum sane mulierem ab se amittere.
   sed transi sodes ad forum atque illud mihi
   argentum rursum iube rescribi, Phormio.

---

905 *sic Σ, personas invertit A*
913 eam nunc extrudi *A*, nunc viduam extrudi Σ

DEM   Don't be absurd!

PHO   Were you afraid that, once I'd given an undertaking, I wouldn't stand by it? Listen, however poor I may be, I've always taken care to be a man of my word.

CHR   (*ironically*) Isn't he the perfect gentleman, just as I said?

DEM   Absolutely.

PHO   And so I've come, Demipho, to announce that I'm ready. You can hand over my bride as soon as you like. I've put off all my other business, as was only proper once I'd realised you were so set on the marriage.

DEM   But he's persuaded me (*indicating Chremes*) not to give you the girl. "What will people say," he said "if you do this? Before, when you could have given her away honourably, you didn't. It would be a scandal to push her out now." He raised more or less the same objections as you did just now when we were talking.[66]

PHO   You're making a fool of me in a pretty high-handed way.

DEM   How do you mean?

PHO   As if you didn't know! Because I won't be able to marry the other girl either. How am I going to go back and face her, after treating her with such contempt?

CHR   (*to Demipho, in a whisper*) Say "Besides, I find that Antipho is unwilling to part with her."

DEM   Besides, I find that my son is unwilling to part with the girl. But come over to the forum, if you will, Phormio, and have the money returned to my account.

---

[66] See lines 413–417.

PHO quodne ego discripsi porro illis quibus debui?

DEM quid igitur fiet?

PHO   si vis mi uxorem dare

925   quam despondisti, ducam. sin est ut velis
manere illam apud te, dos hic maneat, Demipho.
nam non est aequom me propter vos decipi,
quom ego vostri honoris causa repudium alterae
remiserim, quae dotis tantundem dabat.

930 DEM in' hinc malam rem cum istac magnificentia,
fugitive? etiamnunc credis te ignorarier
aut tua facta adeo?

PHO   irritor.

DEM   tune hanc duceres
si tibi daretur?

PHO   fac periclum.

DEM   ut filius
cum illa habitet apud te? hoc vostrum consilium fuit?

935 PHO quaeso, quid narras?

DEM   quin tu mi argentum cedo.

PHO immo vero uxorem tu cedo.

DEM   in ius ambula.

PHO enimvero si porro esse odiosi pergitis—

DEM quid facies?

PHO   egone? vos me indotatis modo
patrocinari fortasse arbitramini.

940   etiam dotatis soleo.

CHR   quid id nostra?

937 in ius? *ante* enimvero *codd, secludunt edd.*

---

67 The implication of the technical language (*rescribere, discribere*)
is that there were bankers in the forum who operated accounts on be-

PHO   You mean the money I've already transferred to my creditors?[67]

DEM   What shall we do, then?

PHO   If you wish me to marry the woman you promised to me, I'll marry her. But if it's the case that you want her to stay with you, the dowry stays with me, Demipho. It's not right for me to lose out on your account, when it was out of regard for you that I broke off my engagement with the other woman, who was offering me a dowry of the same amount.

DEM   You go to hell, you and your arrogant airs, you vagabond! Do you still think we don't know you or your ways of behaving?

PHO   You're provoking me.

DEM   Would you marry her if she was given to you?

PHO   Try me.

DEM   So that my son could live with her in your house? Was that your scheme?

PHO   Excuse me, what did you say?

DEM   Just you hand over the money.

PHO   No, just you hand over the bride.

DEM   (*laying a hand on him*) Come with me to court.

PHO   (*freeing himself*) Really, if you are going to persist in being so unpleasant—(*he turns away*)

DEM   What will you do?

PHO   Me? Perhaps you think I only champion the cause of undowried women. I also do dowried ones.

CHR   What's that to us?

half of their clients. Banking was relatively new at Rome in the days of Plautus and Terence, though there were sophisticated financial systems at Athens in the time of New Comedy.

PHO   nihil.
hic quandam noram quoius vir uxorem—

CHR   hem!

DEM   quid est?

PHO   —Lemni habuit aliam—

CHR   nullus sum!

PHO   —ex qua filiam
suscepit, et eam clam educat.

CHR   sepultus sum!

PHO   haec adeo ego illi iam denarrabo.

CHR   obsecro,

945   ne facias.

PHO   oh! tune is eras?

DEM   ut ludos facit!

CHR   missum te facimus.

PHO   fabulae!

CHR   quid vis tibi?
argentum quod habes condonamus te.

PHO   audio.
quid vos, malum, ergo me sic ludificamini
inepti vostra puerili sententia?

950   nolo, volo; volo, nolo rursum; cape, cedo;
quod dictum indictumst; quod modo erat ratum irri-
    tumst.

CHR   quo pacto aut unde hic haec rescivit?

DEM   nescio,
nisi me dixisse nemini certe scio.

CHR   monstri, ita me di ament, simile.

PHO   inieci scrupulum.

---

949 sententia *codd.*, inconstantia *Bentley edd. nonn.*

PHO   (*with a shrug of the shoulders*) Nothing. I knew a woman
here whose husband had another—

CHR   (*alarmed*) What!

DEM   (*to Chremes*) What's the matter?

PHO   —wife on Lemnos—

CHR   I'm done for!

PHO   —by whom he had a daughter, whom he's brought up in
secret.

CHR   I'm dead and buried!

PHO   This is the news I'm just about to break to her.

CHR   (*in despair*) I implore you, don't do it!

PHO   (*innocently*) Oh! Was it you?

DEM   (*aside*) How he's making fun of us!

CHR   We'll let you off.

PHO   Nonsense!

CHR   What do you want? We'll let you keep the money you
have.

PHO   I note your offer. (*changing his tone*) So why the hell
are you two making fun of me in this silly way with your
puerile attitudes? I will, I won't; I won't, I will again; take
it, give it back; what was said is unsaid; what was agreed
before is cancelled. (*he walks away*)

CHR   (*whispering, to Demipho*) How did he find this out? Who
from?

DEM   (*to Chremes*) I don't know. Only I'm quite sure I've told
nobody.

CHR   (*to Demipho*) Heaven help me, it's unnatural!

PHO   (*aside*) That's put a stone in their shoe.[68]

---

[68] An idiomatic expression that is found also in *The Brothers* (line
228).

123

DEM   hem!

955   hicine ut a nobis hoc tantum argenti auferat
     tam aperte irridens? emori hercle satius est.
     animo virili praesentique ut sis para.
     vides tuom peccatum esse elatum foras
     neque iam id celare posse te uxorem tuam.
960   nunc quod ipsa ex aliis auditura sit, Chreme,
     id nosmet indicare placabilius est.
     tum hunc impuratum poterimus nostro modo
     ulcisci.

PHO   attat! nisi mi prospicio, haereo.
     hi gladiatorio animo ad me affectant viam.

965 CHR   at vereor ut placari possit.

DEM   bono animo's.
     ego redigam vos in gratiam, hoc fretus, Chreme,
     quom e medio excessit unde haec susceptast tibi.

PHO   itane agitis mecum? satis astute aggredimini.
     non hercle ex re istius me instigasti, Demipho.

970   ain tu? ubi quae lubitum fuerit peregre feceris
     neque huius sis veritus feminae primariae
     quin novo modo ei faceres contumeliam,
     venias nunc precibus lautum peccatum tuom?
     hisce ego illam dictis ita tibi incensam dabo
975   ut ne restinguas lacrumis si exstillaveris.

DEM   malum quod isti di deaeque omnes duint!
     tantane affectum quemquam esse hominem audacia!
     non hoc publicitus scelus hinc asportarier
     in solas terras!

CHR   in id redactus sum loci

DEM   (*angrily*) Hey, is he going to make off with all that money and laugh in our faces? By god, I'd rather die! Now show yourself a man and keep your wits about you. As you can see, your misconduct's out, and you can't hide it from your wife any longer. In this situation you're more likely to win her over if we tell her ourselves what she is going to hear from others. Then we'll be able to pay this filthy scoundrel back in our own way.

PHO   (*aside*) Help! If I don't look out, I'm cornered! These two are coming for me like gladiators![69]

CHR   But I'm afraid she can't be won over.

DEM   Don't worry! I'll arrange a reconciliation on the basis that the woman who bore your child has passed away.

PHO   (*returning to them*) Is this how you're going to deal with me? A pretty cunning plan of attack! (*to Demipho*) By god, you haven't done *him* much good (*pointing to Chremes*) by provoking me, Demipho. (*to Chremes*) Answer me. When you took your pleasure overseas and had no scruples about insulting your excellent wife in this unheard of way, do you now come with prayers to wash away your sins? I'll incense her so much by what I'm going to tell her that you won't be able to put out the fire even if you dissolve into tears.

DEM   May all the gods and goddesses damn him! How can a man be possessed of such effrontery? The villain should be deported to some deserted land at public expense.

CHR   (*to Demipho*) I'm reduced to such a state that I have no idea at all what to do.

---

[69] That is, desperately, as Donatus explains. The reference to gladiators, which were unknown in Athens, is a rare Roman allusion on Terence's part.

980   ut quid agam cum illo nesciam prorsum.

DEM   ego scio.

in ius eamus.

PHO   in ius? huc, si quid lubet.

CHR   assequere, retine dum ego huc servos evoco.

DEM   enim nequeo solus. accurre.

PHO   una iniuriast

tecum.

DEM   lege agito ergo.

PHO   alterast tecum, Chreme.

985 DEM rape hunc.

PHO   sic agitis? enimvero vocest opus.

Nausistrata! exi.

DEM   os opprime. impurum vide

quantum valet!

PHO   Nausistrata, inquam!

DEM   non taces?

PHO   taceam?

DEM   nisi sequitur, pugnos in ventrem ingere.

PHO   vel oculum exsculpe. est ubi vos ulciscar probe.

982 assequere . . . evoco *Chremeti dat* A, *Demiphoni* Σ
983 enim . . . accurre *Demiphoni dat* A, *Chremeti* Σ
984 lege . . . ergo *Demiphoni dat* A, *Chremeti* Σ
985 rape hunc *Demiphoni dat* Σ, *Chremeti* A
986–987 os opprime *Demiphoni dedi, Chremeti codd. edd.* impurum
. . . valet *Chremeti continuat* A, *Demiphoni dat* Σ
987 non taces *Demiphoni dant codd. pl., Chremeti* CPD
989 exsculpe A, exclude Σ, excludito *Prisc.*

DEM I have. (*to Phormio*) Let's go to court.

PHO To court? Yes, here, if you like. (*he moves towards Chremes' house*)

CHR (*to Demipho*) After him! Hold him while I call out your slaves. (*he goes to Demipho's door*)

DEM (*grappling with Phormio*) I can't by myself. Hurry up!

PHO (*to Demipho*) That's one case for assault.

DEM Take me to court, then.

PHO (*as Chremes approaches with a slave*) And another against you, Chremes.

DEM (*to the slave*) Haul him off! (*the slave tries to seize Phormio*)

PHO Is this how you want it? Very well, I shall have to use my voice. (*shouting*) Nausistrata! Come out here!

DEM (*to the slave*) Stop his mouth! (*the slave tries to put a hand over Phormio's mouth but is shrugged off*) (*to Chremes*) The strength of the filthy scoundrel!

PHO (*shouting again*) Nausistrata, I say!

DEM (*to Phormio*) Shut your mouth!

PHO (*to Demipho, mockingly*) Me? Shut my mouth?

DEM (*to the slave*) If he won't go with you, punch him in the stomach!

PHO (*nonchalantly*) Gouge out my eye, if you like. (*to Demipho and Chremes*) I'll well and truly get my revenge on you two.[70]

[70] There is some confusion in the MSS about the speaker assignations at the end of the scene. In this version the "stronger" part is given to Demipho, and the "weaker" to Chremes, in keeping with their general characterisation. The emergence of a slave is inferred from line 982 but is not guaranteed by the text. This is a rare scene of knockabout farce for Terence.

V. IX: NAUSISTRATA. CHREMES. DEMIPHO. PHORMIO.

990 NAU   qui nominat me? hem! quid istuc turbaest, obsecro,
mi vir?

PHO   ehem! quid nunc obstipuisti?

NAU   quis hic homost?
non mihi respondes?

PHO   hicine ut tibi respondeat,
qui hercle ubi sit nescit?

CHR   cave isti quicquam creduas.

PHO   abi, tange. si non totus friget, me enica.

995 CHR   nil est.

NAU   quid ergo? quid istic narrat?

PHO   iam scies.
ausculta.

CHR   pergin credere?

NAU   quid ego, obsecro,
huic credam, qui nil dixit?

PHO   delirat miser
timore.

NAU   non pol temerest quod tu tam times.

CHR   egon timeo?

PHO   recte sane. quando nil times,

1000   et hoc nil est quod ego dico, tu narra.

DEM   scelus,
tibi narret?

PHO   ohe tu! factumst abs te sedulo
pro fratre.

NAU   mi vir, non mihi narras?

CHR   at—

NAU   quid "at"?

<hr />

1002 narras Σ, dices A

Enter NAUSISTRATA *from Chremes' house.*

NAU Who's calling me? (*to Chremes*) Hey! For goodness' sake, what's all this brawling, my dear husband?

PHO (*to Chremes, who keeps silent*) Hello! Are you struck dumb all of a sudden?

NAU (*to Chremes*) Who is this fellow? Aren't you going to answer me?

PHO (*to Nausistrata*) Him answer, when he doesn't even know where he is!

CHR (*to Nausistrata*) Don't believe anything he says.

PHO (*to Nausistrata*) Go on, touch him. Strike me dead if he's not stone cold all over.

CHR It's nothing.

NAU What's the matter, then? What's this fellow talking about?

PHO (*to Nausistrata*) You'll soon find out. Listen.

CHR (*to Nausistrata*) Are you going to believe him?

NAU For goodness' sake, how am I supposed to believe him, when he hasn't said a word?

PHO (*aside*) The poor man's out of his mind with fear.

NAU You wouldn't be so afraid for nothing, for heaven's sake.

CHR Me afraid?

PHO Of course not. Since you're not afraid and what I'm saying is nothing, *you* tell her.

DEM (*to Phormio*) You villain, is he to tell the story for you?

PHO That's enough from you! You've done your best for your brother.

NAU (*to Chremes*) Aren't you going to tell me, my dear?

CHR Well—

NAU How do you mean "well"?

129

CHR   non opus est dicto.

PHO   tibi quidem. at scito huic opust.

    in Lemno—

DEM   hem! quid ais?

CHR   non taces?

PHO   —clam te—

CHR   ei mihi!

1005 PHO   —uxorem duxit.

NAU   mi homo, di melius duint!

PHO   sic factumst.

NAU   perii misera!

PHO   et inde filiam

    suscepit iam unam, dum tu dormis.

CHR   quid agimus?

NAU   pro di immortales! facinus miserandum et malum!

PHO   hoc actumst.

NAU   an quicquam hodiest factum indignius?

1010   qui mi, ubi ad uxores ventumst, tum fiunt senes.

    Demipho, te appello. nam cum hoc ipso distaedet loqui.

    haecin erant itiones crebrae et mansiones diutinae

    Lemni? haecin erat ea quae nostros minuit fructus vili-

        tas?

DEM   ego, Nausistrata, esse in hac re culpam meritum non

      nego.

1015   sed ea quin sit ignoscenda?

PHO   verba fiunt mortuo.

DEM   nam neque neglegentia tua neque odio id fecit tuo.

    vinolentus fere abhinc annos quindecim mulierculam

    eam compressit inde haec natast, neque postilla um-

      quam attigit.

CHR I don't need to tell you.

PHO (*to Chremes*) *You* don't, but *she* needs to know. In Lemnos—

DEM Hey! What are you saying?

CHR Can't you shut up?

PHO —unknown to you—

CHR Confound it!

PHO —he married a wife.

NAU My good fellow, heaven preserve us!

PHO It's true.

NAU Poor me! I'm ruined!

PHO And from her he's already had one daughter, while you were fast asleep.

CHR (*to Demipho*) What are we going to do?

NAU By the immortal gods, what a wretched evil deed!

PHO (*to Chremes*) Going to do? It's all done.

NAU Can anything be more outrageous? It's only when they're with their wives that they're elderly. (*to Demipho*) Demipho, I appeal to you: I'm sick of talking to him. Were these his frequent journeys to Lemnos and his lengthy stays there? Was this the slump in prices that reduced our income?

DEM Nausistrata, I don't deny that he's to blame in all this. But isn't it something that can be forgiven?

PHO (*aside*) They're talking about a dead man.

DEM He didn't do it out of disregard or dislike of you. He forced himself on the poor woman when he was drunk, some fifteen years ago, and the girl was born. But he never touched her after that. The mother's now dead,

---

1008 miserandum *A*, indignum Σ
1015 quin *A¹*, quae Σ, qui *A²*

131

ea mortem obiit, e medio abiit qui fuit in re hac scrupu-
lus.

1020 quam ob rem te oro, ut alia facta tua sunt, aequo animo
hoc feras.

NAU quid ego aequo animo? cupio misera in hac re iam defun-
gier.

sed quid sperem? aetate porro minus peccaturum pu-
tem?

iam tum erat senex, senectus si verecundos facit.

an mea forma atque aetas nunc magis expetendast, De-
mipho?

1025 quid mi hic affers quam ob rem exspectem aut sperem
porro non fore?

PHO exsequias Chremeti quibus est commodum ire, em, tem-
pus est.

sic dabo: age nunc, Phormionem qui volet lacessito;

"faxo tali sum mactatum atque hic est infortunio."

redeat sane in gratiam iam; supplici satis est mihi.

1030 habet haec ei quod, dum vivat, usque ad aurem oggan-
niat.

NAU at meo merito credo. quid ego nunc commemorem,
Demipho,

singulatim qualis ego in hunc fuerim?

DEM   novi aeque omnia
tecum.

NAU   merito hoc meo videtur factum?

DEM   minume gentium.

verum iam, quando accusando fieri infectum non potest,

1035 ignosce. orat, confitetur, purgat: quid vis amplius?

1028 sum mactatum *Don. edd.*, eum mactatum *codd. pl.*, sit mactatus
AD¹L¹

and the source of irritation[71] is no longer with us. So I beg
you to put up with this with your usual patience.

NAU Why should I be patient? Poor me! I want to have done
with this sort of thing. But why should I hope so? Should
I suppose that he'll stray any the less in the future with
advancing years? If old age makes men more virtuous—
he was already an old man then. Am I getting any youn-
ger or more attractive now, Demipho? What reason can
you suggest why I should expect or hope this won't hap-
pen again in the future?

PHO (*in a loud voice*) Anyone who is intending to go to
Chremes' funeral, now's the time. This is how I treat
people. Come on now, anyone who wishes to provoke
Phormio, let him do so: I'll have the same misfortunes in-
flicted on him as on our friend here.[72] (*changing his tone*)
All right, then; let him be restored to favour; he's been
punished enough for me. She's got something to whine
about in his ear for the rest of his life.

NAU (*ironically*) I suppose it's all my fault. Do I need to go
over in detail, Demipho, what I've been to him?

DEM I know as well as you do.

NAU Do you think it's all my fault?

DEM Not in the world. But since this can't be undone by re-
criminations, forgive him now. He pleads, he confesses,
he apologises: what more do you want?

[71] There is another allusion here to the "stone in the shoe" idiom
(Latin *scrupulus*); compare line 954.

[72] If the archaic word *sum* for *eum*, vouched for here by Donatus
but not in the MSS, is the correct reading, this line is probably a quota-
tion from a lost tragedy or epic poem.

PHO enimvero prius quam haec dat veniam, mihi prospiciam
  et Phaedriae.

  heus, Nausistrata, prius quam huic respondes temere,
  audi.

NAU   quid est?

PHO ego minas triginta per fallaciam ab illoc abstuli.

  eas dedi tuo gnato. is pro sua amica lenoni dedit.

1040 CHR hem! quid ais?

NAU   adeo hoc indignum tibi videtur, filius
  homo adulescens si habet unam amicam, tu uxores duas?
  nil pudere! quo ore illum obiurgabis? responde mihi.

DEM faciet ut voles.

NAU   immo ut meam iam scias sententiam,
  neque ego ignosco neque promitto quicquam neque res-
   pondeo

1045 prius quam gnatum videro. eius iudicio permitto omnia;
  quod is iubebit faciam.

PHO   mulier sapiens es, Nausistrata.

NAU satis tibin est?

CHR   immo vero pulchre discedo et probe
  et praeter spem.

NAU   tu tuom nomen dic quid est?

PHO   mihin? Phormio.

  vostrae familiae hercle amicus et tuo summus Phaedriae.

1050 NAU Phormio, at ego ecastor posthac tibi quod potero, quae
  voles

  faciamque et dicam.

PHO   benigne dicis.

1047–1048 immo . . . spem *Chremeti dat Bentley, Phormioni codd.*

134

PHO   (*aside*) Well, before she forgives him, I must look after my own interests and Phaedria's. (*aloud*) Hey, Nausistrata, before you give him a hasty answer, listen.

NAU   What is it?

PHO   I got thirty minas out of him by a trick and gave them to your son. He's given them to a pimp to buy his mistress.

CHR   What! What are you saying?

NAU   (*to Chremes*) Does it seem so shocking to you, if your son at his age has one mistress, when you have two wives? Have you no shame? How will you have the face to rebuke him? Answer me that.

DEM   He'll do as you wish.

NAU   (*to Chremes*) No. To make my position clear, I do not forgive you, nor do I make any promises, nor will I give you my answer before I've seen our son. I leave everything to him to decide; I'll do what he says.

PHO   You are a wise woman, Nausistrata.

NAU   (*to Chremes*) Are you satisfied?

CHR   Indeed. I come out of this very well. It's a fair result and better than I could have hoped.[73]

NAU   (*to Phormio*) You, tell me your name.

PHO   Mine? Phormio, a friend to your whole family, god knows, and especially to Phaedria.

NAU   Well, Phormio, after this I swear I will do and say anything I can to fulfil your wishes.

PHO   That's kind of you.

---

[73] Phaedria is unlikely to propose that his father be thrown out of his home (compare line 586), so that this is a relatively favourable outcome for Chremes. The MSS in fact give this line to Phormio, who has achieved the humbling of Chremes, but it is not clear how Nausistrata's decision is "better than he could have hoped."

NAU   pol meritumst tuom.

PHO   vin primum hodie facere quod ego gaudeam, Nausistra-
       ta,
  et quod tuo viro oculi doleant?

NAU   cupio.

PHO   me ad cenam voca.

NAU   pol vero voco.

DEM   eamus intro hinc.

NAU   fiat. sed ubist Phaedria
  iudex noster?

1055 PHO   iam hic faxo aderit.

Ω   vos valete et plaudite.

1054 eamus *Demiphoni dat* Σ, *Phormioni* A. fiat . . . noster *Nau-
sistratae dat* A, *Chremeti* Σ

NAU   Heaven knows, it's what you deserve.

PHO   Well, for a start, would you like to do something today
      which will bring joy to my heart, Nausistrata, and make
      your husband's eyes smart?

NAU   Willingly.

PHO   Invite me to dinner.

NAU   Very well, I invite you.

DEM   Let's go inside.

NAU   All right. But where's Phaedria, our judge?

PHO   I'll have him here right away.

ALL   (*to the audience*) Farewell and give us your applause.[74]

---

[74] All Terence's plays end with a request for applause, which in a
curtainless theatre signifies to the audience the end of the play. In the
MSS this request is preceded by the Greek letter omega, of which the
significance is not at all clear. It is implied by Horace *Ars Poetica* 155
(*donec cantor 'vos plaudite' dicat*) that the final *plaudite* was spoken by
the *cantor* (singer), perhaps the musician who accompanied the play,
but there is no other evidence to corroborate this. It is more likely that
it was spoken either by all the onstage actors, as in several plays of
Plautus', signified in the MSS by *grex* or *caterva*, or by one of the char-
acters (here presumably Phormio), as in the rest of Plautus' plays.

THE MOTHER-IN-LAW

INTRODUCTORY NOTE

The Mother-in-Law, like *Phormio*, was based on a Greek original by Apollodorus. It was Terence's least successful play in his lifetime in that it failed to get a hearing at its first two productions and finally succeeded only through the perseverance of Terence's producer Lucius Ambivius Turpio. Its failures may have been as much to do with the circumstances of the festivals as with the qualities of the play, since we hear of rival entertainers, such as tightrope walkers, boxers, and gladiators, forcing their way into the theatre; but it is true that it is an unusually sombre play surrounded by much doubt and uncertainty in which the path to the happy ending is by no means clear. The degree of uncertainty may be due to Terence if, as is often supposed, the Greek original had a divine prologue which told the audience the true situation from the outset and enabled it to foresee the dénouement.

The essence of the plot (as of Menander's *The Arbitration*) is that a young man (Pamphilus) has married a girl (Philumena) whom he had earlier raped without knowing her identity and is outraged when she bears an "illegitimate" baby which is in fact his own. Pamphilus discovers the newly born baby when he returns from a business trip on which he has been sent by his father; he promises Philumena's mother Myrrina not to reveal the baby's existence but refuses to take Philumena back. This refusal creates problems between Pamphilus and his father Laches and Philumena's father Phidippus, when they discover the baby and assume it to be Pamphilus' own. Pamphilus tries to claim that he is acting out of loyalty to his mother Sostrata, the "mother-in-law" of the title, who had at the beginning of the play been involved in an unexplained quarrel with her daughter-in-law (Philumena, trying to conceal her pregnancy, had gone home to her own mother and they had refused to let Sostrata in), but Sostrata removes this excuse by selflessly offering to go and live on the family farm to keep out of the young couple's way. The problem is resolved when the two fathers, suspecting that Pamphilus' refusal is due to a continuation of his premarital affair with the courtesan Bacchis, summon her to explain the situation. She goes in to tell the womenfolk that this affair is long since over, and Myrrina recognises a ring Bacchis is wearing as belonging to Philumena, having been torn from Philumena by Pamphilus at the time of the rape and then presented to Bacchis. The way is now clear for the resumption of the marriage and the happy ending; it is decided not to tell those who do not need to know (that is, the fathers) the truth of the situation.

The play is unique among Terence's plays in having only a single pair of lovers; the plot is double only to the extent that there are two sets of parents. It is also unique in that the sympathy lies squarely with the female characters. The two mothers do their best for their respective children and are quite unjustly and unpleasantly criticised by their husbands for causing all the friction between the families. Indeed, it is possible to read the play as a criticism of the patriarchal society, whose conventions are preserved only by a fiction; the two *patresfamilias* have no control over what is going on and are in the end kept out of the secret, while the women are shamefully treated and get no redress. Pamphilus has some redeeming features, notably the genuineness of his feelings both for Bacchis and for Philumena and his loyalty to his promise to Myrrina when in the end it would have been easier for him to declare the illegitimacy of the child; but it is hard to sympathise with him when he has committed what must be the most unpleasant rape in comedy and never in the play shows any regret. In this respect he suffers by comparison with his counterpart Charisios in Menander's *The Arbitration*, who has two long expressions of remorse at his treatment of his wife.

Of the minor characters, Parmeno is the most ineffective of Terence's slaves; having been introduced at the beginning as a gossiping source of information about Pamphilus' situation, in the end he has to be sent on various errands to keep him out of the way, possessing as he does the crucial knowledge that Pamphilus did not touch his wife for two months after the wedding, so that the baby cannot possibly be his. Bacchis stands beside Thais of *The Eunuch* as a *bona meretrix*, willing to face opprobrium in order to save the marriage of her former lover; the brief scene of flirtation between her and Pamphilus at the end of the play must be the most charming scene in comedy between a young man and a courtesan.

SELECT BIBLIOGRAPHY

Editions

Carney, T. F. (Pretoria 1963).
Ireland, S. (Warminster 1990).

Criticism

Gilula, D. "Terence's *Hecyra:* A Delicate Balance of Suspense and Dramatic Irony." *Scripta Classica Israelica* 5 (1979–80): 137–157.

Goldberg, S. M. "The Price of Simplicity," in *Understanding Terence.* Princeton, 1986: 149–169.

Konstan, D. "*Hecyra:* Ironic Comedy," in *Roman Comedy.* Ithaca, 1983: 130–141.

Lefèvre. E. *Terenz' und Apollodors Hecyra.* Munich, 1999.

McGarrity, T. "Reputation vs. Reality in Terence's *Hecyra.*" *Classical Journal* 76 (1980–81): 149–156.

Sewart, D. "Exposition in the *Hecyra* of Apollodorus." *Hermes* 102 (1974): 247–260.

Slater, N. W. "The Fictions of Patriarchy in Terence's *Hecyra.*" *Classical World* 81 (1987–88): 249–260.

DIDASCALIA

INCIPIT TERENTI HECYRA
ACTA LVDIS MEGALENSIBUS
SEXTO IVLIO CAESARE CN. CORNELIO DOLABELLA
AEDILIBVS CVRVLIBVS
MODOS FECIT FLACCVS CLAVDI TIBIIS PARIBVS TOTA
GRAECA MENANDRV
FACTA EST V
ACTA PRIMO SINE PROLOGO CN. OCTAVIO TITO MANLIO COS.
RELATA EST LVCIO AEMILIO PAVLO LVDIS FVNERALIBVS
NON EST PLACITA
TERTIO RELATA EST Q. FVLVIO LVC. MARCIO AEDILIBVS
CVRVLIBVS
EGIT LVC. AMBIVIVS LVC. SERGIVS TVRPIO
PLACVIT

C. SULPICI APOLLINARIS PERIOCHA

uxorem ducit Pamphilus Philumenam,
cui quondam ignorans virgini vitium obtulit,
cuiusque per vim quem detraxit anulum
dederat amicae Bacchidi meretriculae.
profectus dein in Imbrum est; nuptam haud attigit.
hanc mater vitio gravidam, ne id sciat socrus,
ut aegram ad sese transfert. revenit Pamphilus,
deprendit partum, celat; uxorem tamen
recipere non volt. pater incusat Bacchidis
amorem. dum se purgat Bacchis, anulum
mater vitiatae forte adgnoscit Myrrina.
uxorem recipit Pamphilus cum filio.

---

1 Founded in 204 B.C. in honour of the Great Mother; held in April.

PRODUCTION NOTICE

Here begins The Mother-in-Law of Terence, acted at the Ludi Megalenses[1] in the curule aedileship of Sex. Iulius Caesar and Cn. Cornelius Dolabella.[2] Music composed by Flaccus, slave of Claudius, for equal pipes throughout. Greek original by Menander.[3] The author's fifth play, performed first without prologue in the consulship of Cn. Octavius and Ti. Manlius. Performed again at the funeral games of L. Aemilius Paulus. A failure. Performed for the third time in the curule aedileship of Q. Fulvius and L. Marcius.[4] The producers were L. Ambivius and L. Sergius Turpio.[5] A success.

SYNOPSIS BY C. SULPICIUS APOLLINARIS

Pamphilus married Philumena, whom he had earlier raped not knowing who she was; he had taken her ring by force and given it to his girlfriend, the courtesan Bacchis. He then departed to Imbros without touching his wife. The girl being pregnant as a result of the rape, her mother takes her home to hide this fact from her mother-in-law, pretending that she is sick. Pamphilus returns, discovers the baby, and keeps it secret; but he refuses to take his wife back. His father blames his love for Bacchis. While Bacchis is clearing herself of this charge, Myrrina, the mother of the raped girl, chances to recognise the ring, and Pamphilus takes his wife back together with his son.

It was the occasion of four of Terence's plays.
[2] That is, in 165 B.C., which makes this Terence's second play. It is his fifth (as stated below) if this unsuccessful first performance is ignored.   [3] In fact by Apollodorus (see *Phormio* note 3).
[4] The second and third performances were in 160. On Aemilius Paullus see Introduction.   [5] L. Sergius is unknown.

PERSONAE

PHILOTIS meretrix
SYRA anus
PARMENO servos
LACHES senex
SOSTRATA matrona
PHIDIPPUS senex
PAMPHILUS adulescens
SOSIA servos
MYRRINA matrona
BACCHIS meretrix

Scaena: Athenis

CHARACTERS

PHILOTIS, a young courtesan
SYRA, an old woman
PARMENO, slave of Laches
LACHES, an old man, husband of Sostrata, father of
   Pamphilus
SOSTRATA, a matron, wife of Laches, mother of Pamphilus
PHIDIPPUS, an old man, husband of Myrrina, father of
   Philumena
PAMPHILUS, a young man, son of Laches and Myrrina, hus-
   band of Philumena
SOSIA, another slave of Laches
MYRRINA, a matron, wife of Phidippus, mother of Philu-
   mena
BACCHIS, a courtesan, lover of Pamphilus

Staging

The stage represents a street in Athens. On it are three houses,
belonging to Laches, Phidippus, and the courtesan Bacchis.
The exit on the audience's right leads to the forum, that on their
left to the harbour and the country.

HECYRA

PROLOGUS (I)

Hecyra est huic nomen fabulae. haec quom datast,
nova, ei novom intervenit vitium et calamitas
ut neque spectari neque cognosci potuerit.
ita populus studio stupidus in funambulo
5   animum occuparat. nunc haec planest pro nova,
et is qui scripsit hanc ob eam rem noluit
iterum referre ut iterum possit vendere.
alias cognostis eius: quaeso hanc noscite.

PROLOGUS (II)

orator ad vos venio ornatu prologi.
10   sinite exorator sim eodem ut iure uti senem
liceat quo iure sum usus adulescentior,
novas qui exactas feci ut inveterascerent,
ne cum poeta scriptura evanesceret.
in eis quas primum Caecili didici novas
15   partim sum earum exactus, partim vix steti.
quia scibam dubiam fortunam esse scaenicam,
spe incerta certum mihi laborem sustuli.

---

2 nova ei *Bentley*, nova *codd. Don.*, novae *Fleckeisen*, (data) novast
Marouzeau   7 possit *codd. pl.*, posset *p Don. edd.*

---

6 This is the prologue to the second performance.

148

THE MOTHER-IN-LAW

The title of this play is The Mother-in-Law. When it was performed as a new play, it suffered a novel form of misfortune, a disaster which prevented it from being watched or given a hearing: the audience took a foolish fancy to a tightrope walker who claimed their attention. Now it is offered as a genuinely new play: it is not the case that the author has chosen to present it a second time in order to sell it a second time. You have given a hearing to his other plays; please give a hearing to this one.

PROLOGUE (2)[7]

I come to you as an advocate in the guise of a prologue. Allow me to succeed in my advocacy; let me enjoy as an old man the same privilege as I did in my younger days, when I ensured that new plays which had been driven off the stage became established and that the scripts did not vanish from sight along with the playwrights. When I first put on new plays by Caecilius,[8] I was driven off the stage in some of them, and struggled to hold my ground in others. I realised that a theatrical career was a precarious one; success was uncertain and the only certainty

---

[7] This is the prologue to the third performance, and was evidently spoken, like the prologue to *The Self-Tormentor*, by Ambivius Turpio himself.

[8] For Caecilius see Introduction.

easdem agere coepi ut ab eodem alias discerem
novas, studiose ne illum ab studio abducerem.
20   perfeci ut spectarentur: ubi sunt cognitae,
placitae sunt. ita poetam restitui in locum
prope iam remotum iniuria advorsarium
ab studio atque ab labore atque arte musica.
quod si scripturam sprevissem in praesentia
25   et in deterrendo voluissem operam sumere,
ut in otio esset potius quam in negotio,
deterruissem facile ne alias scriberet.
nunc quid petam mea causa aequo animo attendite.
Hecyram ad vos refero, quam mihi per silentium
30   numquam agere licitumst; ita eam oppressit calamitas.
eam calamitatem vostra intellegentia
sedabit, si erit adiutrix nostrae industriae.
quom primum eam agere coepi, pugilum gloria
(funambuli eodem accessit exspectatio),
35   comitum conventus, strepitus, clamor mulierum
fecere ut ante tempus exirem foras.
vetere in nova coepi uti consuetudine
in experiundo ut essem; refero denuo.
primo actu placeo. quom interea rumor venit
40   datum iri gladiatores, populus convolat,
tumultuantur, clamant, pugnant de loco.
ego interea meum non potui tutari locum.
nunc turba nullast: otium et silentiumst.
agendi tempus mihi datumst: vobis datur
45   potestas condecorandi ludos scaenicos.
nolite sinere per vos artem musicam
recidere ad paucos. facite ut vostra auctoritas

was toil. But I set myself to revive these same plays in order to obtain other new ones from the same author; I was very eager that he should not be discouraged from his profession. I managed to get the plays performed, and, once they were known, they were a success. In this way I restored the playwright to his place, when the the attacks of his opponents had practically driven him from his profession and from his craft and from the dramatic art. But if I had rejected his works at the time and had chosen to spend my time discouraging him, thus consigning him to idleness rather than to industry, I could easily have discouraged him from writing any further plays.

Now for my sake listen to my request with open minds. I am presenting "The Mother-in-Law" to you again, which I have never been allowed to play in silence; it has been so dogged by disaster. But your good sense, allied to my efforts, can mitigate the disaster. The first time I tried to perform the play, I was forced off the stage early; there was talk of boxers—and added to that a promise of a tightrope walker—crowds of supporters, general uproar, and women screaming. I decided to use my old practice on this new play and continue the experiment: I put it on a second time. The first act[9] went well. But then a rumour arose that there was going to be a gladiatorial show: crowds rushed in, with much confusion, shouting, and fighting for places, and in these circumstances I couldn't preserve my place.

Now there is no disturbance; all is peace and quiet. I have the chance to perform the play, and you the opportunity to add lustre to the dramatic festivals. Do not allow the dramatic art to fall into the hands of a few through your negligence. Make sure

[9] The word "act" is not here used in the technical sense; act divisions, which were unknown to Terence, were inserted in his plays by Renaissance editors.

151

meae auctoritati fautrix adiutrixque sit.
si numquam avare pretium statui arti meae
50   et eum esse quaestum in animum induxi maxumum
quam maxume servire vostris commodis,
sinite impetrare me, qui in tutelam meam
studium suom et se in vostram commisit fidem,
ne eum circumventum inique iniqui irrideant.
55   mea causa causam accipite et date silentium,
ut lubeat scribere aliis mihique ut discere
novas expediat posthac pretio emptas meo.

ACTUS I

I. I: PHILOTIS. SYRA.

PHI   per pol quam paucos reperias meretricibus
fidelis evenire amatores, Syra.
60   vel hic Pamphilus iurabat quotiens Bacchidi,
quam sancte, uti quivis facile posset credere,
numquam illa viva ducturum uxorem domum!
em, duxit!
SYR   ergo propterea te sedulo
et moneo et hortor ne quoiusquam misereat,
65   quin spolies, mutiles, laceres quemque nacta sis.
PHI   utine eximium neminem habeam?
SYR   neminem.
nam nemo illorum quisquam, scito, ad te venit

49–51 = *Hau. 48–50 secludit Tyrrell*
64 misereat Σ Don., misereas A

---

10 The obvious sense of *pretio meo* is "at my own expense," though
Donatus takes it as meaning "at a price set by me," and explains that, if

that your influence aids and abets my influence.

I have never priced my art on the basis of greed; I have adopted the principle that the greatest reward for me is to serve your interests the best. So let me prevail on you not to allow an author who has entrusted his career to my keeping and himself to your protection to be cheated and unfairly derided by unfair critics. For my sake listen to my plea and grant me silence, so that other authors may be encouraged to write and it may be worth my while in the future to put on new plays bought at my own expense.[10]

ACT ONE

Enter PHILOTIS *and* SYRA *from Bacchis' house talking together.*

PHI   Heaven knows, you can find precious few lovers who turn out faithful to their mistresses, Syra. Take Pamphilus here (*pointing to his house*). How often he swore to Bacchis, and how solemnly, so that no one could possibly have doubted him, that he would never take a wife so long as she was alive! Now look, he's taken one!

SYR   And that's why I constantly urge and exhort you never to take pity on a lover but strip, flay, and fleece every one you get.

PHI   Without any exception at all?

SYR   None. Not one of them, I assure you, comes to you with-

the play failed, the aediles would reclaim from the producer the money they had paid to the author. That the aediles ultimately bought the play is implied in the prologue to *The Eunuch* (line 20); it may be that the producer bought the play from the author and sold his production of it to the aediles.

quin ita paret sese abs te ut blanditiis suis
quam minumo pretio suam voluptatem expleat.
70   hiscin tu, amabo, non contra insidiabere?
PHI   tamen pol eandem iniuriumst esse omnibus.
SYR   iniurium autemst ulcisci advorsarios,
aut qua via te captent eadem ipsos capi?
eheu me miseram! quor non aut istaec mihi
75   aetas et formast aut tibi haec sententia?

I. II: PARMENO. PHILOTIS. SYRA.

PAR   senex si quaeret me, modo isse dicito
ad portum percontatum adventum Pamphili.
audin quid dicam, Scirte? si quaeret me, uti
tum dicas; sin non quaeret, nullus dixeris,
80   alias ut uti possim causa hac integra.
sed videon ego Philotium? unde haec advenit?
Philotis, salve multum.
PHI   o salve, Parmeno.
SYR   salve mecastor, Parmeno.
PAR   et tu edepol, Syra.
dic mi ubi, Philotis, te oblectasti tam diu?
85   PHI   minume equidem me oblectavi, quae cum milite
Corinthum hinc sum profecta inhumanissumo.
biennium ibi perpetuom misera illum tuli.
PAR   edepol te desiderium Athenarum arbitror,
Philotium, cepisse saepe et te tuom
consilium contempsisse.

---

11 Parmeno answers Syra's slightly extravagant *mecasto*r (an oath by
Castor) with an equally extravagant *edepol* (an oath by Pollux). Both are
here translated "god bless."

out the intention of talking you into satisfying his desires at the lowest possible price. Are you not going to do some counterplotting against such people, my darling?

PHI But even so, by heaven, it's not fair to treat them all the same.

SYR Not fair to get revenge on your enemies or to catch them out in the same way as they try to catch you? Oh dear, oh dear! If only either I had your youth and beauty or you had my sense!

Enter PARMENO from Laches' house.

PAR (*speaking back inside the house*) If the old man asks for me, say I've just gone to the harbour to find out when Pamphilus is arriving. Do you hear what I'm saying, Scirtus? If he asks for me, then say that; if he doesn't, don't say a word, so that I can keep the excuse to use another time. (*seeing the women*) But is that my dear little Philotis? Where did she come from? Philotis, a very good day to you.

PHI Good day, Parmeno.

SYR (*coming forward*) Good day and god bless, Parmeno.

PAR And to you, Syra, god bless you too.[11] (*turning back to Philotis*) Tell me, Philotis, where have you been enjoying yourself all this time?

PHI I've scarcely been enjoying myself, I tell you, having left here for Corinth with that brute of a soldier and endured two whole years of misery with him.

PAR Yes, by heaven, and I expect you were often homesick for Athens and regretted your decision to leave.

90	PHI	non dici potest

quam cupida eram huc redeundi, abeundi a milite,
vosque hic videndi, antiqua ut consuetudine
agitarem inter vos libere convivium.
nam illi haud licebat nisi praefinito loqui

95 quae illi placerent.

PAR   haud opinor commode
finem statuisse orationi militem.

PHI sed quid hoc negotist? modo quae narravit mihi
hic intus Bacchis! quod ego numquam credidi
fore, ut ille hac viva posset animum inducere

100 uxorem habere.

PAR   habere autem?

PHI   eho tu, an non habet?

PAR habet, sed firmae haec vereor ut sint nuptiae.

PHI ita di deaeque faxint, si in remst Bacchidis.
sed qui istuc credam ita esse dic mihi, Parmeno.

PAR non est opus prolato hoc. percontarier

105 desiste.

PHI   nempe ea causa ut ne id fiat palam?
ita me di amabunt, haud propterea te rogo,
uti hoc proferam, sed ut tacita mecum gaudeam.

PAR numquam tam dices commode ut tergum meum
tuam in fidem committam.

PHI   ah! noli, Parmeno.

110 quasi tu non multo malis narrare hoc mihi
quam ego quae percontor scire.

PAR   vera haec praedicat
et illud mihi vitiumst maxumum. si mihi fidem
das te tacituram, dicam.

156

PHI   I can't tell you how eager I was to come back here, to get away from the soldier, and see all of you here, and freely enjoy your company just as in the old days. There I wasn't allowed to say anything except what would please him, and that was strictly defined.

PAR   I don't imagine you enjoyed having the soldier regulate your speech.

PHI   But what's going on? What a story Bacchis just told me inside! It's something I never believed could happen, that he could bring himself to take a wife while she was alive.

PAR   Take a wife?

PHI   Oh, come on! Hasn't he taken a wife?

PAR   He has, but I'm afraid it isn't a secure marriage.

PHI   May all the gods and goddesses grant it so, if that will benefit Bacchis! But tell me, Parmeno, why I should believe what you're telling me.

PAR   (*evasively*) It's not something to make public. Don't question me further.

PHI   You mean, you don't want it to come out into the open? As heaven is my witness, I'm not asking you so I can make it public; I just want to enjoy it quietly by myself.

PAR   You're a clever talker but you'll never persuade me to risk my back on your word.

PHI   Oh, don't, Parmeno! As if you weren't much more eager to tell me the story than I am to have my questions answered!

PAR   (*aside*) She's right. It's my greatest failing. (*aloud*) If you give me your word you'll keep it quiet, I'll tell you.

157

	PHI	ad ingenium redis.
		fidem do: loquere.
	PAR	ausculta.
	PHI	istic sum.
	PAR	hanc Bacchidem
115		amabat ut quom maxume tum Pamphilus,
		quom pater uxorem ut ducat orare occipit
		et haec communia omnium quae sunt patrum,
		sese senem esse dicere, illum autem unicum,
		praesidium velle se senectuti suae.
120		ill' primo se negare, sed postquam acrius
		pater instat, fecit animi ut incertus foret
		pudorin anne amori obsequeretur magis.
		tundendo atque odio denique effecit senex:
		despondit ei gnatam huius vicini proxumi.
125		usque illud visumst Pamphilo ne utiquam grave
		donec iam in ipsis nuptiis, postquam videt
		paratas nec moram ullam quin ducat dari,
		ibi demum ita aegre tulit ut ipsam Bacchidem,
		si adesset, credo ibi eius commisereceret.
130		ubiquomque datum erat spatium solitudinis
		ut colloqui mecum una posset, "Parmeno,
		perii! quid ego egi! in quod me conieci malum!
		non potero ferre hoc, Parmeno. perii miser!"
	PHI	at te di deaeque perduint cum isto odio, Lache!
135	PAR	ut ad pauca redeam, uxorem deducit domum.
		nocte illa prima virginem non attigit.
		quae consecutast nox eam, nihilo magis.
	PHI	quid ais? cum virgine una adulescens cubuerit
		plus potus, sese illa abstinere ut potuerit?
140		non veri simile dicis neque verum arbitror.

PHI   That's more like you. I give you my word. Say on.

PAR   Listen.

PHI   I'm all yours.

PAR   Pamphilus was as much in love with Bacchis as ever,
when his father began to beg him to get himself a wife,
using the standard arguments that all fathers use. He was
an old man, he said; he had only one son; and he needed
some security for his old age. Pamphilus at first refused;
but, when his father pressed him harder, he became
quite uncertain whether to obey his sense of duty or his
love. In the end his father was so insistent and tiresome
that he prevailed, and he arranged for Pamphilus to
marry the daughter of our next-door neighbour here
(*pointing to Phidippus' house*). This didn't seem particu-
larly serious to Pamphilus right up to the actual time of
the wedding. But when he saw everything was ready and
that there was no reason now to postpone the marriage,
then finally he was so upset that I believe even Bacchis
herself would have pitied him, had she been present.
Whenever he found a moment to himself in which he
could confide in me, he'd say, "Parmeno, damn it! What
have I done! What have I let myself in for? I won't be able
to bear it, Parmeno. Poor me, I'm ruined!"

PHI   May all the gods and goddeses destroy you, Laches, you
and your tiresome behaviour!

PAR   To cut the story short, he married the girl and took her
home. On that first night he didn't touch her. The follow-
ing night, the same.

PHI   What are you saying? A young man went to bed with a girl
after plenty to drink and was able to keep his hands off
her? It's an unlikely story. I don't believe it.

PAR credo ita videri tibi. nam nemo ad te venit
nisi cupiens tui: ille invitus illam duxerat.
PHI quid deinde fit?
PAR   diebus sane pauculis
post Pamphilus me solum seducit foras
145 narratque ut virgo ab se integra etiam tum siet,
seque ante quam eam uxorem duxisset domum,
sperasse eas tolerare posse nuptias.
"sed quam decrerim me non posse diutius
habere, eam ludibrio haberi, Parmeno,
150 quin integram itidem reddam, ut accepi ab suis,
neque honestum mihi neque utile ipsi virginist."
PHI pium ac pudicum ingenium narras Pamphili.
PAR "hoc ego proferre incommodum mi esse arbitror.
reddi patri autem, quoi tu nil dicas viti,
155 superbumst. sed illam spero, ubi hoc cognoverit
non posse se mecum esse, abituram denique."
PHI quid interea? ibatne ad Bacchidem?
PAR   cotidie.
sed ut fit, postquam hunc alienum ab sese videt,
maligna multo et magis procax facta ilicost.
160 PHI non edepol mirum.
PAR   atque ea res multo maxume
diiunxit illum ab illa, postquam et ipse se
et illam et hanc quae domi erat cognovit satis,
ad exemplum ambarum mores earum existumans.
haec, ita uti liberali esse ingenio decet,

PAR   I'm sure it seems so to you. Nobody comes to you who doesn't desire you, whereas he'd married her against his will.

PHI   What happened then?

PAR   Well, a few days afterwards, Pamphilus took me aside in private and told me that, as far as he was concerned, the girl was still a virgin. He had hoped, before he married her, he would be able to reconcile himself to the marriage. "But, when I decided that I couldn't keep her any longer," he said, "it seemed neither honourable for me nor in the girl's best interest to treat her as a plaything rather than restoring her intact to her family in the state in which I received her."

PHI   You make Pamphilus sound like a decent responsible young man.

PAR   "I can see that it won't do me any good to make this public," he said. "On the other hand it would be insulting to return a bride to her father when there's no fault you can allege in her. I'm hoping that, when she realises that it's impossible for us to live together, she'll end up by leaving me of her own accord."

PHI   What happened in the meantime? Did he continue seeing Bacchis?

PAR   Every day. But, as tends to happen, when she saw that he now belonged to someone else, she immediately became much more grudging and demanding.

PHI   Heaven knows, it's not surprising.

PAR   But the thing that most of all caused him to part from her was when he came to a proper understanding of himself and her and the wife he had at home, judging the characters of both of them from the way they each behaved. The wife, as you would expect from a respectable lady,

165   pudens, modesta, incommoda atque iniurias
         viri omnis ferre et tegere contumelias.
         hic animus partim uxoris misericordia
         devinctus, partim victus huius iniuriis
         paullatim elapsust Bacchidi atque huc transtulit
170   amorem, postquam par ingenium nactus est.
         interea in Imbro moritur cognatus senex
         horunc. ea ad hos redibat lege hereditas.
         eo amantem invitum Pamphilum extrudit pater.
         reliquit cum matre hic uxorem. nam senex
175   rus abdidit se, huc raro in urbem commeat.

PHI   quid adhuc habent infirmitatis nuptiae?

PAR   nunc audies. primo dies complusculos
         bene convenibat sane inter eas. interim
         miris modis odisse coepit Sostratam,
180   neque lites ullae inter eas, postulatio
         numquam.

PHI   quid igitur?

PAR   si quando ad eam accesserat
         confabulatum, fugere e conspectu ilico,
         videre nolle. denique, ubi non quit pati,
         simulat se ad matrem accersi ad rem divinam, abit.
185   ubi illic dies est compluris, accersi iubet:
         dixere causam tum nescioquam. iterum iubet:
         nemo remisit. postquam accersunt saepius,
         aegram esse simulant mulierem. nostra ilico
         it visere ad eam: admisit nemo. hoc ubi senex
190   rescivit, heri ea causa rure huc advenit.

---

12 An island in the northeast Aegean Sea, off the coast of Thrace.

was modest and restrained: she put up with all her husband's unkindness and ill-treatment, and she said nothing of his insulting behaviour. At this point, his heart being partly won over by compassion for his wife, and partly worn down by Bacchis' unpleasantness, he gradually withdrew from Bacchis and transferred his love to his wife, having found a similar nature to his own. Meanwhile an elderly relative of the family died on Imbros,[12] and his property by law reverted to us. Pamphilus was forced to go out there by his father against his will, being in love. He left his wife here with his mother. The old man has buried himself in the country and rarely comes here into town.

PHI So where's the insecurity in the marriage so far?

PAR I'll tell you. At first for several days the two women did get on very well together. But presently the young woman conceived an inexplicable hatred for Sostrata. There wasn't any dispute between them or any complaint.

PHI What then?

PAR Whenever Sostrata went up to her for a chat, she would immediately disappear from sight and refuse to see her. In the end, when she couldn't stand it any longer, she pretended that her mother had sent for her to take part in a religious ceremony, and off she went home. When she'd been there several days, Sostrata sent for her. The family made some excuse. She sent for her again, still no response. After several more attempts, they pretended the young woman was sick. So our mistress went at once to pay a visit, but they wouldn't let her in. Yesterday, when the old man found out, he came in from the country to deal with the matter, and immediately called upon

patrem continuo convenit Philumenae.
quid egerint inter se nondum etiam scio,
nisi sane curaest quorsum eventurum hoc siet.
habes omnem rem. pergam quo coepi hoc iter.

195 PHI et quidem ego. nam constitui cum quodam hospite
me esse illum conventurum.

PAR   di vortant bene
quod agas!

PHI   vale.

PAR   et tu bene vale, Philotium.

ACTUS II

II. I: LACHES. SOSTRATA.

LAC pro deum atque hominum fidem, quod hoc genus est,
    quae haec est coniuratio!
utin omnes mulieres eadem aeque studeant nolintque
    omnia,

200 neque declinatam quicquam ab aliarum ingenio ullam
    reperias!
itaque adeo uno animo omnes socrus oderunt nurus.
viris esse advorsas aeque studiumst, similis pertinaciast,
in eodemque omnes mihi videntur ludo doctae ad mali-
    tiam. et
ei ludo, si ullus est, magistram hanc esse satis certo scio.

205 SOS me miseram! quae nunc quam ob rem accuser nescio.

LAC   hem!
tu nescis?

SOS   non, ita me di bene ament, mi Lache,
itaque una inter nos agere aetatem liceat.

---

201 *secludunt Bentley edd. nonn. et metrum et sensum suspicantes*

Philumena's father. What passed between them I haven't yet discovered, though naturally I'm concerned how this is going to turn out. There you have the whole story. I'll go on my way.

PHI So will I. I've an appointment to meet a client from overseas.

PAR Heaven bless your enterprise!

PHI Goodbye.

PAR Goodbye to you, Philotis dear. (*Parmeno exits left in the direction of the harbour and Philotis and Syra right in the direction of the forum, leaving the stage empty*)

ACT TWO

Enter LACHES from his house, followed by SOSTRATA.

LAC (*to himself*) In the name of gods and men, what a breed they are, what a gang of conspirators! All women have identical likes and dislikes about everything! You can't find a single one whose character differs in any respect from the others! In particular, all mothers-in-law with one accord hate their daughters-in-law; and they're all just as keen to oppose their husbands and just as determined. I reckon that they've all been schooled to wickedness in the same school, and I'm quite sure that, if there is such a school, (*pointing to Sostrata*) she's the headmistress.

SOS Oh dear! I've no idea what I'm being accused of now.

LAC What! You've no idea?

SOS No, heaven help me, Laches dear; let us live out our lives together in peace.

165

LAC   di mala prohibeant!

SOS   meque abs te immerito esse accusatam postmodo rescis-
        ces, scio.

LAC   te immerito? an quicquam pro istis factis dignum te dici
        potest?

210   quae me et te et familiam dedecoras, filio luctum paras.

          tum autem ex amicis inimici ut sint nobis affines facis,

          qui illum decrerunt dignum suos quoi liberos committe-
          rent.

          tu sola exorere quae perturbes haec tua impudentia.

SOS   egon?

LAC   tu inquam, mulier, quae me omnino lapidem, non
        hominem putas.

215   an, qui ruri esse crebro soleo, nescire arbitramini

          quo quisque pacto hic vitam vostrarum exigat?

          multo melius hic quae fiunt quam illi ubi sum assidue
          scio,

          ideo quia, ut vos mihi domi eritis, proinde ego ero fama
          foris.

          iampridem equidem audivi cepisse odium tui Philume-
          nam.

220   minumeque adeo mirum, et ni id fecisset magis mirum
          foret.

          sed non credidi adeo ut etiam totam hanc odisset do-
          mum.

          quod si scissem, illa hic maneret potius, tu hinc isses
          foras.

          at vide quam immerito aegritudo haec oritur mi abs te,
          Sostrata.

225   rus habitatum abii concedens vobis et rei serviens,

          sumptus vostros otiumque ut nostra res posset pati,

166

LAC   Heaven forbid!

SOS   Some day you'll come to realise your accusations against me are unjustified, I'm sure.

LAC   Unjustified? Against you? There are no words fit to describe you after what you've done. You've brought disgrace on me and yourself and the family, and you've created sorrow for our son. And on top of that you've turned his wife's family from friends into enemies, when they'd judged him good enough to be entrusted with their daughter. You came along and ruined all this single-handed by your shameless behaviour.

SOS   Me?

LAC   Yes you, woman! You seem to think I'm solid stone, not flesh and blood. Or do you women imagine that, just because I spend most of my time in the country, I don't know how all of you live your lives in town? I know what goes on here much better than in the place where I spend my time, precisely because my reputation abroad depends on your behaviour at home. I heard in fact some time ago that Philumena had taken a dislike to you. I'm not exactly surprised; it would have been more surprising if she hadn't. But I never believed that her hatred would extend to the whole household. If I'd known that, she would have been the one to remain here and you the one to pack your bags.[13] Can't you see how unfair it is that I should suffer this distress on your account, Sostrata? I went away to live in the country out of consideration for you and to look after our estate, so that our income could

[13] There is an implied threat here of divorce.

---

208 scio *Sostratae continuant Bentley edd. pl.*, *Lacheti dant codd.*

meo labori haud parcens praeter aequom atque aetatem
    meam.
non te pro his curasse rebus ne quid aegre esset mihi!

SOS   non mea opera neque pol culpa evenit.

LAC   immo maxume.
sola hic fuisti, in te omnis haeret culpa sola, Sostrata.

230   quae hic erant curares, quom ego vos curis solvi ceteris.
cum puella anum suscepisse inimicitias non pudet?
illius dices culpa factum?

SOS   haud equidem dico, mi Lache.

LAC   gaudeo, ita me di ament, gnati causa. nam de te quidem
satis scio peccando detrimenti nil fieri potest.

235 SOS   qui scis an ea causa, mi vir, me odisse assimulaverit
ut cum matre plus una esset?

LAC   quid ais? non signi hoc sat est,
quod heri nemo voluit visentem ad eam te intro admit-
    tere?

SOS   enim lassam oppido tum esse aibant: eo ad eam non
    admissa sum.

LAC   tuos esse ego illi mores morbum magis quam ullam aliam
    rem arbitror,

240   et merito adeo. nam vostrarum nullast quin gnatum velit
ducere uxorem. et quae vobis placitast condicio datur:
ubi duxere impulsu vostro, vostro impulsu easdem exi-
    gunt.

      II. II: PHIDIPPUS. LACHES. SOSTRATA.

PHI   etsi scio ego, Philumena, meum ius esse ut te cogam

support your expenditure and your life of leisure. I've laboured unsparingly beyond what could be expected of a man of my age. In return you might have taken some care not to cause me any distress.

SOS   It's not my doing or my fault, for heaven's sake.

LAC   It is, very much so. You were here alone, and you alone must bear the whole blame, Sostrata. You should have looked after things here, since I had relieved you of all other responsibilities. Aren't you ashamed, at your age, to have started a quarrel with a girl? Are you going to say it was her fault?

SOS   No, certainly not, Laches dear.

LAC   I'm delighted to hear it, heaven help me, for our son's sake. As for you, I'm quite sure you won't do your reputation any harm however badly you behave.

SOS   (*ignoring this insult*) How do you know, husband dear, that she didn't just pretend to hate me, so that she could spend more time with her mother?

LAC   What are you saying? Isn't it proof enough that they refused to let you in yesterday when you tried to visit her?

SOS   As a matter of fact, they said she was extremely tired at the time. That's why I wasn't let in.

LAC   I reckon it's your behaviour which is making her sick rather than anything else. And no wonder. All you women want your sons to marry, and you get the match you want. Then, having pushed them into marriage, you push them out again.

Enter PHIDIPPUS from his house.

PHI   (*speaking back inside the house*) I know I have the right, Philumena, to compel you to obey my orders. But in

169

		quae ego imperem facere, ego tamen patrio animo victus faciam
245		ut tibi concedam neque tuae lubidini advorsabor.
	LAC	atque eccum Phidippum optume video. hinc iam scibo hic quid sit.
		Phidippe, etsi ego meis me omnibus scio esse apprime obsequentem,
		sed non adeo ut mea facilitas corrumpat illorum animos.
		quod tu si idem faceres, magis in rem et vostram et nostram id esset.
250		nunc video in illarum potestate esse te.
	PHI	heia vero?
	LAC	adii te heri de filia: ut veni, itidem incertum amisti.
		haud ita decet, si perpetuam hanc vis esse affinitatem,
		celare te iras. si quid est peccatum a nobis, profer:
		aut ea refellendo aut purgando vobis corrigemus
255		te iudice ipso. sin east causa retinendi apud vos
		quia aegrast, te mihi iniuriam facere arbitror, Phidippe,
		si metuis satis ut meae domi curetur diligenter.
		at ita me di ament, haud tibi hoc concedo—etsi illi pater es—
		ut tu illam salvam magis velis quam ego. id adeo gnati causa,
260		quem ego intellexi illam haud minus quam se ipsum magni facere.
		neque adeo clam mest quam esse eum graviter laturum credo,
		hoc si rescierit. eo domum studeo haec prius quam ille redeat.
	PHI	Laches, et diligentiam vostram et benignitatem
		novi et quae dicis omnia esse ut dicis animum induco,

deference to my paternal feelings I shall give in to you
and not oppose your whims.

LAC   (*to himself*) There's Phidippus. Excellent! I'll find out
from him what this is all about. (*addressing him*) Phidip-
pus, I know that I'm extremely indulgent to all my family,
but not to the extent that my generosity corrupts their
characters. If you acted in the same way, it would be to
your advantage and to ours. But, as it is, I see that you are
under the thumb of your womenfolk.

PHI   Come on now! Is that so?

LAC   I approached you yesterday about your daughter, and
you sent me away just as uncertain as when I came. If you
want this marriage relationship to be lasting, you mustn't
conceal the reasons for your anger in this way. If we have
done anything wrong, bring it out into the open. We'll ei-
ther disprove the allegation or apologise, and we'll make
amends to your satisfaction. But if the reason for keeping
your daughter at home is that she's sick, I reckon you are
doing me an injustice, Phidippus, if you're worried she
may not be looked after well enough in my house. But,
heaven knows, I don't accept—even if you are her fa-
ther—that you are more concerned for her welfare than I
am. I'm concerned for my son's sake, knowing as I do that
he values her no less highly than himself. And I'm very
well aware how upset he'll be if he finds out about this;
that's why I'm keen that she return home before he does.

PHI   Laches, I know both your concern and your good will,
and I'm persuaded that everything you say is as you say.

171

265 et te hoc mihi cupio credere: illam ad vos redire studeo
si facere possim ullo modo.

LAC   quae res te id facere prohibet?
eho, numquidnam accusat virum?

PHI   minume. nam postquam attendi
magis et vi coepi cogere ut rediret, sancte adiurat
non posse apud vos Pamphilo se absente perdurare.

270 aliud fortasse aliis vitist: ego sum animo leni natus,
non possum advorsari meis.

LAC   em, Sostrata.

SOS   heu me miseram!

LAC certumne est istuc?

PHI   nunc quidem, ut videtur. sed numquid vis?
nam est quod me transire ad forum iam oportet.

LAC   eo tecum una.

II. III: SOSTRATA.

SOS edepol ne nos sumus inique aeque omnes invisae viris

275 propter paucas, quae omnes faciunt dignae ut videamur
malo.

nam ita me di ament, quod me accusat nunc vir, sum ex-
tra noxiam.

sed non facilest expurgatu, ita animum induxerunt so-
crus

omnis esse iniquas. haud pol mequidem. nam numquam
secus

habui illam ac si ex me esset nata, nec qui hoc mi eveniat
scio;

280 nisi pol filium multimodis exspecto ut redeat domum.

172

In turn I want you to believe this of me, that I am eager
for her to return to you if I can achieve it by any means.

LAC So what's stopping you? Hey! Surely she's not making
some complaint against her husband?

PHI Not at all. When I pressed her further and tried to com-
pel her forcibly to return, she swore on oath that she
couldn't endure living in your house in Pamphilus' ab-
sence. I suppose everyone has his own failing: in my case
I was born with an easygoing nature, and I can't oppose
my family.

LAC (*turning to Sostrata*). There you are, Sostrata.

SOS Oh! What a misery!

LAC (*to Phidippus*) Is that settled then?

PHI It seems so, for the present at least. But was that all? I've
some business I must attend to now in the forum.

LAC I'll come with you. (*they exit right in the direction of the
forum*)

SOSTRATA is left on stage alone.

SOS Heaven knows, it really is unfair that we women are all
equally hated by our husbands because of a few who
make it seem that we all deserve such treatment. As
heaven is my witness, I am not guilty of what my husband
now accuses me. But it's not easy to clear myself, when
they're so convinced that all mothers-in-law are unrea-
sonable. But not me, for heaven's sake. I've never treated
her otherwise than as if she were my own daughter, and
I don't know why this is happening to me. Heaven knows,
I'm really looking forward to my son's return. (*she exits
into her house*)

ACTUS III

III. I: PAMPHILUS. PARMENO. (MYRRINA.)

PAM nemini plura acerba credo esse ex amore homini um-
quam oblata

quam mi. heu me infelicem! hancin ego vitam parsi
perdere!

hacin causa ego eram tanto opere cupidus redeundi do-
mum! hui!

quanto fuerat praestabilius ubivis gentium agere aetatem

285 quam huc redire atque haec ita esse miserum me rescis-
cere!

nam nos omnes quibus est alicunde aliquis obiectus
labos,

omne quod est interea tempus prius quam id rescitumst
lucrost.

PAR at sic citius qui te expedias his aerumnis reperias:

si non rediisses, haec irae factae essent multo ampliores.

290 sed nunc adventum tuom ambas, Pamphile, scio reveri-
turas.

rem cognosces, iram expedies, rursum in gratiam resti-
tues.

levia sunt quae tu pergravia esse in animum induxti
tuom.

PAM quid consolare me? an quisquam usquam gentiumst
aeque miser?

prius quam hanc uxorem duxi habebam alibi animum
amori deditum.

295 tamen numquam ausus sum recusare eam quam mi
obtrudit pater.

174

ACT THREE

Enter PAMPHILUS *and* PARMENO *left from the direction of the harbour.*

PAM I don't believe anyone has ever had more anguish in-
flicted on him by love than I have. Oh! What an evil fate!
Was this the life I refrained from destroying? Was it for
this I was so eager to return home? Oh! How much pref-
erable it would have been to live out my days anywhere
else in the world than to come back here and discover
this awful situation! For all of us who have some trouble
coming our way from somewhere, the time intervening
before we discover it is all gain.

PAR But this way you'll get to free yourself from these worries
all the sooner. If you hadn't come back, their quarrels
would have become far more serious. As it is, I know
your return will bring them both back to their senses,
Pamphilus. You'll ascertain the facts, settle their quar-
rels, and effect a reconciliation. Things that you've per-
suaded yourself are very serious are actually trifles.

PAM Why try to console me? Is there anyone in the whole
world as miserable as I am? Before I married, my affec-
tions were engaged in another affair, but I never dared
refuse the wife my father thrust upon me. And in such a

---

283 hui *Fleckeisen*, cui *codd.*

iam in hac re, ut taceam, quoivis facile scitust quam fue-
    rim miser.

vix me illim abstraxi atque impeditum in ea expedivi ani-
    mum meum,

vixque huc contuleram: em, nova res ortast porro ab hac
    quae me abstrahat.

tum matrem ex ea re me aut uxorem in culpa inventurum
    arbitror.

300   quod quom ita esse invenero, quid restat nisi porro ut
    fiam miser?

nam matris ferre iniurias me, Parmeno, pietas iubet;

tum uxori obnoxius sum: ita olim suo me ingenio pertulit,

tot meas iniurias quae numquam in ullo patefecit loco.

sed magnum nescioquid necessest evenisse, Parmeno,

305   unde ira inter eas intercessit quae tam permansit diu.

PAR   haud quidem hercle: parvom. si vis vero veram rationem
    exsequi,

non maxumas quae maxumae sunt interdum irae iniurias

faciunt. nam saepe est quibus in rebus alius ne iratus qui-
    demst,

quom de eadem causast iracundus factus inimicissumus.

310   pueri inter sese quam pro levibus noxiis iras gerunt!

quapropter? quia enim qui eos gubernat animus eum
    infirmum gerunt.

itidem illae mulieres sunt ferme ut pueri levi sententia.

fortasse unum aliquod verbum inter eas iram hanc conci-
    visse.

PAM   abi, Parmeno, intro ac me venisse nuntia.

PAR   hem! quid hoc est?

---

313 concivisse *edd.*, conscivisse *Don. in comm.*, concivisset A^2,
conciverit Σ, consciverit *Don.*, concluserit A^1

situation, without my uttering a word, it must be obvious to anyone how miserable I was. I'd hardly torn myself away, disentangled my affections, and transferred them to my wife here, when, lo and behold, some new development has arisen to tear me away from her as well. What's more, I suppose that at the end of all this I'll find either my mother or my wife to be at fault; and, when I do find this out, what's left for me but still more misery? Filial duty bids me bear with any wrongs done by my mother, Parmeno; on the other hand, I am in debt to my wife, who good-naturedly put up with me at the time and has never breathed a word of my many wrongdoings to anyone. But something terrible must have happened, Parmeno, to cause a quarrel between them which has lasted so long.

PAR   Good god, no. It's a minor matter. If you really want the true explanation, sometimes the greatest quarrel doesn't imply the greatest wrongdoing. It often happens that in a given situation one man isn't even angry, while with the same justification a hot-tempered person becomes an enemy for life. Look at children, who quarrel among themselves over trivial complaints, and why? Because they are unable to control their impulses. It's the same with these women: they change their minds, just like children. It's likely it was a single word which stirred up this quarrel between them.

PAM   Go inside, Parmeno, and announce my return.

PAR   (*startled by a noise from Phidippus' house*) Hello! What's that?

PAM   tace!

315   trepidari sentio et cursari rursum prorsum.

PAR   agedum, ad fores
accedo propius. em, sensistin?

PAM   noli fabularier.
pro Iuppiter, clamorem audivi.

PAR   tute loqueris, me vetas.

MYR   (*intus*) tace, obsecro, mea gnata!

PAM   matris vox visast Philumenae.
nullus sum!

PAR   quidum?

PAM   perii!

PAR   quam ob rem?

PAM   nescioquod magnum malum

320   profecto, Parmeno, me celant.

PAR   uxorem Philumenam
pavitare nescioquid dixerunt. id si forte est nescio.

PAM interii! quor mihi id non dixti?

PAR   quia non poteram una omnia.

PAM quid morbist?

PAR   nescio.

PAM   quid? nemon medicum adduxit?

PAR   nescio.

PAM cesso hinc ire intro ut hoc quam primum quidquid est
certo sciam?

325   quonam modo, Philumena mea, nunc te offendam affec-
tam?
nam si periclum ullum in te inest, perisse me una haud
dubiumst.

---

316 accedo *AD¹p¹*, accede *cett.*
320 celant *codd. pl.*, celas *AD¹p¹*

PAM   Hush! I can hear sounds of panic and people rushing to and fro.

PAR   Come on, I'm going up closer to the door. (*he does so and listens*) There! Did you hear?

PAM   (*coming up beside him*) Don't speak a word. (*changing his tone as he hears a cry from inside*) Great Jupiter! I heard a scream.

PAR   You're speaking: you told me not to.

MYR   (*inside*) Hush, for goodness' sake, my daughter!

PAM   That sounded like Philumena's mother. I'm done for!

PAR   How so?

PAM   I'm ruined!

PAR   Why?

PAM   There must be some terrible trouble they're hiding from me, Parmeno.

PAR   They said that your wife Philumena had some sort of a fever. I don't know: perhaps that's it.

PAM   I'm lost! Why didn't you tell me?

PAR   (*defensively*) I couldn't tell you everything at once.

PAM   What's the matter with her?

PAR   I don't know.

PAM   What! Has nobody sent for a doctor?

PAR   I don't know.

PAM   Why don't I go straight inside and find out for sure what's going on? (*turning to go*) In what state will I find you now, Philumena, my darling? If you're in any danger, there's no doubt it's the end of me as well. (*he exits into Phidippus' house, leaving Parmeno on stage alone*)

179

PAR non usus factost mihi nunc hunc intro sequi.
      nam invisos omnis nos esse illis sentio:
      heri nemo voluit Sostratam intro admittere.
330   si forte morbus amplior factus siet
      (quod sane nolim, maxume eri causa mei),
      servom ilico introisse dicent Sostratae,
      aliquid tulisse comminiscentur mali
      capiti atque aetati illorum morbus qui auctu' sit.
335   era in crimen veniet, ego vero in magnum malum.

III. II: SOSTRATA. PARMENO. PAMPHILUS.

SOS nescioquid iamdudum audio hic tumultuari misera.
      male metuo ne Philumenae magis morbus aggravescat,
      quod te, Aesculapi, et te, Salus, ne quid sit huius oro.
      nunc ad eam visam.

PAR   heus, Sostrata!
SOS   hem!
PAR   iterum istinc excludere.
340 SOS ehem, Parmeno, tun hic eras? perii! quid faciam misera?
      non visam uxorem Pamphili, quom in proxumo hic sit ae-
        gra?
PAR non visas? ne mittas quidem visendi causa quemquam.
      nam qui amat quoi odio ipsus est, bis facere stulte duco:
      laborem inanem ipsus capit et illi molestiam affert.
345   tum filius tuos intro iit videre, ut venit, quid agat.
SOS quid ais? an venit Pamphilus?
PAR   venit.

---

14 Sostrata here prays to Aesculapius (Greek Asclepius), the god of
healing, and Salus (Greek Hygieia), the goddess of good health.

THE MOTHER-IN-LAW

PAR (*to himself*) There's no point in me following him inside now. I can see that none of us is welcome there: yesterday nobody would let Sostrata in. If for some reason the illness gets more serious, which I certainly hope it doesn't, especially for my master's sake, they'll immediately say that a slave of Sostrata's was inside the house and claim that he brought in something harmful to their health and well-being which made the illness worse. My mistress will be blamed, and I'll be in for a thrashing.

Enter SOSTRATA *from Laches' house.*

SOS (*to herself*) Oh dear, I've been hearing sounds of commotion here for some time. I'm terribly afraid that Philumena's illness is getting worse. Oh gods of Health and Healing,[14] I pray it is nothing of that sort. I'll go in and see her now. (*she moves towards Phidippus' door*)

PAR Hey, Sostrata!

SOS (*not yet seeing him*) What's that?

PAR You'll be refused admittance again.

SOS (*turning round*) Oh Parmeno, is that you? Damn it! What can I do, poor me? Am I not to visit Pamphilus' wife, when she is lying sick next door to us here?

PAR Not visit her? Don't even send anyone to ask about a visit. To love someone who's taken a dislike to you is stupid twice over, if you ask me: you're wasting your own time and you're causing annoyance to the other person. Besides, your son went inside as soon as he arrived to see how she's doing.

SOS (*surprised*) What are you saying? Is Pamphilus back?

PAR Yes, he is.

181

SOS   dis gratiam habeo.
         hem! istoc verbo animus mihi redit et cura ex corde ex-
            cessit.

PAR   iam ea te causa maxume nunc hoc intro ire nolo.
         nam si remittent quippiam Philumenae dolores,

350   omnem rem narrabit, scio, continuo sola soli
         quae inter vos intervenerit, unde ortumst initium irae.
         atque eccum video ipsum egredi. quam tristist!

SOS   o mi gnate!

PAM   mea mater, salve.

SOS   gaudeo venisse salvom. salvan
        Philumenast?

PAM   meliusculast.

SOS   utinam istuc ita di faxint!

355   quid tu igitur lacrimas? aut quid es tam tristis?

PAM   recte, mater.

SOS   quid fuit tumulti? dic mihi. an dolor repente invasit?

PAM   ita factumst.

SOS   quid morbist?

PAM   febris.

SOS   cotidiana?

PAM   ita aiunt.
         i sodes intro. consequar iam te, mea mater.

SOS   fiat.

PAM   tu pueris curre, Parmeno, obviam atque eis onera adiuta.

360 PAR   quid? non sciunt ipsi viam domum qua veniant?

PAM   cessas?

---

15 Literally, one recurring daily (quotidian), hence chronic rather than acute.

SOS Thank heaven! Oh! That news has restored my spirit and banished the cares from my heart.

PAR That's why I particularly don't want you to go in there now. If Philumena's pain eases at all, I'm sure she'll tell him the whole story at once while they're alone together, and explain what came between you, and how this quarrel began. But there he is coming out. How gloomy he looks!

Enter *PAMPHILUS from Phidippus' house in a disturbed state.*

SOS My son!

PAM Mother dear, good day.

SOS I'm glad you're safely back. Is Philumena all right?

PAM She's a little bit better.

SOS The gods grant it so! But why are you weeping? Why do you look so gloomy?

PAM It's all right, mother.

SOS What was the commotion about? Tell me, did she have a sudden attack of pain?

PAM Yes, that was it.

SOS What sort of illness is it?

PAM A fever.

SOS A mild one?[15]

PAM So they say. But go back inside, if you will, mother dear. I'll follow in a moment.

SOS All right. (*she goes back into her house*)

PAM (*to Parmeno*) You run and meet the slaves, Parmeno, and help them wih the baggage.

PAR (*rudely*) What? Don't they know the way home for themselves?

PAM What are you waiting for? (*Parmeno exits left in the direction of the harbour*)

III. III: PAMPHILUS.

PAM nequeo mearum rerum initium ullum invenire idoneum
unde exordiar narrare quae necopinanti accidunt,
partim quae perspexi hisce oculis, partim quae accepi
    auribus,
qua me propter exanimatum citius eduxi foras.

365 nam modo intro me ut corripui timidus, alio suspicans
morbo me visurum affectam ac sensi esse uxorem, ei
    mihi!
postquam me aspexere ancillae advenisse, ilico omnes
    simul
laetae exclamant "venit," id quod me repente aspexerant.
sed continuo voltum earum sensi immutari omnium,

370 quia tam incommode illis fors obtulerat adventum
    meum.
una illarum interea propere praecucurrit nuntians
me venisse. ego eius videndi cupidus recta consequor.
postquam intro adveni, extemplo eius morbum cognovi
    miser.
nam neque ut celari posset tempus spatium ullum dabat

375 neque voce alia ac res monebat ipsa poterat conqueri.
postquam aspexi, "o facinus indignum" inquam et corri-
    pui ilico
me inde lacrumans, incredibili re atque atroci percitus.
mater consequitur. iam ut limen exirem, ad genua accidit
lacrumans misera. miseritumst. profecto hoc sic est, ut
    puto:

380 omnibus nobis ut res dant sese, ita magni atque humiles
    sumus.
hanc habere orationem mecum principio institit:

PAMPHILUS remains onstage alone.

PAM I can't think of a suitable point from which to begin to tell the things that have befallen me so unexpectedly—some seen with these very eyes, others heard with these ears—and have sent me rushing out of the house so distraught. I dashed inside just now full of anxiety, expecting to see my wife suffering from an illness very different from the one I found, but oh dear! As soon as the maids saw I was back, they all cried out in one voice "He's come," full of joy because they had not expected to see me.

But the next moment I noticed a change in all their expressions, because my return happened to have come at a most inconvenient time. Presently one of them ran ahead in a hurry to report my arrival. I followed straight behind her, eager to see my wife. When I got inside the room, I immediately recognised to my dismay what was wrong with her. The situation allowed them no time to cover it up, and she herself could only utter cries prompted by her pains. When I saw her, I cried out "It's outrageous!" and dashed out from the room at once in tears, overwhelmed by the terrible unbelievable turn of events.

Her mother came after me. As I was going out of the door, she fell to her knees, weeping miserably. I was stirred to pity. It's quite true, if you ask me, that we are all proud or humble according to our circumstances. Then

"o mi Pamphile, abs te quam ob rem haec abierit causam
 vides.
nam vitiumst oblatum virgini olim a nescioquo improbo.
nunc huc confugit te atque alios partum ut celaret
 suom."

385 sed quom orata huius reminiscor nequeo quin lacrumem
 miser.
"quaeque fors fortunast" inquit "nobis quae te hodie
 obtulit,
per eam te obsecramus ambae, si ius, si fas est, uti
advorsa eius per te tecta tacitaque apud omnis sient.
si umquam erga te animo esse amico sensisti eam, mi
 Pamphile,

390 sine labore hanc gratiam te uti sibi des pro illa nunc rogat.
ceterum de redducenda id facias quod in rem sit tuam.
parturire eam nec gravidam esse ex te solus consciu's.
nam aiunt tecum post duobus concubuisse mensibus.
tum, postquam ad te venit, mensis agitur hic iam septi-
 mus:

395 quod te scire ipsa indicat res. nunc si potis es, Pamphile,
maxume volo doque operam ut clam partus eveniat pa-
 trem
atque adeo omnis. sed si id fieri non potest quin sentiant,
dicam abortum esse. scio nemini aliter suspectum fore
quin, quod veri similest, e te recte eum natum putent.

---

16 Literally, "as a virgin," the assumption being that respectable girls
preserved their virginity until marriage.
17 There is an allusion here in the Latin to Fors Fortuna, the god-
dess of good luck (see *Phormio* note 63).

she began to plead with me: "Oh my dear Pamphilus, you see the reason why she's left you. She was raped a while ago before her marriage[16] by some reprobate. Now she's taken refuge here to conceal the birth from you and everyone else." When I recall her pleas, I can't help weeping, I'm so distressed.

"Whatever stroke of luck has brought you to us today," she continued, "by that[17] we both implore you, if the laws of men and gods permit, to hide her misfortunes and keep them secret from everybody. If ever you have recognised the love towards you in her heart, my dear Pamphilus, she begs you in return to grant her this favour, which will cost you nothing. As for taking her back, you must do what you think fit. You're the only person who knows that she's having a baby and that it is not yours. I'm told that she slept with you only after two months, and this is now the seventh month since she came to live with you.[18] You know all this perfectly well, as the events show. Now, if it's possible, Pamphilus, what I want above all and am trying to achieve is that the birth should be kept secret from her father and indeed from everybody. But if its discovery can't be prevented, I'll say that there's been a miscarriage. I'm sure that nobody will suspect anything; they'll come to the natural conclusion

[18] Since the marriage took place seven months ago, a baby born from it would be premature but possible; on the other hand those who know that Pamphilus did not touch his wife for two months after the marriage will be aware that the child cannot be his.

400   continuo exponetur. hic tibi nil est quicquam incommo-
            di,
        et illi miserae indigne factam iniuriam contexeris."
        pollicitus sum et servare in eo certumst quod dixi fidem.
        nam de redducenda, id vero ne utiquam honestum esse
            arbitror
        nec faciam, etsi amor me graviter consuetudoque eius
            tenet.
405   lacrumo quae posthac futurast vita quom in mentem
            venit
        solitudoque. o fortuna, ut numquam perpetuo's data!
        sed iam prior amor me ad hanc rem exercitatum reddidit,
        quem ego tum consilio missum feci. idem huic operam
            dabo.

        adest Parmeno cum pueris. hunc minumest opus
410   in hac re adesse. nam olim soli credidi
        ea me abstinuisse in principio quom datast.
        vereor, si clamorem eius hic crebro exaudiat,
        ne parturire intellegat. aliquo mihist
        hinc ablegandus dum parit Philumena.

            III. IV: PARMENO. SOSIA. PAMPHILUS.

415 PAR   ain tu tibi hoc incommodum evenisse iter?
    SOS   non hercle verbis, Parmeno, dici potest
          tantum quam re ipsa navigare incommodumst.
    PAR   itan est?

        406 data *Don. in comm. edd. pl.*, bona *codd. Don.*

        ---

        19 The exposure of unwanted babies is common in New Comedy
        and no doubt reflects real-life practice. Illegitimate babies were partic-
        ularly at risk. If the father was unwilling to raise the child, the mother

that you were the father. I'll have the baby exposed[19] at once. That way there'll be no problem for you, and you'll have covered up the dreadful wrong done to the poor girl."

I gave my promise and I'm determined to honour my undertaking. As for taking her back, I don't believe that would be at all honourable, and I won't do it, in spite of the love and intimacy which bind me so strongly to her. I weep when I think of the life ahead of me and the loneliness. Oh fortune, how impermanent a gift you are! But my previous love affair has given me good practice in this sort of thing. I managed to get over that one through reason. I'll see if I can do the same with this one.

(*looking down the street*) Here comes Parmeno with the slaves. He's the last person we want involved in the situation. He's the only person I let know at the time that I didn't touch the girl when we were first married. I'm afraid that, if he hears these repeated cries, he'll realise that Philumena's in labour. I must send him away somewhere until the baby is born. (*he stands aside*)

Enter PARMENO *left from the direction of the harbour together with* SOSIA *and other slaves carrying baggage.*

PAR (*to Sosia*) You say it turned out to be an unpleasant journey?

SOS God knows, Parmeno, words really can't express quite how unpleasant it actually is to travel by sea.

PAR Is that so?

might, as here and often elsewhere in drama (compare *The Self-Tormentor* lines 626–643), give the baby to someone else to expose, in the hope that it might in fact be spared.

SOS	o fortunate, nescis quid mali
	praeterieris qui numquam's ingressus mare.
420	nam alias ut mittam miserias, unam hanc vide.
	dies triginta aut plus eo in navi fui,
	quom interea semper mortem exspectabam miser.
	ita usque advorsa tempestate usi sumus.
PAR	odiosum.
SOS	haud clam mest. denique hercle aufugerim
425	potius quam redeam, si eo mihi redeundum sciam.
PAR	olim quidem te causae impellebant leves,
	quod nunc minitare facere, ut faceres, Sosia.
	sed Pamphilum ipsum video stare ante ostium.
	ite intro. ego hunc adibo, si quid me velit.
430	ere, etiam tu hic stas?
PAM	et quidem te exspecto.
PAR	quid est?
PAM	in arcem transcurso opus est.
PAR	quoi homini?
PAM	tibi.
PAR	in arcem? quid eo?
PAM	Callidemidem hospitem
	Myconium, qui mecum una vectust, conveni.
PAR	perii! vovisse hunc dicam, si salvos domum
435	redisset umquam, ut me ambulando rumperet.
PAM	quid cessas?
PAR	quid vis dicam? an conveniam modo?

---

[20] Myconos, a Cycladic island not far from Delos, is not on the direct route from Imbros (line 171) to Athens, but a ship making this journey by the more sheltered route could well have called in there.

SOS You lucky devil, you don't know what misery you've missed by never going to sea. To say nothing of other sufferings, consider this one aspect. I was on the voyage for thirty days or more, and all the time I was in misery, expecting death at any moment; the weather we had was so foul all the way.

PAR How tiresome!

SOS Don't I know it? In the end, by god, I would rather run away than come back home if I knew I had to go back there again.

PAR (*with a smile*) In the old days it didn't take much to make you do what you're threatening to do now, Sosia. (*seeing Pamphilus*) But there's Pamphilus himself standing in front of the door. (*to Sosia and the slaves*) You go inside. (*they exit into Laches' house*) I'll go up and see if there's anything he wants from me. (*approaching Pamphilus*) Master, are you still standing here?

PAM Yes, and I've been looking for you.

PAR What for?

PAM I need someone to run over to the acropolis.

PAR (*without enthusiasm*) And who might that be?

PAM You.

PAR To the acropolis? Why there?

PAM Go and find Callidemides, my host from Myconos,[20] who travelled with me.

PAR (*aside*) Damn it! I bet he made a vow[21] that, if he ever got home safely, he'd burst my guts with running errands.

PAM What are you waiting for?

PAR What do you want me to say? Or do I just find him?

---

[21] It was common practice for travellers to vow a sacrifice or dedication to an appropriate deity if they returned safely home from their trip.

PAM immo quod constitui me hodie conventurum eum,
non posse, ne me frustra illi exspectet. vola.
PAR at non novi hominis faciem.
PAM   at faciam ut noveris.
440 magnus, rubicundus, crispus, crassus, caesius,
cadaverosa facie.
PAR   di illum perduint!
quid si non veniet? maneamne usque ad vesperum?
PAM maneto. curre.
PAR   non queo: ita defessu' sum.
PAM ille abiit. quid agam infelix? prorsus nescio
445 quo pacto hoc celem quod me oravit Myrrina,
suae gnatae partum. nam me miseret mulieris.
quod potero faciam, tamen ut pietatem colam.
nam me parenti potius quam amori obsequi
oportet. attat! eccum Phidippum et patrem
450 video. horsum pergunt. quid dicam hisce incertu' sum.

III. V: LACHES. PHIDIPPUS. PAMPHILUS.

LAC dixtin dudum illam dixisse se exspectare filium?
PHI factum.
LAC   venisse aiunt. redeat.
PAM   causam quam dicam patri
quam ob rem non redducam nescio.
LAC   quem ego hic audivi loqui?
PAM certum offirmarest viam me quam decrevi persequi.

192

PAM No. I made an appointment to meet him today. Tell him I can't, so he doesn't waste his time waiting for me there. Off you go.

PAR But I don't know what he looks like.

PAM I'll tell you how to recognise him. (*inventing wildly*) He's tall, ruddy, curly-haired, fat, grey-eyed, and with a face like a corpse.

PAR (*aside*) To hell with him! (*to Pamphilus*) What if he doesn't come? Am I to stay there right until evening?

PAM Yes, stay. Now run.

PAR I can't. I'm so tired. (*he goes off right reluctantly, leaving Pamphilus on stage alone*)

PAM That's got rid of him! What am I going to do, poor me? I've no idea how to keep the secret Myrrina begged me to keep, the fact that her daughter's having a baby. I'm sorry for the woman, so I'll do what I can, so long as I maintain my duty as a son. I must put my mother first before my love. (*looking down the street to the right*) Oh no! There are Phidippus and my father. They're coming this way. I just don't know what to say to them.

Enter LACHES *and* PHIDIPPUS *right from the direction of the forum.*

LAC Didn't you just tell me she said she was waiting for my son's return?

PHI Yes, I did.

LAC I'm told he's arrived. So she can come back.

PAM (*aside*) I don't know what reason to give my father for not taking her back.

LAC (*to Phidippus*) Who was that speaking?

PAM (*aside*) I'm determined to persist in following the path I've chosen.

455 LAC ipsus est de quo hoc agebam tecum.
    PAM   salve, mi pater.
    LAC gnate mi, salve.
    PHI   bene factum te advenisse, Pamphile;
        atque adeo, id quod maxumumst, salvom atque validum.
    PAM   creditur.
    LAC advenis modo?
    PAM   admodum.
    LAC   cedo, quid reliquit Phania
        consobrinus noster?
    PAM   sane hercle homo voluptati obsequens
460   fuit dum vixit; et qui sic sunt haud multum heredem
               iuvant,
        sibi vero hanc laudem relinquont "vixit, dum vixit, bene."
    LAC tum tu igitur nil attulisti plus una hac sententia?
    PAM quidquid est id quod reliquit, profuit.
    LAC   immo obfuit.
        nam illum vivom et salvom vellem.
    PHI   impune optare istuc licet.
465   ill' revivescet iam numquam. et tamen utrum malis scio.
    LAC heri Philumenam ad se accersi hic iussit. dic iussisse te.
    PHI noli fodere. iussi.
    LAC   sed eam iam remittet.
    PHI   scilicet.
    PAM omnem rem scio ut sit gesta. adveniens audivi modo.
    LAC at istos invidos di perdant qui haec lubenter nuntiant.

194

LAC   (*to Phidippus*) It's the very person we were talking about.

PAM   (*to Laches*) Good day, my dear father.

LAC   My dear son, good day.

PHI   It's good news that you're back, Pamphilus, and safe and well too, which is the important thing.

PAM   Quite so.

LAC   Have you just arrived?

PAM   Just now.

LAC   (*eagerly*) Tell me, how much did our cousin Phania leave?

PAM   Well actually, he was a great pursuer of pleasure while he lived, and men of that type don't do much for their heirs. What they do leave is an epitaph for themselves: "He lived, while he lived, well."

LAC   You mean you've brought back nothing except one single well turned phrase?

PAM   However little he did leave, it's a profit.

LAC   (*self-righteously*) No, it's a loss. I'd rather he was safe alive.

PHI   It's easy enough for you to express that wish. He's never going to return from the dead. (*aside*) And I know which you'd prefer.

LAC   (*to Pamphilus*) Yesterday Phidippus here ordered Philumena to be brought over to him. (*aside to Phidippus*). Say you ordered her.

PHI   (*aside to Laches*) Don't nudge me. (*aloud*) Yes I did.

LAC   Now he'll send her back straightaway.

PHI   Of course.

PAM   I know the whole story. I heard it just now when I arrived.

LAC   Confound those spiteful people who take delight in spreading gossip!

470	PAM	ego me scio cavisse ne ulla merito contumelia
		fieri a vobis posset; idque si nunc memorare hic velim
		quam fideli animo et benigno in illam et clementi fui,
		vere possum, ni te ex ipsa haec magis velim resciscere.
		namque eo pacto maxume apud te meo erit ingenio fides,
475		quom illa, quae nunc in me iniquast, aequa de me dixerit.
		neque mea culpa hoc discidium evenisse, id testor deos.
		sed quando sese esse indignam deputat matri meae
		quae concedat huiusque mores toleret sua modestia,
		neque alio pacto componi potest inter eas gratia,
480		segreganda aut mater a mest, Phidippe, aut Philumena.
		nunc me pietas matris potius commodum suadet sequi.
	LAC	Pamphile, haud invito ad auris sermo mi accessit tuos,
		quom te postputasse omnis res prae parente intellego.
		verum vide ne impulsus ira prave insistas, Pamphile.
485	PAM	quibus iris pulsus nunc in illam iniquo' sim,
		quae numquam quicquam erga me commeritast, pater,
		quod nollem, et saepe quod vellem meritam scio?
		amoque et laudo et vehementer desidero.
490		nam fuisse erga me miro ingenio expertu' sum,
		illique exopto ut relicuam vitam exigat
		cum eo viro me qui sit fortunatior,
		quandoquidem illam a me distrahit necessitas.
	PHI	tibi id in manust ne fiat.
	LAC	si sanus sies,
		iube illam redire.

478 huiusque *scripsi*, eiusque *Bothe*, cuiusque *codd*.

196

PAM (*slowly and deliberately*) I'm conscious of having taken every care not to give your family any just grounds for complaint. If I cared to recall here and now how loyal and kind and understanding I've been to her, I could do it quite truthfully, except that I should prefer you to hear it from her own lips. That will be the best way to give you confidence in my character, when she who now does me wrong speaks out and does me justice. I call the gods to witness that this separation has not come about through any fault of mine. Since she thinks it beneath her dignity to defer to my mother and to tolerate her ways with some proper restraint on her own part, and since there is no other way in which they can be reconciled, I must give up either my mother, Phidippus, or Philumena. In this situation my duty as a son bids me give preference to my mother's interests.

LAC Pamphilus, I was not displeased to hear what you had to say. I appreciate that you have put your mother before everything else. But mind that resentment doesn't lead you to pursue the wrong course, Pamphilus.

PAM (*with passion*) What resentment could make me treat her unjustly now, father, when she has never done anything against my wishes and I know she has often done things just to please me? I have nothing but love and praise for her and I miss her desperately, knowing from experience how wonderfully well disposed she was towards me. And I pray that she may pass the rest of her life with a husband more fortunate than I am, since she's torn away from me by fate.

PHI It's in your power to prevent it.

LAC If you have any sense, tell her to come back.

	PAM	non est consilium, pater.
495		matris servibo commodis.
	LAC	quo abis? mane!
		mane, inquam! quo abis?
	PHI	quae haec est pertinacia?
	LAC	dixin, Phidippe, hanc rem aegre laturum esse eum?
		quam ob rem te orabam filiam ut remitteres.
	PHI	non credidi edepol adeo inhumanum fore.
500		ita nunc is sibi me supplicaturum putat?
		sist ut velit redducere uxorem, licet;
		sin aliost animo, renumeret dotem huc, eat.
	LAC	ecce autem, tu quoque proterve iracundus es.
	PHI	percontumax redisti huc nobis, Pamphile.
505	LAC	decedet iam ira haec, etsi merito iratus est.
	PHI	quia paullum vobis accessit pecuniae,
		sublati animi sunt.
	LAC	etiam mecum litigas?
	PHI	deliberet renuntietque hodie mihi
		velitne an non, ut alii, si huic non est, siet.
510	LAC	Phidippe, ades, audi paucis. abiit. quid mea?
		postremo inter se transigant ipsi ut lubet,
		quando nec gnatus neque hic mi quicquam obtemperant,
		quae dico parvi pendunt. porto hoc iurgium
		ad uxorem quoius haec fiunt consilio omnia,
515		atque in eam hoc omne quod mihi aegrest evomam.

495 mane $\gamma D^2 L$, ades *cett.* (*nisi* ades mane $D^1 p^1$) *edd. pl.*

PAM That's not my intention, father. I shall devote myself to my mother's happiness. (*he turns to go*)

LAC Where are you going? Stop! Stop, I say! Where are you going? (*Pamphilus rushes into his house*)

PHI (*to Laches*) Why is he so stubborn?

LAC Didn't I tell you, Phidippus, that he would take this badly? That's why I begged you to send your daughter back.

PHI I didn't believe, for god's sake, he would be so lacking in human feeling. Does he really suppose I'll now go down on my knees to him? If in fact he wants to take his wife back, he can. But if he intends otherwise, he must return the dowry to me and go his way.

LAC Listen to that! You're another person being perverse and bad-tempered!

PHI (*shouting offstage*) You've returned to us in a very defiant mood, Pamphilus.

LAC He'll soon get over his resentment, even if it is justified.

PHI (*stung by this last remark*) You people are getting above yourselves, just because you've come into a bit of money.

LAC Are you picking a quarrel with me as well?

PHI (*formally*) He must consider his position and let me know today whether he wants her or not, so that someone else can have her if he doesn't. (*he makes to leave*)

LAC Phidippus, come here, listen a moment. (*Phidippus stalks off into his house*) (*to himself*) He's gone. What do I care? In the end they can sort it out for themselves to their own liking; neither he nor my son takes any notice of me or attaches any importance to what I say. I'll report this dispute to my wife, since all of this is due to her scheming, and vent all my annoyance on her. (*he exits into his house*)

ACTUS IV

IV. I: MYRRINA. PHIDIPPUS.

MYR   perii! quid agam? quo me vortam? quid viro meo respon-
       debo

       misera? nam audivisse vocem pueri visust vagientis:

       ita corripuit derepente tacitus sese ad filiam.

       quod si rescierit peperisse eam, id qua causa clam me
       habuisse

520   dicam non edepol scio.

       sed ostium concrepuit. credo ipsum exire ad me. nulla
       sum!

PHI   uxor ubi me ad filiam ire sensit, se duxit foras.

       atque eccam video. quid ais, Myrrina? heus, tibi dico.

MYR   mihine, vir?

PHI   vir ego tuos sim? tu virum me aut hominem deputas adeo
       esse?

525   nam si utrumvis horum, mulier, umquam tibi visus fo-
       rem,

       non sic ludibrio tuis factis habitus essem.

MYR   quibus?

PHI   at rogitas?

       peperit filia. hem! taces? ex qui?

MYR   istuc patrem rogarest aequom?

       perii! ex quo censes nisi ex illo quoi datast nuptum, ob-
       secro?

PHI   credo, neque adeo arbitrari patris est aliter. sed demiror

---

22 See *Phormio* note 62.

ACT FOUR

Enter MYRRINA *from her house in an agitated state.*

MYR (*to herself*) Damn it all! What am I going to do? Which way can I turn? Oh dear, what shall I tell my husband? He must have heard the baby crying: he dashed into our daughter's room so suddenly without saying a word. If he discovers she's had a child, heaven help me, I've no idea what reason I can give him for keeping it secret. But there's the door.[22] I suppose he's coming out to find me. I'm done for! (*she moves away from the door*)

Enter PHIDIPPUS *from his house.*

PHI When my wife realised I was going in to see my daughter, she ran outside. (*seeing Myrrina*) And there she is. What do have to say for yourself, Myrrina? Hey, I'm talking to you.

MYR (*with assumed innocence*) To me, husband?

PHI (*furiously*) Your husband, am I? Do you reckon me a husband or even a human being? If you'd ever seen me as either of these, woman, you wouldn't have made a fool of me like this by your doings.

MYR What doings?

PHI Do you need to ask? Our daughter has had a baby. (*Myrrina averts her eyes*) What! Not a word? Whose child is it?

MYR Is that a proper question for her father to ask? Damn it all! Whose child do you suppose it is other than her husband's, for heaven's sake?

PHI (*calming down*) I believe you. Indeed it's not for her father to think otherwise. But I can't imagine why it is

201

530   quid sit quam ob rem hunc tanto opere omnis nos celare
            volueris
        partum, praesertim quom et recte et tempore suo pepe-
            rerit.
        adeon pervicaci esse animo ut puerum praeoptares pe-
            rire,
        ex quo firmiorem inter nos fore amicitiam posthac scires,
        potius quam advorsum animi tui lubidinem esset cum illo
            nupta!
535   ego etiam illorum esse hanc culpam credidi, quae test
            penes.

MYR   misera sum.
PHI   utinam sciam ita esse istuc! sed nunc mi in mentem venit
        de hac re quod locuta's olim, quom illum generum cepi-
            mus.
        nam negabas nuptam posse filiam te tuam pati
        cum eo qui meretricem amaret, qui pernoctaret foris.
540 MYR   quamvis causam hunc suspicari quam ipsam veram ma-
            volo.
PHI   multo prius scivi quam tu illum habere amicam, Myrrina.
        verum id vitium numquam decrevi esse ego adules-
            centiae.
        nam id innatumst. at pol iam aderit se quoque etiam
            quom oderit.
        sed ut olim te ostendisti, eadem esse nil cessavisti usque
            adhuc
545   ut filiam ab eo abduceres neu quod ego egissem esset
            ratum.

[543] nam id *metro consulentes Bentley edd.*, nam id omnibus *codd.*

that you were so anxious to keep the birth from all of us, especially when it was a normal birth and at the right time.[23] (*a thought strikes him*) Can it be that you are so perverse? Do you prefer to see the death of a baby[24] who you knew would create a stronger bond of friendship between our two families for the future rather than the continuation of a marriage which was not to your liking? I actually thought the fault lay with them, when it lies with you.

MYR   I'm so unhappy!

PHI   If only I believed you![25] But I've just remembered what you said on the subject at the time when we took him as our son-in-law. You said you couldn't bear to see your daughter married to a man who kept a mistress and spent his nights away from home.

MYR   (*aside*) Better he suspect any other reason than the true one.

PHI   I knew he had a lover long before you did, Myrrina. But I've never considered this a vice in a young man. It's natural. For heaven's sake, the time will soon come when he even hates himself for it. But you've never to this day made any change to the attitude you revealed then, that you wanted to get your daughter away from him and

[23] Phidippus has evidently seen a normal healthy baby and not bothered to calculate the length of the gestation period (see note 18).

[24] Phidippus infers from the concealment of the birth that Myrrina is intending to expose the baby.

[25] That is, "that you are unhappy because you are being falsely accused," which is the implication of Myrrina's preceding remark.

id nunc res indicium haec facit quo pacto factum volue-
   ris.

MYR adeon me esse pervicacem censes, quoi mater siem,
ut eo essem animo, si ex usu esset nostro hoc matrimo-
   nium?

PHI tun prospicere aut iudicare nostram in rem quod sit
   potes?

550   audisti ex aliquo fortasse qui vidisse eum diceret
exeuntem aut intro euntem ad amicam. quid tum postea?
si modeste ac raro haec fecit, nonne ea dissimulare nos
magis humanumst quam dare operam id scire qui nos
   oderit?
nam si is posset ab ea sese derepente avellere

555   quicum tot consuesset annos, non eum hominem duce-
   rem
nec virum satis firmum gnatae.

MYR   mitte adulescentem, obsecro,
et quae me peccasse ais. abi, solus solum conveni,
roga velitne an non uxorem. sist ut dicat velle se,
redde; sin est autem ut nolit, recte ego consului meae.

560 PHI siquidem ille ipse non volt et tu sensti in eo esse, Myr-
   rina,
peccatum, aderam quoius consilio fuerat ea par prospici.
quam ob rem incendor ira esse ausam facere haec te
   iniussu meo.
interdico ne extulisse extra aedis puerum usquam velis.
sed ego stultior meis dictis parere hanc qui postulem.

565   ibo intro atque edicam servis ne quoquam efferri sinant.

---

558 an non uxorem Σ, uxorem an non A *metro incerto*

undo my arrangement. What has happened here makes it clear enough what your intentions were.

MYR   Do you suppose me so perverse that I would treat my own daughter like that, if this marriage was to our benefit?

PHI   Are you capable of looking ahead or judging what is to our advantage? Maybe you heard someone claiming to have seen him coming away from his mistress or going in to see her. What of it? If his visits were discreet and not too frequent, surely it is more human for us to turn a blind eye than to make it our business to find them out and make him hate us? If he was able to tear himself away at a moment's notice from an affair that had lasted for so many years, I would see him as lacking in human feeling and not a very stable husband for our daughter.

MYR   Never mind the young man, for goodness' sake, and the misdeeds which you say I have committed. Go and speak to him in private, and ask him whether he wants his wife or not. If it turns out that he says yes, give her back to him. If he says no, then I've done the right thing by my daughter.

PHI   Even if he is unwilling and you felt that the wrong was on his side, Myrrina, I was here and the decision should have been taken on my advice. So I'm incensed that you've ventured to act without my permission. I forbid you to take the baby anywhere outside the house. (*aside*) But I'd be a fool to expect her to do what I tell her! I'll go inside and give instructions to the slaves not to let it be taken out anywhere. (*he exits into his house, leaving Myrrina onstage alone*)

MYR nullam pol credo mulierem me miseriorem vivere.

nam ut hic laturus hoc sit, si ipsam rem ut siet resciverit,

non edepol clam mest, quom hoc quod leviust tam animo
irato tulit,

nec qua via sententia eius possit mutari scio.

570 hoc mi unum ex plurumis miseriis relicuom fuerat ma-
lum,

si puerum ut tollam cogit, quoius nos qui sit nescimus
pater.

nam quod compressast gnata, forma in tenebris nosci
non quitast,

neque detractum ei tum quicquamst qui posset post
nosci qui siet;

ipse eripuit vi, in digito quem habuit virgini abiens anu-
lum.

575 simul vereor Pamphilum ne orata nostra nequeat diutius

celare, quom sciet alienum puerum tolli pro suo.

IV. II: SOSTRATA. PAMPHILUS.

SOS non clam mest, gnate mi, tibi me esse suspectam, uxorem
tuam

propter meos mores hinc abisse, etsi ea dissimulas sedu-
lo.

verum ita me di ament itaque obtingant ex te quae ex-
optem mihi ut

580 numquam sciens commerui merito ut caperet odium
illam mei,

teque ante quod me amare rebar, ei rei firmasti fidem.

nam mi intus tuos pater narravit modo quo pacto me
habueris

praepositam amori tuo. nunc tibi me certumst contra
gratiam

MYR   (*to herself*) For heaven's sake, I don't think there's a more
miserable woman alive than me. If he finds out the true
state of affairs, it's only too clear to me how he's going to
react, when he's lost his temper at a less serious thing like
this. And I don't know how I can make him change his
mind. After all my countless miseries, it will be the last
straw if he forces me to raise a child whose father's iden-
tity we don't know. When my daughter was raped, she
couldn't recognise her assailant in the darkness, and she
didn't snatch any possession of his at the time by which
he could be identified later; in fact he himself as he left
stole a ring from her, which she was wearing on her
finger. At the same time I'm afraid that Pamphilus won't
be able to keep the secret I asked of him any longer, when
he finds out that someone else's child is being raised as
his. (*she exits into her house, leaving the stage empty*)

Enter SOSTRATA *and* PAMPHILUS *from their house.*

SOS   I'm well aware, my son, that you suspect that it's because
of my behaviour that your wife has left us, even though
you're doing your best to disguise the fact. But I swear by
the favour of heaven and every hope I have of you that
I've never consciously done anything to deserve her dis-
like. As for yourself, I always imagined that you loved me
and now you've confirmed my belief. Your father told me
inside just now how you've put consideration for me
above your love. Now I've decided to repay your kind-

referre, ut apud me praemium esse positum pietati scias.

585   mi Pamphile, hoc et vobis et meae commodum famae arbitror:

ego rus abituram hinc cum tuo me esse certo decrevi patre,

ne mea praesentia obstet neu causa ulla restet relicua

quin tua Philumena ad te redeat.

PAM   quaeso, quid istuc consilist?

illius stultitia victa ex urbe tu rus habitatum migres?

590   haud facies, neque sinam ut qui nobis, mater, male dictum velit,

mea pertinacia esse dicat factum, haud tua modestia.

tum tuas amicas te et cognatas deserere et festos dies

mea causa nolo.

SOS   nil pol iam istaec mihi res voluptatis ferunt.

dum aetatis tempus tulit, perfuncta satis sum. satias iam tenet

595   studiorum istorum. haec mihi nunc curast maxuma ut ne quoi mea

longinquitas aetatis obstet mortemve exspectet meam.

hic video me esse invisam immerito: tempust me concedere.

sic optume, ut ego opinor, omnis causas praecidam omnibus:

et me hac suspicione exsolvam et illis morem gessero.

600   sine me, obsecro, hoc effugere volgus quod male audit mulierum.

PAM   quam fortunatus ceteris sum rebus, absque una hac foret,

hanc matrem habens talem, illam autem uxorem!

ness, to show you how highly I value a son's loyalty. Pamphilus my dear, this is what I consider best for the pair of you and for my reputation. I've made up my mind to go and live on the farm with your father. Then I won't be in your way, and there'll be no remaining reason why your Philumena should not come back to you.

PAM   For heaven's sake, what kind of a scheme is this? You abandon the city for the country just because of her stupidity? You'll do nothing of the sort. And I won't have slander-mongers saying that all this is due to my obstinacy rather than to your unselfishness, mother. Besides, I don't want you to abandon your friends and relatives and your public festivals[26] for my sake.

SOS   Heaven knows, those things don't give me any pleasure nowadays. While my time of life allowed it, I had my fill of them, but now I'm bored with such pursuits. My chief concern now is not to be a nuisance to anybody in my old age or have people looking forward to my death. I see that I'm hated here, though it's not my fault. It's time for me to withdraw. As I see it, this is the best way to put an end to all these problems: I'll clear myself of suspicion and I'll let them (*pointing to Phidippus' house*) have their way. I implore you, let me escape the common reproach of womankind.[27]

PAM   How lucky I am in everything, apart from one matter,[28] having a mother like you and a wife like her!

[26] The religious festivals were one of the attractions of life in the city, and provided women in particular with the opportunity to socialise.   [27] That is, the charge that mothers-in-law hate their daughters-in-law.   [28] That is, the existence of the child.

SOS   obsecro, mi Pamphile,
non tute incommodam rem, ut quaequest, in animum in-
duces pati?
si cetera ita sunt ut vis itaque uti esse ego illa existumo,

605   mi gnate, da veniam hanc mihi, redduc illam.

PAM   vae misero mihi!

SOS   et mihi quidem! nam haec res non minus me male habet
quam te, gnate mi.

IV. III: LACHES. SOSTRATA. PAMPHILUS.

LAC   quem cum istoc sermonem habueris procul hinc stans
accepi, uxor.
istuc est sapere, qui ubiquomque opus sit animum possis
flectere,
quod sit faciundum fortasse post, idem hoc nunc si fece-
ris.

610 SOS   fors fuat pol.

LAC   abi rus ergo hinc. ibi ego te et tu me feres.

SOS   spero ecastor.

LAC   i ergo intro et compone quae tecum simul
ferantur. dixi.

SOS   ita ut iubes faciam.

PAM   pater!

LAC   quid vis, Pamphile?

PAM   hinc abire matrem? minume.

LAC   quid ita istuc vis?

PAM   quia de uxore incertus sum etiam quid sim facturus.

LAC   quid est?

615   quid vis facere nisi redducere?

---

604 illa *Erasmus edd.*, illam *codd. Don.* (illam *retinet Marouzeau* ea
post itaque *addito*)

SOS   I beg you, my dear Pamphilus, can't you bring yourself to put up with that problem, whatever it is? If everything else is as you wish and things are as I believe them to be, grant me this favour, my son, and take her back.

PAM   Oh dear! I'm so miserable!

SOS   So am I! This situation is as distressing to me as it is to you, my son.

LACHES has entered from his house unseen during the previous scene.

LAC   (*to Sostrata*) I've been standing over here, my dear, and I overheard your conversation from a distance. It shows good sense to be willing to change your mind when the need arises, and to do now what you might well have to do later.

SOS   Heaven grant you're right!

LAC   So off you go to the farm, where I'll put up with you and you with me.

SOS   I certainly hope we will.

LAC   Go inside then, and get together what you need to take with you. That's all. (*he turns away*)

SOS   I'll do as you suggest. (*she exits into her house*)

PAM   Father!

LAC   What do you want, Pamphilus?

PAM   Is mother to go away? No, on no account.

LAC   How do you mean?

PAM   Because I'm still uncertain what to do about my wife.

LAC   What's this? What else do you want but to take her back?

PAM   equidem cupio et vix contineor.
        sed non minuam meum consilium. ex usu quod est id
           persequar.
        credo ea gratia concordes, si non redducam, fore.

LAC   nescias. verum id tua refert nil utrum illaec fecerint
        quando haec aberit. odiosa haec est aetas adulescentulis.

620   e medio aequom excederest. postremo nos iam fabulae
        sumus, Pamphile, "senex atque anus."
        sed video Phidippum egredi per tempus. accedamus.

IV. III: PHIDIPPUS. LACHES. PAMPHILUS.

PHI   tibi quoque edepol sum iratus, Philumena,
        graviter quidem. nam hercle factumst abs te turpiter.

625   etsi tibi causast de hac re: mater te impulit.
        huic vero nullast.

LAC   opportune te mihi,
        Phidippe, in ipso tempore ostendis.

PHI   quid est?

PAM   quid respondebo his? aut quo pacto hoc aperiam?

LAC   dic filiae rus concessuram hinc Sostratam,

630   ne revereatur minus iam quo redeat domum.

PHI   ah!
        nullam de his rebus culpam commeruit tua.
        a Myrrina haec sunt mea uxore exorta omnia.

PAM   mutatio fit.

PHI   ea nos perturbat, Lache.

---

617 credo *codd. Don.*, non credo *edd. nonn.* concordes *CP¹D²LE*,
concordes magis *cett. Don.* si non *codd. Don.*, si *edd. nonn.*
633 mutatio fit *Pamphilo dat A²*, Phidippo *cett.*

PAM   (*aside*) That's what I want, and I can scarcely restrain myself. But I won't alter my decision. I'll persist with the proper course. (*to Laches*) I believe it will help to reconcile them, if I don't take her back.

LAC   You can't tell. But it makes no difference to you what they do, once your mother's gone away. Old people are irksome to the young. It's the right thing for her to get out of your way. (*smiling ruefully*) In the end we're just the old couple in the story,[29] Pamphilus. (*as Phidippus' door opens*) But here's Phidippus coming out, just when we want him. Let's approach him.

Enter PHIDIPPUS *from his house.*

PHI   (*speaking back to Philumena inside*) In heaven's name, Philumena, I'm angry with you too, exceedingly so. By god, you've acted disgracefully. You do have an excuse, though: your mother put you up to it. She has none.

LAC   (*accosting him*) You've appeared very conveniently, Phidippus, just at the right moment.

PHI   How so?

PAM   (*aside*) What shall I tell them? How can I explain the situation?

LAC   Tell your daughter that Sostrata is going to retire to the farm, so she needn't be afraid to come home any more.

PHI   Oh! Your wife's not at all to blame for this. It all started with my wife Myrrina.

PAM   (*aside*) That's a change!

PHI   She's the one who's stirred up this trouble, Laches.

---

[29] The reference is uncertain. Donatus suggests that "The Old Man and the Old Woman" (*senex atque anus*) was the title of a story.

213

	PAM	dum ne redducam, turbent porro quam velint.
635	PHI	ego, Pamphile, esse inter nos, si fieri potest,
		affinitatem hanc sane perpetuam volo.
		sin est ut aliter tua siet sententia,
		accipias puerum.
	PAM	sensit peperisse. occidi!
	LAC	puerum? quem puerum?
	PHI	natus est nobis nepos.
640		nam abducta a vobis praegnas fuerat filia,
		neque fuisse praegnatem umquam ante hunc scivi diem.
	LAC	bene, ita me di ament, nuntias; et gaudeo
		natum illum et tibi illam salvam. sed quid mulieris
		uxorem habes aut quibus moratam moribus?
645		nosne hoc celatos tam diu! nequeo satis
		quam hoc mihi videtur factum prave proloqui.
	PHI	non tibi illud factum minus placet quam mihi, Lache.
	PAM	etiamsi dudum fuerat ambiguom hoc mihi,
		nunc non est quom eam sequitur alienus puer.
650	LAC	nulla tibi, Pamphile, hic iam consultatiost.
	PAM	perii!
	LAC	hunc videre saepe optabamus diem
		quom ex te esset aliquis qui te appellaret patrem.
		evenit. habeo gratiam dis.
	PAM	nullu' sum!
	LAC	redduc uxorem ac noli advorsari mihi.
655	PAM	pater, si ex me illa liberos vellet sibi

<hr>

643 *sic* δ *Don.* natum filium *A.* tibi et γ*D²L*

PAM (*aside*) As long as I don't have to take her back, they can stir up all the trouble they like.

PHI (*to Pamphilus*) Pamphilus, my own wish is for the family connection between us to be a truly lasting one, if that's possible. But if in fact you have other ideas, you must take the child.[30]

PAM (*aside*) He's found out about the birth. I'm lost!

LAC Child? What child?

PHI We have a grandson. Our daughter was pregnant when she was removed from your house, though I didn't find out about the pregnancy until today.

LAC Heaven help me! That's good news. I'm delighted a child's been born and your daughter's safe and well. But what sort of a woman do you have for a wife? Is this how she usually behaves? To think we've been kept in the dark for so long! I can hardly express in words how perverse her conduct strikes me as being.

PHI I am just as displeased at her actions as you are, Laches.

PAM (*aside*) Whatever doubts I had before, I've none now, if she's bringing someone else's child with her.

LAC (*to Pamphilus*) You've no longer any room for deliberation, Pamphilus.

PAM (*aside*) I'm ruined!

LAC This is the day we often longed to see, when you would have a child to call you father. It's come, and I give thanks to the gods.

PAM (*aside*) I'm done for!

LAC Do what I tell you and take back your wife.

PAM Father, if she wanted to have children by me and remain

[30] In case of a divorce (which is implied in the phrase "other ideas"), the custody of the child reverted to the father.

aut se esse mecum nuptam, satis certo scio,
non clam me haberet quae celasse intellego.
nunc quom eius alienum esse animum a me sentiam

nec conventurum inter nos posthac arbitror,

660 quam ob rem redducam?

LAC   mater quod suasit sua
adulescens mulier fecit. mirandumne id est?
censen te posse reperire ullam mulierem
quae careat culpa? an quia non delincunt viri?

PHI vosmet videte iam, Lache et tu Pamphile,

665 remissan opus sit vobis redductan domum.
uxor quid faciat in manu non est mea:
neutra in re vobis difficultas a me erit.
sed quid faciemus puero?

LAC   ridicule rogas.
quicquid futurumst, huic suom reddas scilicet

670 ut alamus nostrum.

PAM   quem ipse neglexit pater,
ego alam?

LAC   quid dixti? eho! an non alemus, Pamphile?
prodemus, quaeso, potius? quae haec amentiast?
enimvero prorsus iam tacere non queo.
nam cogis ea quae nolo ut praesente hoc loquar.

675 ignarum censes tuarum lacrimarum esse me
aut quid sit id quod sollicitare ad hunc modum?
primum hanc ubi dixti causam, te propter tuam
matrem non posse habere hanc uxorem domi,
pollicitast ea se concessuram ex aedibus.

680 nunc postquam ademptam hanc quoque tibi causam
     vides,
puer quia clam test natus, nactus alteram's.

my wife, I'm quite sure she would not have kept from me what I see she has kept secret. It's clear that she's turned against me, and I don't think we'll be able to live together in the future: why should I take her back?

LAC She's young and she did what her mother urged her to do. Is that surprising? Do you suppose you can find a perfect woman? Or is it that men have no failings?

PHI You two, Laches and Pamphilus, must decide whether you want to send her back to us or take her back home. What my wife does is not in my control, but either way I won't create any difficulties. But what shall we do with the child?

LAC That's a ridiculous question. Whatever happens, you must of course give Pamphilus his child back, so that we can bring it up as ours.

PAM (*forgetting himself*) Bring up a child which its own father has disowned?

LAC (*not quite comprehending*) What did you say? Oh! Shall we not bring it up, Pamphilus? Would you rather we abandoned it, if you please? What sort of a madness is this? (*changing his tone*) Really, I can't hold my tongue any longer. You're forcing me to say what I don't want to say in front of him (*pointing to Phidippus*). Do you suppose I haven't noticed your tears or realised what it is that is upsetting you so? Originally you gave the excuse that you couldn't keep your wife at home because of your mother; so your mother undertook to leave the house. Now, when you see this excuse removed from you, you've found yourself another one, that she had a baby without

217

erras tui animi si me esse ignarum putas.
aliquando tandem huc animum ut adiungas tuom,
quam longum spatium amandi amicam tibi dedi!
685   sumptus quos fecisti in eam quam animo aequo tuli!
egi atque oravi tecum uxorem ut duceres,
tempus dixi esse. impulsu duxisti meo.
quae tum obsecutus mihi fecisti ut decuerat.
nunc animum rursum ad meretricem induxti tuom,
690   quoi tu obsecutus facis huic adeo iniuriam.
nam in eandem vitam te revolutum denuo
video esse.

PAM   mene?

LAC   te ipsum. et facis iniuriam:
confingis falsas causas ad discordiam,
ut cum illa vivas, testem hanc quom abs te amoveris;
695   sensitque adeo uxor. nam ei causa alia quae fuit
quam ob rem abs te abiret?

PHI   plane hic divinat. nam id est.

PAM   dabo iusiurandum nil esse istorum mihi.

LAC   ah!
redduc uxorem aut quam ob rem non opus sit cedo.

PAM   non est nunc tempus.

LAC   puerum accipias. nam is quidem
700   in culpa non est. post de matre videro.

PAM   omnibu' modis miser sum nec quid agam scio.
tot nunc me rebus miserum concludit pater.
abibo hinc, praesens quando promoveo parum.
nam puerum iniussu, credo, non tollent meo,
705   praesertim in ea re quom sit mi adiutrix socrus.

your knowledge. If you think I don't know what's in your mind, you're mistaken. How long I allowed you to carry on an affair with a mistress, so that you might some day in the end turn your mind in the direction of marriage! How patiently I bore the expense of that affair! I begged and implored you to take a wife. I said it was time. You took one in response to my prompting. You did the proper thing then in complying with my wishes. But now you've turned your attention to your mistress again; you're complying with *her* wishes and committing a wrong against your wife. I see you've relapsed once more into your old way of life.

PAM   (*indignantly*) Me?

LAC   Yes, you. And you're doing her a wrong. You're inventing false excuses for a quarrel, so that you can live with your mistress without your wife looking over your shoulder. And in fact your wife has realised this. What other reason could she have for leaving you?

PHI   (*aside*) The man must have second sight. That's exactly it.

PAM   I will swear on oath that none of this is true.

LAC   Oh! Take your wife back then or tell us why you don't want to.

PAM   Now's not the time.

LAC   Well, take the child. It's certainly not to blame. I'll see about the mother later.

PAM   (*aside*) I'm thoroughly miserable, and I don't know what to do. Oh dear, my father has me cornered with all these arguments. I'll be off, since I'm not achieving anything by staying here. They won't raise the child without my permission, I'm sure, especially since my mother-in-law is on my side in this. (*he rushes off left*)

219

LAC   fugis? hem! nec quicquam certi respondes mihi?
        num tibi videtur esse apud sese? sine.
        puerum, Phidippe, mihi cedo. ego alam.

PHI   maxume.
        non mirum fecit uxor si hoc aegre tulit.

710   amarae mulieres sunt: non facile haec ferunt.
        propterea haec irast. nam ipsa narravit mihi.
        id ego hoc praesente tibi nolueram dicere,
        neque illi credebam primo. nunc verum palamst.
        nam omnino abhorrere animum huic video a nuptiis.

715 LAC quid ergo agam, Phidippe? quid das consili?

PHI   quid agas? meretricem hanc primum adeundam censeo.
        oremus, accusemus, gravius denique
        minitemur si cum illo habuerit rem postea.

LAC   faciam ut mones. eho puere, curre ad Bacchidem hanc

720   vicinam nostram: huc evoca verbis meis.
        at te oro porro in hac re adiutor sis mihi.

PHI   ah!
        iamdudum dixi idemque nunc dico, Lache.
        manere affinitatem hanc inter nos volo,
        si ullo modost ut possit, quod spero fore.

725   sed vin adesse me una dum istam convenis?

LAC   immo vero abi, aliquam puero nutricem para.

719 puere curre *Erasmus*, curre puer *F*, puer curre *cett*.

LAC (*shouting after him*) Are you running away? Hey! Aren't you going to give me a definite answer? (*to Phidippus*) Do you think he's all right? But never mind him. Give me the child, Phidippus. I'll bring it up.

PHI By all means. No wonder my wife has taken this badly. Women are prickly creatures: they don't take these things easily. This *is* what's caused all the ill-feeling: she told me herself.[31] I didn't want to say it in your son's presence, and I didn't believe her at first. But now the truth is out. I can see that he's temperamentally quite unsuited to married life.

LAC What shall I do then, Phidippus? What's your advice?

PHI What should you do? I suggest that we approach this mistress of his first. Let's appeal to her, put the accusation in front of her, and finally threaten some firm action if she has anything to do with him in the future.

LAC I'll do as you suggest. (*calling inside*) Hey, boy! Run next door to Bacchis' house and tell her I want her out here. (*a slave emerges and departs on this errand*) (*to Phidippus*) And please continue to stand by me in this.

PHI Well, I've said it all the time and I say it again now, Laches. I want this marriage alliance between us to last, if it's at all possible, and I hope it will. But do you want me to be present when you speak to her?

LAC No. You go off and find a nurse for the baby. (*Phidippus exits right in the direction of the forum*)

---

[31] See lines 536–540.

ACTUS V

V. I: BACCHIS. LACHES.

BAC   non hoc de nihilost quod Laches me nunc conventam
     esse expetit.

       nec pol me multum fallit quin quod suspicor sit quod
     velit.

LAC   videndumst ne minus propter iram hinc impetrem quam
     possiem,

730   aut ne quid faciam plus quod post me minus fecisse satiu'
     sit.

       aggrediar. Bacchis, salve.

BAC   salve, Lache.

LAC   credo edepol te non nil mirari, Bacchis,
     quid sit quapropter te huc foras puerum evocare iussi.

BAC   ego pol quoque etiam timida sum quom venit mi in men-
     tem quae sim,

735   ne nomen mihi quaesti obsiet. nam mores facile tutor.

LAC   si vera dices, nil tibist a me pericli, mulier.

       nam iam aetate ea sum ut non siet peccato mi ignosci
     aequom.

       quo magis omnes res cautius ne temere faciam accuro.

       nam si id facis facturave's bonas quod par est facere,

740   inscitum offerre iniuriam tibi immerenti iniquomst.

BAC   est magna ecastor gratia de istac re quam tibi habeam.

       nam qui post factam iniuriam se expurget parum mi pro-
     sit.

       sed quid istuc est?

LAC   meum receptas filium ad te Pamphilum.

BAC   ah!

ACT FIVE

Enter BACCHIS *from her house, accompanied by two maids.*

BAC   (*to herself*) It's not for nothing that Laches wants to get in touch with me now. And, unless I'm much mistaken, I've a good idea of what he's after.

LAC   (*to himself*) I must be careful not to lose my temper and so achieve less than I might have, or overdo things and then regret it afterwards. I'll approach her. (*to Bacchis*) Good day, Bacchis.

BAC   Good day, Laches.

LAC   I suppose you must really be quite puzzled, Bacchis, why I sent my slave to call you out here.

BAC   I'm also rather apprehensive, heaven knows, when I remember what I am. I hope the reputation of my profession won't count against me; my behaviour I can easily defend.

LAC   (*awkwardly polite*) If you tell the truth, you're in no danger from me, my good woman. I'm now at an age where I can't expect any indiscretion to be excused, so I'm all the more careful in all situations not to act too hastily. If you are behaving as an honest woman should and intend to go on doing so, it would be wrong of me to offer you a clumsy insult when you don't deserve it.

BAC   (*amused*) Lord knows, I should be very grateful to you for that remark. An apology *after* an insult wouldn't do much for me. But what is this about?

LAC   You're receiving visits from my son Pamphilus.

BAC   Oh?

---

[729] hinc *Bentley*, hanc *codd*.   [736] dices *Dp Don*., dicis *cett*.

LAC sine dicam. uxorem hanc prius quam duxit, vostrum
  amorem pertuli.

745 mane. nondum etiam dixi id quod volui. hic nunc uxorem
  habet.

quaere alium tibi firmiorem dum tibi tempus consulen-
  dist.

nam neque ille hoc animo erit aetatem neque pol tu ea-
  dem istac aetate.

BAC quis id ait?

LAC   socrus.

BAC   mene?

LAC   te ipsam. et filiam abduxit suam

puerumque ob eam rem clam voluit, natus quist, exstin-
  guere.

750 BAC aliud si scirem qui firmare meam apud vos possem fidem
sanctius quam iusiurandum, id pollicerer tibi, Lache,
me segregatum habuisse, uxorem ut duxit, a me Pamphi-
  lum.

LAC lepida's. sed scin quid volo potius sodes facias?

BAC   quid vis? cedo.

LAC eas ad mulieres huc intro atque istuc iusiurandum idem

755 pollicere illis. exple animum eis teque hoc crimine ex-
  pedi.

BAC faciam quod pol, si esset alia ex hoc quaestu, haud face-
  ret, scio,

ut de tali causa nuptae mulieri se ostenderet.

sed nolo esse falsa fama gnatum suspectum tuom,

nec leviorem vobis, quibus est minume aequom, eum
  viderier

---

746 firmiorem *edd.*, firmiorem amicum Σ, amicum firmiorem A

LAC   Let me speak. Before he took a wife, I put up with your love affair. (*Bacchis begins to protest*) Wait! I haven't yet said what I wanted to say. He now has a wife. So find yourself a more permanent lover, while you have time to do what's best for yourself. He won't feel the way he does for ever, and you won't always be of the same age.

BAC   (*returning to Laches' accusation*) Who says so?

LAC   His mother-in-law.

BAC   Of me?

LAC   Yes, you. And she's taken her daughter back, and for the same reason has decided to do away with the baby that's been born without anybody being told.

BAC   (*earnestly*) If I knew a more solemn way to convince you of my truthfulness than by swearing an oath, I would use it, Laches, to assure you I have had no dealings with Pamphilus since the day he married.[32]

LAC   That's very nice of you! But do you know what I'd rather you did, if you will?

BAC   What? Tell me.

LAC   Go inside to the women and give them the same solemn assurance. Put their minds at rest and clear yourself of this accusation.

BAC   All right. I'll do what I'm sure nobody else of my profession would do: face up to a married woman for such a purpose. But I don't want your son to come under suspicion through a false rumour, nor you of all people to think

---

[32] This statement contradicts that of Parmeno at lines 157–159. Either Bacchis is lying here to protect herself and Pamphilus, or Parmeno was embellishing his story there in order to impress Philotis.

760   immerito. nam meritus de mest quod queam illi ut com-
        modem.

LAC   facilem benivolumque lingua tua iam tibi me reddidit.

    nam non sunt solae arbitratae haec: ego quoque etiam
        credidi.

    nunc quam ego te esse praeter nostram opinionem com-
        peri,

    fac eadem ut sis porro. nostra utere amicitia ut voles.

765   aliter si facies—reprimam me ne aegre quicquam ex me
        audias.

    verum hoc moneo unum: qualis sim amicus aut quid pos-
        siem

    potius quam inimicus, periclum facias.

        V. II: PHIDIPPUS. BACCHIS. LACHES.

PHI   nil apud me tibi
    defieri patiar, quin quod opus sit benigne praebeatur.

    sed quom tu satura atque ebria eris, puer ut satur sit faci-
        to.

770 LAC   noster socer, video, venit. puero nutricem adducit.

    Phidippe, Bacchis deierat persancte—

PHI   haecin east?

LAC   haec est.

PHI   nec pol istae metuont deos neque eas respicere deos opi-
        nor.

BAC   ancillas dedo: quolubet cruciatu per me exquire.

    haec res hic agitur. Pamphilo me facere ut redeat uxor

775   oportet. quod si perficio non paenitet me famae,

---

[33] The evidence of slaves was admissible in a court of law only when
obtained under torture.

him irresponsible when he doesn't deserve it. From me he deserves all the help I can give him.

LAC Your words have filled me with generosity and good will towards you. The women weren't the only ones who believed the story: I did so too. Now that I've found you a different person from what we expected, just go on being that way, and you may make what use of our friendship you will. If you don't—but I'll refrain from saying anything that might upset you. However, I'll give you one piece of advice: try me and see what sort of a friend I am and what I can do for you as a friend rather than as an enemy.

Enter PHIDIPPUS *right bringing a* NURSE *for the baby.*

PHI (*to the nurse*) I'll see you don't lack anything in my house; whatever you need will be generously provided. But when you've had enough to eat and drink, make sure the baby is satisfied. (*the nurse exits into Phidippus' house*)

LAC (*to himself*) I see our father-in-law's back. He's bringing a nurse for the baby. (*to Phidippus*) Phidippus, Bacchis has sworn a most solemn oath—

PHI (*looking at Bacchis with some distaste*) Is that her?

LAC Yes, it is.

PHI Their sort don't fear the gods, for heaven's sake, and I don't expect the gods take any notice of them.

BAC (*with dignity*) My maids are at your disposal; you have my permission to examine them under whatever torture you like.[33] What's happening here is this. I see it as my duty to ensure that Pamphilus' wife goes back to him. If I succeed in that, I don't mind it being said of me that I am

227

solam fecisse id quod aliae meretrices facere fugitant.

LAC Phidippe, nostras mulieres suspectas fuisse falso
nobis in re ipsa invenimus. porro hanc nunc experiamur.
nam si compererit crimini tua se uxor credidisse,

780 missam iram faciet. sin autemst ob eam rem iratus gna-
tus,
quod peperit uxor clam, id levest. cito ab eo haec ira
abscedet.
profecto in hac re nil malist quod sit discidio dignum.

PHI velim quidem hercle.

LAC   exquire: adest. quod satis sit faciet ipsa.

PHI quid mihi istaec narras? an quia non tute ipse dudum
audisti

785 de hac re animus meus ut sit, Laches? illis modo explete
animum.

LAC quaeso edepol, Bacchis, quod mihi's pollicita tute ut ser-
ves.

BAC ob eam rem vin ergo intro eam?

LAC   i atque exple animum eis; coge ut credant.

BAC eo, etsi scio pol eis fore meum conspectum invisum
hodie.
nam nupta meretrici hostis est, a viro ubi segregatast.

790 LAC at haec amicae erunt, ubi quam ob rem adveneris rescis-
cent.

792 nam illas errore et te simul suspicione exsolves.

779 credidisse *D¹p Don.*, falso credidisse *codd. pl.*, se credidisse A
791 PH. at easdem amicas fore tibi promitto rem ubi cognorint *codd.
pl., versum omittit A, post 783 habent Dp*

the only woman in my profession to have done what the others wouldn't dream of doing.

LAC Phidippus, we've discovered that in fact we've suspected our wives wrongly; let's now give Bacchis a hearing in her turn. If your wife finds out that she has believed a mere accusation, she'll put aside her anger. And if my son resents the fact that his wife has had a child without telling anybody, it's no great matter; he'll soon get over it. It's quite clear there's nothing here that justifies a separation.

PHI By god, I hope so.

LAC Well, examine her (*pointing to Bacchis*): she's at your service. I'm sure she'll give you satisfaction.

PHI Why are you saying this to me? Didn't you hear me telling you just now how I feel in this, Laches?[34] It's just the women you need to satisfy. (*he exits into his house*)

LAC (*to Bacchis*) I beg you in heaven's name, keep the promise you made me.

BAC You want me to go inside for that purpose?

LAC Yes, go and satisfy them. Make them believe you.

BAC I'll go, though I know they're going to hate the sight of me, by heaven. When a bride's parted from her husband, there's no love lost between her and his mistress.

LAC But they'll become your friends, once they find out why you've come.[35] You'll have saved them from error and yourself from suspicion.

---

[34] Phidippus has stated that he is keen to preserve the marriage relationship between the two families (see lines 722–724).

[35] The Calliopian MS (Σ) preserve an extra line here (791) in which Phidippus virtually repeats what Laches has just said. The line looks like a doublet of 790 and is here omitted: it would be out of keeping with Phidippus' hostile attitude to Bacchis.

BAC   perii! pudet Philumenae. me sequimini huc intro ambae.

LAC   quid est quod mihi malim quam quod huic intellego eve-
       nire,

795   ut gratiam ineat sine suo dispendio et mihi prosit?
       nam sist ut haec nunc Pamphilum vere ab se segregarit,
       scit sibi nobilitatem ex eo et rem natam et gloriam esse.
       referet gratiam ei unaque nos sibi opera amicos iunget.

V. III: PARMENO. BACCHIS.

PAR   edepol ne meam erus esse operam deputat parvi preti,

800   qui ob rem nullam misit frustra ubi totum desedi diem,
       Myconium hospitem dum exspecto in arce Callidemi-
          dem.
       itaque ineptus hodie dum illi sedeo, ut quisque venerat,
       accedebam: "adulescens, dic dum, quaeso, mi, es tu My-
          conius?"
       "non sum." "at Callidemides?" "non." "hospitem ecquem
          Pamphilum

805   hic habes?" omnes negabant, neque eum quemquam
          esse arbitror.
       denique hercle iam pudebat: abii. sed quid Bacchidem
       ab nostro affine exeuntem video? quid huic hic est rei?

BAC   Parmeno, opportune te offers. propere curre ad Pamphi-
       lum.

PAR   quid eo?

BAC   dic me orare ut veniat.

BAC (*to herself*) Damnation! I'm embarrassed to face Philu-
mena. (*pulling herself together*) You two, follow me in-
side. (*she exits into Phidippus' house with her maids*)

LAC (*to himself*) There's nothing I'd rather see happen than
what I see happening to her: she's earning herself grati-
tude at no cost and doing me me a good turn. If it's true
that she's now broken off with Pamphilus, she knows that
fame and fortune and glory all await her as a result. She'll
be repaying his kindness and at the same time winning
our friendship. (*he exits into his house, leaving the stage
empty*)

Enter PARMENO *right from the direction of the forum, looking
hot and tired.*

PAR (*to himself*) Believe me, my master doesn't put much
value on my services. For no reason at all he sent me on a
pointless errand: I've been sitting around the whole day
on the acropolis waiting for Callidemides, this visitor
from Myconos. I sat there like a fool, and, whenever any-
one came past, I went up to him and said: "Excuse me,
young man, are you from Myconos?" "Not me." "Are you
Callidemides?" "No." "Do you have a friend here called
Pamphilus?" They all said no. I don't think any such per-
son exists. In the end, for god's sake, I got embarrassed
and left. (*seeing Bacchis emerging from Phidippus'
house*) But why's Bacchis coming out of our in-laws'
house? What's she up to there?

BAC Parmeno, you're just in time. Run off and find Pam-
philus, and look sharp about it.

PAR What for?

BAC Tell him, I beg him to come.

	PAR	ad te?
	BAC	immo, ad Philumenam.
810	PAR	quid reist?
	BAC	tua quod nil refert percontari desinas.
	PAR	nil aliud dicam?
	BAC	etiam: cognosse anulum illum Myrrinam

gnatae suae fuisse quem ipsus olim mi dederat.

	PAR	scio.

tantumnest?

	BAC	tantum. aderit continuo hoc ubi ex te audiverit.

sed cessas?

	PAR	minume equidem. nam hodie mihi potestas non datast.
815		ita cursando atque ambulando totum hunc contrivi diem.

	BAC	quantam obtuli adventu meo laetitiam Pamphilo hodie!

quot commodas res attuli! quot autem ademi curas!

gnatum ei restituo, qui paene harunc ipsiusque opera
    periit;

uxorem, quam numquamst ratus posthac se habiturum,
    reddo.

820 qua re suspectus suo patri et Phidippo fuit, exsolvi.

hic adeo his rebus anulus fuit initium inveniundis.

nam memini abhinc mensis decem fere ad me nocte
    prima

confugere anhelantem domum sine comite, vini plenum,

cum hoc anulo. extimui ilico. "mi Pamphile," inquam
    "amabo,

825 quid exanimatu's, obsecro? aut unde anulum istum nac-
    tu's?

dic mi." ille alias res agere se simulare. postquam id
    video,

PAR To you?

BAC No, to Philumena.

PAR What's this about?

BAC (*rudely*) Stop asking questions. It's not your business.

PAR No further message?

BAC Yes. Say that Myrrina has recognised the ring he once gave me. It had belonged to her daughter.

PAR I see. Is that all?

BAC That's all. He'll come at once when he hears what you have to say. (*Parmeno lingers*) What are you waiting for?

PAR I'm not waiting at all. I haven't been allowed to wait all day. I've wasted the whole time running around doing errands. (*he exits left, leaving Bacchis onstage alone*)

BAC (*to herself*) How much happiness I've given Pamphilus by coming here today! How many blessings I've brought him, and how many worries I've removed! I'm restoring to him a son, who almost lost his life thanks to the women and himself, and I'm giving him back a wife, whom he never imagined he'd have again. And I've cleared away the suspicions which his father and Phidippus had of him. It was in fact this ring (*pointing to her finger*) which led to the recognition of the truth. I remember that about ten months ago[36] he came rushing to my house as night fell, out of breath, all by himself,[37] the worse for wine, with this ring. I was frightened out of my wits. "My dear Pamphilus," I said, "my darling, why are you in such a state, for goodness' sake? And where did you get that ring? Tell me." He pretended he hadn't heard me. When

---

[36] That is, ten lunar months, equivalent to nine calendar months.

[37] A young man out on the town would normally have been accompanied by a slave.

nescioquid suspicarier magis coepi, instare ut dicat.
homo se fatetur vi in via nescioquam compressisse,
dicitque sese illi anulum, dum luctat, detraxisse.
830 eum haec cognovit Myrrina in digito modo me haben-
tem.
rogat unde sit. narro omnia haec. inde est cognitio facta
Philumenam compressam esse ab eo et filium inde hunc
natum.
haec tot propter me gaudia illi contigisse laetor,
etsi hoc meretrices aliae nolunt. neque enimst in rem
nostram
835 ut quisquam amator nuptiis laetetur. verum ecastor
numquam animum quaesti gratia ad malas adducam par-
tis.
ego dum illo licitumst usa sum benigno et lepido et comi.
incommode mihi nuptiis evenit, factum fateor.
at pol me fecisse arbitror ne id merito mi eveniret.
840 multa ex quo fuerint commoda, eius incommoda ae-
quomst ferre.

V. III: PAMPHILUS. PARMENO. BACCHIS.

PAM vide, mi Parmeno, etiam sodes ut mi haec certa et clara
attuleris.
ne me in breve conicias tempus gaudio hoc falso frui.
PAR visumst.
PAM   certen?
PAR   certe.
PAM   deus sum si hoc itast.
PAR   verum reperies.

830 habentem *codd.*, habente *Bentley edd. pl.*

I saw that, my suspicions increased and I insisted on an answer. The fellow admitted he'd raped some girl in the street, and said he'd snatched the ring off her in the struggle. Well, just now Myrrina here recognised the ring, which I was wearing on my finger. She asked where I had got it, and I told her the whole story. That's how it came out that it was Philumena who had been raped by him and it is his son who has now been born. I am delighted to have been the cause of so much joy for him, though this is not how other women of my sort feel. It's not in our interest for any lover to be happily married. But I swear I'll never bring myself to behave meanly for the sake of my profession. While circumstances allowed us to be together, I found him kind, charming, and generous. His marriage was a blow to me, I have to admit. But, heavens, I don't think I did anything to deserve it. When you've had so many good times from a man, it's only right to put up with the bad ones.

Enter PAMPHILUS *left with* PARMENO.

PAM   My dear Parmeno, make sure once more, if you will, that what you're telling me is clear and definite, and that you're not condemning me to momentary enjoyment of a spurious happiness.

PAR   I *have* made sure.

PAM   Absolutely?

PAR   Absolutely.

PAM   I'm a god, if this is right.

PAR   You'll find it's true.

PAM   manedum sodes. timeo ne aliud credam atque aliud nun-
ties.

845 PAR maneo.

PAM   sic te dixe opinor, invenisse Myrrinam
Bacchidem anulum suom habere.

PAR   factum.

PAM   eum quem olim ei dedi,
eaque hoc te mihi nuntiare iussit. itanest factum?

PAR   ita, inquam.

PAM   quis mest fortunatior venustatisque adeo plenior?
egon pro hoc te nuntio qui donem? qui? qui? nescio.

850 PAR at ego scio.

PAM   quid?

PAR   nihilo enim.
nam neque in nuntio neque in me ipso tibi boni quid sit
scio.

PAM   egon qui ab Orco mortuom me reducem in lucem feceris
sinam sine munere a me abire? ah, nimium me ignavom
putas.

sed Bacchidem eccam video stare ante ostium.

855   me exspectat, credo. adibo.

BAC   salve, Pamphile.

PAM   o Bacchis, o mea Bacchis, servatrix mea!

BAC   bene factum et volup est.

PAM   factis ut credam facis,
antiquamque adeo tuam venustatem obtines

845 dixe *Bentley edd. pl.*, dixisse (= *iamb. oct.*) *codd. Don.*
853 ignavom *A*, ingratum Σ

PAM Wait a moment, if you don't mind. I'm worried that you're telling me one thing and I'm believing another.

PAR I'm waiting.

PAM This is what I think you said. Myrrina has discovered Bacchis wearing *her* ring.

PAR Exactly.

PAM The one I gave her some time ago? And she told you to tell me the news? Is that it?

PAR Yes, that's it, I'm telling you.

PAM (*ecstatically*) Who is more fortunate than me or indeed luckier in love? (*hugging Parmeno*) What reward shall I give you in return for this news? What? What? I've no idea.

PAR (*disengaging himself*) Well, *I* have.

PAM What?

PAR Nothing. I can't see what good I or my news have done you.

PAM (*expansively*) I was dead and you brought me back from hell into the light of day. Can I let you go off after that without a reward? Oh, you must think I'm a despicable wretch! (*suddenly seeing Bacchis*) But look, there's Bacchis standing in front of our door. I suppose she's looking for me. I'll go up to her. (*he does so, while Parmeno keep his distance*)

BAC Good day, Pamphilus.

PAM (*throwing his arms round her*) Oh Bacchis, oh my darling Bacchis, my salvation!

BAC You're welcome. It's a pleasure.

PAM Your deeds speak for you. (*stepping back and looking at her fondly*) And you still retain your old charm! It will al-

ut voluptati obitus, sermo, adventus tuos, quoquomque
adveneris,

860 semper siet.

BAC at tu ecastor morem antiquom atque ingenium obtines,
ut unus hominum homo te vivat numquam quisquam
blandior.

PAM hahahae! tun mihi istuc?

BAC recte amasti, Pamphile, uxorem tuam.
nam numquam ante hunc diem meis oculis eam quod
nossem videram.

perliberalis visast.

PAM dic verum.

BAC ita me di ament, Pamphile.

865 PAM dic mi, harum rerum numquid dixti iam patri?

BAC nil.

PAM neque opus est.
adeo muttito. placet non fieri hic itidem ut in comoediis
omnia omnes ubi resciscunt. hic quos par fuerat rescis-
cere
sciunt. quos non autem aequomst scire neque resciscent
neque scient.

BAC immo etiam qui hoc occultari facilius credas dabo.

870 Myrrina ita Phidippo dixit iureiurando meo
se fidem habuisse et propterea te sibi purgatum.

PAM optumest,
speroque hanc rem esse eventuram nobis ex sententia.

PAR ere, licetne scire ex te hodie quid sit quod feci boni?
aut quid istuc est quod vos agitis?

PAM non licet.

ways be a delight to meet you, talk with you, have a visit from you, wherever it may be.

BAC And *you're* still your old self with your old ways, I swear it. There's not a man alive with a smoother tongue than yours.

PAM Hahaha! Are *you* saying that to *me*?

BAC (*more seriously*) You were right to fall in love with your wife, Pamphilus. As far as I know, I'd never set eyes on her before today. She seems a very nice lady.

PAM (*a little embarrassed*) Tell me the truth.

BAC (*laughing*) It is the truth, as heaven is my witness, Pamphilus.

PAM Tell me, have you told my father[38] anything about this?

BAC Not a thing.

PAM There's no need to, not even a whisper. I don't want what happens in comedies to happen here, where everybody finds out everything. In this case those who need to know know already; those who don't must not find out or ever know.

BAC Well, I'll give you a reason to believe we can keep the secret fairly easily. Myrrina told Phidippus that she was convinced by my oath and that you're therefore cleared in her eyes.

PAM That's excellent. And I hope this whole situation will turn out to our liking. (*Bacchis exits into her house*)

PAR (*coming up to Pamphilus*) Master, am I allowed to know what good thing I've done today? Or what exactly you all are up to?

PAM No, you're not.

---

[38] Or "her father"; the Latin is not specific.

PAR   tamen suspicor:

875   ego hunc ab Orco mortuom? quo pacto?

PAM   nescis, Parmeno,

quantum hodie profueris mihi et ex quanta aerumna
    extraxeris.

PAR   immo vero scio, neque imprudens feci.

PAM   ego istuc satis scio.

PAR   an

temere quicquam Parmeno praetereat quod facto usu'
    sit?

PAM   sequere me intro, Parmeno.

PAR   sequor. equidem plus hodie boni

880   feci imprudens quam sciens ante hunc diem umquam.

Ω   plaudite!

877 an . . . sit *Parmenoni dant codd. pl. Don., Pamphilo Ap[1], Bacchidi
Don. in comm.*

PAR   Well, I have my suspicions. (*musing to himself*) I brought him back from hell when he was dead? How?

PAM   You've no idea, Parmeno, what a good turn you've done me today and what distress you've rescued me from.

PAR   (*bluffing*) Yes, I have. I knew perfectly well what I was doing.

PAM   (*also bluffing*) I'm sure you did.

PAR   Would Parmeno be so careless as to pass by anything which needed to be done?

PAM   Follow me inside, Parmeno.

PAR   I'm coming. (*to himself*) Truly, I've done more good to-day unwittingly than I've ever done on purpose before.

ALL   (*to the audience*) Give us your applause.[39]

---

[39] See *Phormio* note 74.

THE BROTHERS

INTRODUCTORY NOTE

The Brothers, based on a Greek original of the same name by Menander, is in many ways Terence's most interesting play. Its theme is the same as that of *The Self-Tormentor*, the father-son relationship, but it puts the two rival methods of education, the strict and the lenient, in starker opposition to each other and by an unexpected volte-face at the end invites the audience to judge between them. Of the two fathers, Micio, who argues on philosophical grounds for a lenient approach, is in the ascendancy for most of the play, but it is the strict Demea who wins out in the end. This raises the question whether Terence adapted Menander's ending and if so why: it is interesting that the vast majority of subsequent adaptations of Terence have in fact allowed the Micio figure to triumph. It is possible that Menander, who was a pupil in the Peripatetic school after Aristotle, favoured Micio as an embodiment of Aristotle's "reasonable man," and that Terence, influenced by the Roman concept of the strict *paterfamilias*, shifted the balance in favour of Demea. But since very little remains of Menander's play, this can only be speculation.

The play begins with a monologue by Micio outlining his philosophy of education (this is the only play of Terence's which opens with a monologue), after which Demea bursts in with the news that Aeschinus (Demea's older son,

245

adopted by Micio and now being brought up by him) has broken into a pimp's house and abducted a music girl. Aeschinus then arrives with the girl, pursued by the pimp, and blows are struck as she is bustled into Micio's house; the obvious intention of the scene is to add a slapstick element after the long verbal debate between Micio and Demea. It is made clear in Terence's prologue that this scene was not in Menander's *The Brothers*, but had been taken by Terence from a play by Menander's contemporary Diphilus; this is a clear case of "contamination" which Terence does not deny. Next Ctesipho (Demea's younger son) arrives, and we learn to our surprise that Aeschinus has abducted the girl for his brother, not for himself. Even more surprising is the revelation in the following scene that Aeschinus has got the daughter of the widow next door pregnant and has been ashamed to confess this to his father, so that we have to revise our opinion of Aeschinus and of the efficacy of Micio's educational methods. It is commonly believed that in Menander's version a divine prologue would have told the audience the truth of the situation from the beginning, thus eliminating the surprise element.

One of the best scenes of the play is the one where Micio, now in possession of the true facts, catches Aeschinus on the doorstep of the house next door, trying to pluck up courage to knock, and teases him with a false tale about a relative from Miletus, who (in accordance with Athenian law about orphan heiresses) has come to carry away the daughter and marry her. After this Micio rebukes Aeschinus for the rape of the girl and for not having told him the situation before, but then reveals that he has arranged for them to marry, leaving Aeschinus overjoyed at having such a wonderful father. At this point Micio's educational methods seem to be vindicated; conversely, Demea seems quite out of touch with Ctesipho, fondly believing that his son is a paragon of virtue when nothing could be further from the truth. However, at the end of the play, Aeschinus transfers his allegiance to Demea, who has decided to embark on a campaign of affability and wins Aeschinus over by a proposal to hasten the marriage by destroying the garden wall between the two houses and bringing the bride across. Moreover, Demea asserts himself over Micio, persuading him very much against his will and his better judgment to marry his son's new mother-in-law and to perform various other acts of generosity. The play ends with Micio discomfited and Demea offering his two sons advice and reproof as appropriate.

The play makes good use of the "duality method" with a contrasted pair of fathers and a contrasted pair of sons all closely involved in each other's problems. Micio and Demea are in fact brothers, Micio an easygoing wealthy bachelor living in town and Demea a tight-fisted married farmer living in the country; the exchanges between them illuminate the differences in their characters as well as in their educational principles. Of the two sons, Aeschinus is by far the more attractive; Ctesipho is by contrast feckless and irresponsible. Among the minor characters Syrus stands out, not a tricky slave in the Plautine sense, but an extremely smooth operator, who flatters Demea shamelessly with false tales about Ctesipho's propriety and then sends him on a wild goose chase around the town in search of Micio. Syrus also gets the better of the pimp Sannio, whom he persuades to accept the bare purchase price for the music girl. Hegio, a relative of the widow Sostrata, is introduced as a man of old-fashioned principles and displays a fierce loyalty to her and her family; it is interesting from a social and ethical standpoint that he is prepared to condone the rape so long as Aeschinus recognises his responsibility and marries the girl. Sostrata herself has a small but sympathetic part. Her loneliness as a widow is emphasised, and she shows spirit in refusing to hush up her daughter's condition and proclaiming herself ready to take Aeschinus to court when he has (apparently) abandoned the girl.

SELECT BIBLIOGRAPHY

Editions

Gratwick, A. S. (Warminster, 2nd edn 2000).
Martin, R. H. (Cambridge 1976).

Criticism

Fantham, E. "*Heautontimoroumenos* and *Adelphoe:* A Study of Fatherhood in Terence and Menander." *Latomus* 30 (1971): 970–998.

Goldberg, S. M. *Understanding Terence.* Princeton, 1986: 22–29, 97–105, 211–216.

Grant, J. N. "The Ending of Terence's *Adelphoe* and the Menandrian Original." *American Journal of Philology* 96 (1975): 42–60.

Johnson, W. R. "Micio and the Perils of Perfection." *California Studies in Classical Antiquity* 1 (1968): 171–186.

Lord, C. "Aristotle, Menander, and the *Adelphoe* of Terence." *Transactions of the American Philological Association* 107 (1977): 183–202.

Rieth, O. *Die Kunst Menanders in den Adelphen des Terenz.* Hildesheim, 1964.

DIDASCALIA

INCIPIT TERENTI ADELPHOE
ACTA LVDIS FUNEBRIBVS L. AEMELIO PAULO
QUOS FECERE Q. FABIVS MAXVMVS P. CORNELIVS AFRICANVS
EGERE L. AMBIVIVS TURPIO L. HATILIVS PRAENESTINVS
MODOS FECIT FLACCVS CLAVDI TIBIIS SARRANIS TOTA
GRAECA MENANDRV
FACTA VI M CORNELIO CETHEGO L. ANICIO GALLO COS

C. SULPICI APOLLINARIS PERIOCHA

duos cum haberet Demea adulescentulos
dat Micioni fratri adoptandum Aeschinum,
sed Ctesiphonem retinet. hunc citharistriae
lepore captum sub duro et tristi patre
frater celabat Aeschinus. famam rei,
amorem in sese transferebat, denique
fidicinam lenoni eripit. vitiaverat
idem Aeschinus civem Atticam pauperculam
fidemque dederat hanc sibi uxorem fore.
Demea iurgare, graviter ferre. mox tamen
ut veritas patefactast, ducit Aeschinus
vitiatam, potitur Ctesipho citharistriam.

PRODUCTION NOTICE

Here begins The Brothers of Terence, acted at the Funeral Games given in honour of Aemilius Paullus by Q. Fabius Maximus and P. Cornelius Africanus.[1] Produced by L. Ambivius Turpio and L. Atilius of Praeneste. Music composed by Flaccus, slave of Claudius, for Sarranian pipes throughout.[2] Greek original by Menander. The author's sixth play, performed in the consulship of M. Cornelius Cethegus and L. Anicius Gallus.[3]

SYNOPSIS BY C. SULPICIUS APOLLINARIS

Having two young sons, Demea gave Aeschinus to his brother Micio to adopt but kept Ctesipho for himself. The latter while under the eye of his strict stern father was captivated by the charms of a music girl, but his secret was kept by his brother Aeschinus, who took upon himself the infamy of the love affair and in the end abducted the girl from the pimp. Aeschinus for his part had raped a poor Athenian citizen girl, and had promised to make her his wife. Demea is upset at this and a quarrel ensues. But presently the truth comes out, Aeschinus marries the girl he had raped, and Ctesipho is allowed to keep the music girl.

[1] This was the same festival at which *The Mother-in-Law* failed for the second time. Q. Fabius Maximus and P. Cornelius Africanus (= Scipio Aemilianus) were in fact the sons of Aemilius Paullus: their names reflect the families into which they were adopted.

[2] Sarranian (i.e. Tyrian) pipes were apparently equal; it is not clear how they differed from other equal pipes.

[3] That is, in 160 B.C.

PERSONAE

MICIO senex
DEMEA senex
SANNIO leno
AESCHINUS adulescens
SYRUS servos
CTESIPHO adulescens
SOSTRATA matrona
CANTHARA anus
GETA servos
HEGIO senex
DROMO puer

Scaena: Athenis

252

CHARACTERS

MICIO, an old man, adoptive father of Aeschinus

DEMEA, an old man, brother of Micio and father of
    Aeschinus and Ctesipho

SANNIO, a pimp

AESCHINUS, a young man, son of Demea and adoptive son
    of Micio, lover of Pamphila

SYRUS, slave of Micio

CTESIPHO, a young man, son of Demea and lover of the
    courtesan Bacchis

SOSTRATA, a matron, mother of Pamphila

CANTHARA, an old woman, nurse in Sostrata's household

GETA, slave of Sostrata

HEGIO, an old man, friend and relative of Sostrata

DROMO, another slave of Micio

Staging

The stage represents a street in Athens. On it are two houses,
that of Micio to the audience's left and that of Sostrata to their
right.[4] The exit on the right leads to the forum; that on the left
leads to the country.

---

[4] The location of the two stage houses is conjectural. The reason for
placing Micio's house to the left is that Demea at his entry from the
right at line 543 fails to see Ctesipho and Syrus in front of it.

ADELPOE

postquam poeta sensit scripturam suam
ab iniquis observari et advorsarios
rapere in peiorem partem quam acturi sumus,
indicio de se ipse erit, vos eritis iudices
5 laudin an vitio duci factum oporteat.
Synapothnescontes Diphili comoediast.
eam Commorientis Plautus fecit fabulam.
in Graeca adulescens est qui lenoni eripit
meretricem in prima fabula. eum Plautus locum
10 reliquit integrum, eum hic locum sumpsit sibi
in Adelphos, verbum de verbo expressum extulit.
eam nos acturi sumus novam. pernoscite
furtumne factum existumetis an locum
reprehensum qui praeteritus neglegentiast.
15 nam quod isti dicunt malevoli, homines nobilis
hunc adiutare assidueque una scribere,
quod illi maledictum vehemens esse existumant,
eam laudem hic ducit maxumam quom illis placet
qui vobis univorsis et populo placent,
20 quorum opera in bello, in otio, in negotio
suo quisque tempore usust sine superbia.

THE BROTHERS

PROLOGUE

The playwright is aware that his works are being subjected to unfair criticism and that his opponents are misrepresenting the play we are about to perform. He will himself present the evidence in his own trial, and you shall judge whether what he has done merits praise or censure. *Synapothescontes* is a comedy by Diphilus,[5] on which Plautus based his play *Commorientes*.[6] At the beginning of the Greek version there is a young man who abducts a girl from a pimp. Plautus left that scene out, and our author has taken it over for his *The Brothers*, reproducing it word for word. We are presenting this as a brand new play. It is for you to decide whether you deem us guilty of plagiarism or of the reclaiming of a scene which had been carelessly omitted.

As for the malicious accusation that members of the nobility assist our author and collaborate with him in his writing all the time, which his enemies consider a serious reproach, he regards it as a great compliment, if he finds favour with men who find favour with all of you and the people at large, men whose services have been freely available to everyone in time of need in war, in peace, and in their daily affairs.

---

[5] Diphilus was an older contemporary of Menander's and was acknowledged as one of the three leading writers of New Comedy.
[6] Both titles mean "Joined in Death."

dehinc ne exspectetis argumentum fabulae:
senes qui primi venient, ii partem aperient,
in agendo partem ostendent. facite aequanimitas
25 poetae ad scribendum augeat industriam.

ACTUS I

I. I: MICIO.

MIC Storax! non rediit hac nocte a cena Aeschinus
neque servolorum quisquam qui advorsum ierant.
profecto hoc vere dicunt: si absis uspiam
aut ibi si cesses, evenire ea satius est
30 quae in te uxor dicit et quae in animo cogitat
irata quam illa quae parentes propitii.
uxor, si cesses, aut te amare cogitat
aut tete amari aut potare atque animo obsequi
et tibi bene esse soli, quom sibi sit male.
35 ego quia non rediit filius quae cogito et
quibus nunc sollicitor rebus! ne aut ille alserit
aut uspiam ceciderit aut praefregerit
aliquid. vah! quemquamne hominem in animo instituere
     aut
parare quod sit carius quam ipsest sibi!
40 atque ex me hic natus non est sed ex fratre. is adeo
dissimili studiost iam inde ab adulescentia.
ego hanc clementem vitam urbanam atque otium
secutus sum et, quod fortunatum isti putant,
uxorem numquam habui. ille contra haec omnia.
45 ruri agere vitam, semper parce ac duriter
se habere. uxorem duxit, nati filii
duo. inde ego hunc maiorem adoptavi mihi,

THE BROTHERS

After this don't expect an outline of the plot. The old men who come on first will in part explain it and in part reveal it in the course of the action. See that you give the play a fair hearing and encourage the author to continue with the task of writing.

ACT ONE

Enter MICIO *from his house.*

MIC (*calling down the street to a slave*) Storax! (*getting no reply, to himself*) Aeschinus hasn't come back from that dinner party last night, nor any of the slaves who went to fetch him. It's quite true what they say: if you're out somewhere and get home late, you're better off with what an angry wife accuses you of or imagines than what fond parents do. If you're late, your wife imagines that you're in love or that someone has fallen in love with you or else that you're drinking and enjoying yourself and having fun on your own while she isn't. But in my case, when my son hasn't returned, what dreadful things I imagine, what anxieties I entertain! I only hope he hasn't caught a cold or fallen somewhere or broken something. Oh! Why does anybody want or acquire something that will prove dearer to him than his own self? In fact, he's not my own son by birth but my brother's. Now *he's* been a totally different character from me ever since we were young. I've pursued an easygoing life of leisure in the city, and I've never had a wife, which they reckon is a blessing. He's been exactly the opposite. He's lived in the country, choosing a life of thrift and hardship. He married and had two sons. Of these I adopted the elder one and have brought him up since he was a small child. I've

257

eduxi e parvolo, habui, amavi pro meo.
in eo me oblecto, solum id est carum mihi.
50 ille ut item contra me habeat facio sedulo.
do, praetermitto, non necesse habeo omnia
pro meo iure agere. postremo, alii clanculum
patres quae faciunt, quae fert adulescentia,
ea ne me celet consuefeci filium.
55 nam qui mentiri aut fallere institerit patrem aut
audebit, tanto magis audebit ceteros.
pudore et liberalitate liberos
retinere satius esse credo quam metu.
haec fratri mecum non conveniunt neque placent.
60 venit ad me saepe clamitans "quid agis, Micio?
quor perdis adulescentem nobis? quor amat?
quor potat? quor tu his rebus sumptum suggeris,
vestitu nimio indulges? nimium ineptus es."
nimium ipsest durus praeter aequomque et bonum,
65 et errat longe mea quidem sententia
qui imperium credat gravius esse aut stabilius
vi quod fit quam illud quod amicitia adiungitur.
mea sic est ratio et sic animum induco meum:
malo coactus qui suom officium facit,
70 dum id rescitum iri credit, tantisper cavet;
si sperat fore clam, rursum ad ingenium redit.
ill' quem beneficio adiungas ex animo facit,
studet par referre, praesens absensque idem erit.
hoc patriumst, potius consuefacere filium
75 sua sponte recte facere quam alieno metu:
hoc pater et dominus interest. hoc qui nequit,
fateatur nescire imperare liberis.

55 institerit *Kauer-Lindsay*, insueverit *A*, insuerit Σ

treated him and loved him as my own. In him I find my pleasure; he's the only thing I really care about. And I do my best to see that he returns my affection. I'm generous, I turn a blind eye, I don't find it necessary to exert my authority all the time. In short I've accustomed my son not to hide from me those youthful escapades which others get up to behind their fathers' backs. A boy who sets out to lie and deceive his father and is bold enough to do that will be all the more bold with others. I believe that it is better to discipline children by gaining their respect and showing generosity than through fear. My brother doesn't agree with me on this; he just doesn't approve. He often comes to me shouting "What are you doing, Micio? Why are you ruining our boy? Why is he having a love affair? Why is he drinking? Why are you supplying him with money for these things? Why are you spoiling him with expensive clothes? You're being all too silly about it." Well, he's being all too strict, well beyond what is fair or right; and he's making a big mistake, in my opinion at least, if he thinks that authority imposed by force is stronger or surer than one based on affection. This is my philosophy and the principle I've adopted. A person who acts as he ought under threat of punishment watches his step only as long as he believes he'll be found out; if he thinks he can go undiscovered, he reverts to his natural tendencies. A person who is won over by kindness acts from the heart. He is eager to repay you; he will be the same whether he is with you or not. A father's duty is to accustom his son to do right of his own accord rather than through fear of someone else. That's the difference between a father and a master. Anyone who can't see this should admit he has no idea how to manage children.

sed estne hic ipsus de quo agebam? et certe is est.
nescioquid tristem video. credo, iam ut solet
80   iurgabit.

I. II: MICIO. DEMEA.

MIC   salvom te advenire, Demea,
gaudemus.

DEM   ehem, opportune! te ipsum quaerito.

MIC   quid tristis es?

DEM   rogas me, ubi nobis Aeschinus
siet, quid tristis ego sim?

MIC   dixin hoc fore?
quid fecit?

DEM   quid ille fecerit? quem neque pudet
85   quicquam nec metuit quemquam neque legem putat
tenere se ullam. nam illa quae antehac facta sunt
omitto: modo quid dissignavit?

MIC   quidnam id est?

DEM   fores effregit atque in aedis irruit
alienas. ipsum dominum atque omnem familiam
90   mulcavit usque ad mortem. eripuit mulierem
quam amabat. clamant omnes indignissume
factum esse. hoc advenienti quot mihi, Micio,
dixere! in orest omni populo. denique,
si conferendum exemplumst, non fratrem videt
95   rei dare operam, ruri esse parcum ac sobrium?
nullum huius simile factum. haec quom illi, Micio,
dico, tibi dico. tu illum corrumpi sinis.

---

7 The antecedents of the plot are not very clear in Terence's version.
Though the play apparently opens in the early morning (line 26),
Demea has had time to come in from the country and go into town,
where he has heard rumours of Aeschinus' escapade.

(*looking down the street*) But isn't that the very man I was talking about? I'm sure it is. He's looking gloomy about something. I suppose he'll pick a quarrel as usual.

Enter DEMEA *right from the direction of the forum.*[7]

MIC (*civilly*) Glad to see you back all right, Demea.

DEM (*ignoring the greeting*) Oh, good! I've been looking for you.

MIC Why so gloomy?

DEM You ask me why I'm gloomy, when we've Aeschinus on our hands?

MIC (*aside*) Didn't I tell you he'd be like this? (*aloud*) What's he done?

DEM What's he done? A boy who has no shame or fear and believes he's above the law? To say nothing of what he's done in the past, look at his latest exploit.

MIC What on earth is it?

DEM He's broken down a door and forced his way into someone else's house. He's beaten the master and the whole household practically to death. And he's abducted a girl he'd taken a fancy to. Everybody is protesting that it's outrageous behaviour. The number of people who spoke of it, Micio, as I came into town! The whole population is talking about it. All I can say is, if he needs an example, why doesn't he look at his brother, who is devoting himself to work and living a sober frugal life on the farm? Their behaviour's totally different. And when I complain about Aeschinus, I'm complaining about you, Micio. You're the one who're letting him go to the bad.

MIC   homini imperito numquam quicquam iniustiust,
        qui nisi quod ipse fecit nil rectum putat.
100 DEM quorsum istuc?
MIC   quia tu, Demea, haec male iudicas.
        non est flagitium, mihi crede, adulescentulum
        scortari neque potari, non est, neque fores
        effringere. haec si neque ego neque tu fecimus,
        non siit egestas facere nos. tu nunc tibi
105   id laudi ducis quod tum fecisti inopia?
        iniuriumst. nam si esset unde fieret,
        faceremus. et tu illum tuom, si esses homo,
        sineres nunc facere dum per aetatem licet
        potius quam, ubi te exspectatum eiecisset foras,
110   alieniore aetate post faceret tamen.
DEM   pro Iuppiter, tu homo adigis me ad insaniam.
        non est flagitium facere haec adulescentulum?
MIC   ah!
        ausculta, ne me optundas de hac re saepius.
        tuom filium dedisti adoptandum mihi.
115   is meus est factus. si quid peccat, Demea,
        mihi peccat. ego illi maxumam partem fero.
        opsonat, potat, olet unguenta? de meo.
        amat? dabitur a me argentum dum erit commodum;
        ubi non erit, fortasse excludetur foras.
120   fores effregit? restituentur. discidit
        vestem? resarcietur. et—dis gratia—
        est unde haec fiant; et adhuc non molesta sunt.
        postremo aut desine aut cedo quemvis arbitrum.

---

[8] This was not one of the accusations made by Demea: Micio is concentrating on matters which can easily be put right.

MIC There's nothing more unreasonable than a man with no experience of the world who doesn't think anything right except what he's done himself.

DEM And what's that supposed to mean?

MIC That you've got this quite wrong, Demea. It's not a scandal, believe me, for a young lad to chase after girls or go drinking. It really isn't, nor to break down a door. If you and I didn't do these things, it was because we couldn't afford them. Are you now claiming credit for behaviour forced on you by poverty? That's not reasonable. If we'd had the means to do these things, we would have done them. And, if you had any humanity, you would allow that son of yours to do them while he has the excuse of youth, rather than have him do them at a less appropriate age when he has at long last seen you to your grave.

DEM Jupiter! You're driving me crazy. Not a scandal for a young lad to behave like this?

MIC Oh! Listen to me and stop battering my ears with these complaints. You gave me your son to adopt. He's now mine, and, if he does anything wrong, Demea, I'm the one who's affected, I'm the one who bears the brunt of it. He wines and dines and smells of perfume: it's at my expense. He's in love: I'll keep him in funds as long as it suits me; when it doesn't, maybe he'll be thrown out. He's broken down a door: it can be repaired. He's torn some clothes:[8] they can be mended. I have the means to pay, thank heaven, and so far it isn't a problem. So in the end either shut up or name an arbitrator:[9] I'll demonstrate

---

[9] Both Greek and Roman law provided for civil disputes to be settled by an arbitrator acceptable to both sides. Menander's *The Arbitration* takes its name from just such a scene.

te plura in hac re peccare ostendam.

DEM   ei mihi!

125   pater esse disce ab illis qui vere sciunt.

MIC   natura tu illi pater es, consiliis ego.

DEM   tun consiliis quicquam?

MIC   ah! si pergis, abiero.

DEM   sicin agis?

MIC   an ego totiens de eadem re audiam?

DEM   curaest mihi.

MIC   et mihi curaest. verum, Demea,

130   curemus aequam uterque partem. tu alterum,
ego item alterum. nam ambos curare propemodum
reposcere illumst quem dedisti.

DEM   ah, Micio!

MIC   mihi sic videtur.

DEM   quid istic? si tibi istuc placet,
profundat, perdat, pereat. nil ad me attinet.

135   iam si verbum unum posthac—

MIC   rursum, Demea,
irascere?

DEM   an non credis? repeto quem dedi?
aegrest. alienus non sum. si obsto—em, desino.
unum vis curem: curo. et est dis gratia
quom ita ut volost. iste tuos ipse sentiet

140   posterius—nolo in illum gravius dicere.

MIC   nec nil neque omnia haec sunt quae dicit. tamen
non nil molesta haec sunt mihi. sed ostendere
me aegre pati illi nolui. nam itast homo:
quom placo, advorsor sedulo et deterreo,

127 consiliis *A*, consulis Σ *Don.*

that you're the one who is more at fault here.

DEM Oh dear! Learn how to be a father from those who really know.

MIC You're his father by birth, I by counsel.

DEM You couldn't counsel anything!

MIC Oh! If you're going to carry on, I'm leaving. (*he turns to go*)

DEM Is that your attitude?

MIC Am I supposed to go on listening to the same old story?

DEM (*changing his tone*) I'm concerned for him.

MIC So am I. But, Demea, let's divide the concern equally between us. You take one son, I'll take the other. If you're going to concern yourself with both, you might as well demand the return of the one you gave me.

DEM Oh, Micio!

MIC That's how I see it.

DEM All right then. If that's what you want, let him squander, waste, go to the bad. It's not my business. But if I hear one word in the future—

MIC Losing your temper again, Demea?

DEM You don't believe me? Is this asking back the boy I gave you? It's difficult. He's my flesh and blood. If I interfere—Very well, I give up. You want me to concern myself with one son? I'll do just that, and thank heaven he's a boy after my own heart. That one of yours will come to his senses in due course. But I don't want to be too harsh on him. (*he exits left in the direction of the country, leaving Micio onstage alone*)

MIC (*to himself*) There's something in what he says, but it's not the whole story. I *am* rather annoyed by all this, but I wasn't going to show him I'm upset. He's that sort of man: when I want to calm him down, though I do my best to

265

145   tamen vix humane patitur. verum si augeam
      aut etiam adiutor sim eius iracundiae,
      insaniam profecto cum illo. etsi Aeschinus
      non nullam in hac re nobis facit iniuriam.
      quam hic non amavit meretricem? aut quoi non dedit
150   aliquid? postremo nuper (credo iam omnium
      taedebat) dixit velle uxorem ducere.
      sperabam iam defervisse adulescentiam.
      gaudebam. ecce autem de integro! nisi, quidquid est,
      volo scire atque hominem convenire, si apud forumst.

ACTUS II

II. I: SANNIO. AESCHINUS. (PARMENO.) (BACCHIS.)

155 SAN   obsecro, populares, ferte misero atque innocenti auxi-
              lium,
            subvenite inopi.

    AES   otiose. nunciam ilico hic consiste.
            quid respectas? nil periclist. numquam dum ego adero
              hic te tanget.

    SAN   ego istam invitis omnibus.

    AES   quamquamst scelestus non committet hodie umquam
              iterum ut vapulet.

160 SAN   Aeschine, audi, ne te ignarum fuisse dicas meorum
              morum.
            leno ego sum.

    AES   scio.

---

[10] This is the scene that is stated in the prologue (lines 6–11) to have
been taken by Terence from Diphilus and inserted into Menander's *The
Brothers*. It lasts to line 195, since a comment by Donatus makes it clear
that the monologue by Sannio that follows thereafter is from Menander.

oppose his arguments and dissuade him, he doesn't react like a sensible human being. If I fuelled his bad temper and encouraged it, I'm sure I'd go insane with him. But it's true that Aeschinus is treating me pretty badly in this. Is there a girl in town he hasn't taken a fancy to and spent money on? In the end, just recently—I suppose he was getting bored with the lot of them—he told me he wanted to take a wife. I hoped that the flames of youthful passion had died down, and I was delighted. But here he goes all over again! Well, whatever the facts are, I want to know. I'll go and find him, if he's in the forum. (*he exits right in the direction of the forum, leaving the stage empty*)

ACT TWO

Enter AESCHINUS *left with* PARMENO, *escorting the music girl Bacchis and pursued by* SANNIO.[10]

SAN (*shouting*) Fellow citizens, for goodness' sake come to the rescue of a poor innocent man. Help me! I'm defenceless!

AES (*to the girl, who is looking round anxiously at Sannio's approach*) Relax! Just stay where you are now. Don't look round. There's no danger. He'll never touch you while I'm here.

SAN Yes I will. Just you try to stop me.

AES (*to the girl*) He may be a villain, but he won't risk a second thrashing today.

SAN Listen, Aeschinus, so you can't say you're unaware of my character. I'm a pimp.

AES I know.

267

SAN   at ita ut usquam fuit fide quisquam optuma.
tu quod te posterius perges hanc iniuriam mi nolle
factam esse, huius non faciam. crede hoc, ego meum ius
    persequar
neque tu verbis solves umquam quod mihi re male fece-
    ris.

165   novi ego vostra haec: "nollem factum." iusiurandum
    dabitur te esse
indignum iniuria hac, indignis quom egomet sim accep-
    tus modis.

AES   abi prae strenue ac fores aperi.
SAN   ceterum hoc nihili facis?
AES   i intro nunciam.
SAN   enim non sinam.
AES   accede illuc, Parmeno.
nimium istuc abisti. hic propter hunc adsiste. em sic volo.

170   cave nunciam oculos a meis oculis quoquam demoveas
    tuos,
ne mora sit, si innuerim, quin pugnus continuo in mala
    haereat.

SAN   istuc volo ergo ipsum experiri.
AES   em serva. omitte mulierem.
SAN   o facinus indignum!
AES   geminabit nisi caves.
SAN   ei miseriam!
AES   non innueram, verum in istam partem potius peccato
    tamen.

175   i nunciam.

172 em . . . mulierem *Aeschino dant* C¹P¹E¹GD², em serva *Aeschino*
omitte mulierem *Parmenoni dat* A, em . . . mulierem *Parmenoni dant*
cett.   173 ei miseriam Σ, ei misero mihi A

SAN   But as honest a one as ever there was. As for you, if you defend yourself later by saying that you regret this assault on me, (*snapping his fingers*) I won't give that much. Believe me, I'll pursue my rights. You'll never talk your way out of the harm you've done me. I know your sort and your "I sincerely regret." You'll swear on oath that the assault was quite out of character, when the fact is I've been treated quite outrageously.[11]

AES   (*to Parmeno*) Go on ahead, quickly now, and open the door. (*Parmeno opens the door of Micio's house*)

SAN   Aren't you taking me seriously?

AES   (*to the girl*) Now! In you go!

SAN   (*pushing forward and grabbing the girl*) Oh no you don't!

AES   (*to Parmeno*) Over here, Parmeno! You're too far away! Stand right beside him! That's it! Now make sure you don't take your eyes off mine. If I nod, don't wait. Plant your fist in his jaw instantly.

SAN   I'd just like to see him try. (*he begins to drag the girl away*)

AES   (*to Parmeno*) Watch him! (*to Sannio*) Let the girl go! (*he nods to Parmeno, who strikes Sannio*)

SAN   It's outrageous!

AES   He'll do it again if you don't look out.

SAN   (*as Parmeno strikes him again*) Ow! That hurts! (*he loosens his grip on the girl*)

AES   (*to Parmeno*) I didn't nod. But it's a fault in the right direction. (*to the girl*) In you go now. (*she exits into Micio's house with Parmeno*)

---

[11] There is a play here on two senses of *indignus*, "undeserving" (of people) and "improper" (hence "outrageous") of actions.

SAN	quid hoc reist? regnumne, Aeschine, hic tu possides?
AES	si possiderem, ornatus esses ex tuis virtutibus.
SAN	quid tibi rei mecumst?
AES	nil.
SAN	quid? nostin qui sim?
AES	non desidero.
SAN	tetigin tui quicquam?
AES	si attigisses, ferres infortunium.
SAN	qui tibi magis licet meam habere pro qua ego argentum dedi?

180 responde.

AES	ante aedis non fecisse erit melius hic convicium.

nam si molestus pergis esse, iam intro abripiere atque ibi
usque ad necem operiere loris.

SAN	loris liber?
AES	sic erit.
SAN	o hominem impurum! hicin libertatem aiunt esse aequam omnibus?
AES	si satis iam debacchatus es, leno, audi, si vis, nunciam.

185 SAN egon debacchatus sum autem an tu in me?

AES	mitte ista atque ad rem redi.
SAN	quam rem? quo redeam?
AES	iamne me vis dicere id quod ad te attinet?
SAN	cupio, modo aequi aliquid.
AES	vah! leno iniqua me non volt loqui.
SAN	leno sum, fateor, pernicies communis adulescentium,

periurus, pestis. tamen tibi a me nullast orta iniuria.

190 AES nam hercle etiam hoc restat.

SAN	illuc, quaeso, redi quo coepisti, Aeschine.

THE BROTHERS

SAN   What's going on here? Are you the king of this place, Aeschinus?

AES   If I were, you'd be decorated according to your deserts.

SAN   Do you have something against me?

AES   Nothing.

SAN   Well, do you know who I am?

AES   I have no desire to know.

SAN   Have I ever touched anything of yours?

AES   If you had, it would be your misfortune.

SAN   How can you have a prior claim to a girl I paid for? Answer me that.

AES   You'd be wiser not to make a scene in front of my house. If you go on being a nuisance, you'll be carried off inside and whipped to the point of death.

SAN   Whipped? A free man?

AES   That's right.

SAN   You filthy scoundrel! And they say that everybody here is equal before the law!

AES   If you've finished raging and ranting,[12] pimp, kindly listen to me.

SAN   Me raging and ranting? What about you?

AES   Forget it. Let's get back to business.

SAN   What business? Get back where?

AES   Do you want me to tell you something to your advantage?

SAN   I'm keen, so long as it's reasonable.

AES   Huh! A pimp doesn't want me to be unreasonable!

SAN   I'm a pimp, I admit it, the bane of all young men, a perjurer, a plague. But I haven't done you any wrong.

AES   No, by god! That's still to come.

SAN   Please, can you go back to where you started, Aeschinus?

---

[12] Literally, "playing the bacchanal."

AES   minis viginti tu illam emisti—quae res tibi vortat male!
argenti tantum dabitur.

SAN   quid si ego tibi illam nolo vendere?
coges me?

AES   minume.

SAN   namque id metui.

AES   neque vendundam censeo
quae liberast. nam ego liberali illam assero causa manu.

195   nunc vide utrum vis, argentum accipere an causam me-
ditari tuam.

delibera hoc dum ego redeo, leno.

SAN   pro supreme Iuppiter,

minume miror qui insanire occipiunt ex iniuria.

domo me eripuit, verberavit, me invito abduxit meam;

200   homini misero plus quingentos colaphos infregit mihi.

199   ob male facta haec tantidem emptam postulat sibi tra-
dier.

verum enim, quando bene promeruit, fiat: suom ius pos-
tulat.

age, iam cupio si modo argentum reddat. sed ego hoc ha-
riolor:

ubi me dixero dare tanti, testis faciet ilico

vendidisse me. de argento, somnium: "mox, cras redi."

205   id quoque possum ferre si modo reddat, quamquam iniu-
riumst.

verum cogito id quod res est: quando eum quaestum oc-
ceperis,

accipiunda et mussitanda iniuria adulescentiumst.

sed nemo dabit. frustra egomet mecum has rationes
puto.

199–200 *ordinem invertunt edd.*

AES   You bought the girl for twenty minas[13]—and much good may it do you! We'll give you the same amount for her.

SAN   What if I refuse to sell her to you? Will you compel me?

AES   No, not at all.

SAN   (*ironically*) I was afraid you might.

AES   I take the view you can't sell a girl who's freeborn. (*formally*) I hereby assert her claim to freedom. So choose which you like: accept the money or prepare your case. Ponder that until I come back, pimp. (*he exits into Micio's house, leaving Sannio onstage alone*)

SAN   (*to himself*) Almighty Jupiter! No wonder that victims of injustice are driven insane. This fellow dragged me from my house, beat me up, took away a girl without my consent, and rained more than five hundred blows on my poor head. All I get for my pains is a demand that she be handed over at cost price. (*ironically*) But, since he's deserving, so be it; he's only demanding his rights. (*shrugging his shoulders*) All right, I'll accept the offer, if only he does pay up. But I foresee that, once I've agreed to let him have her at that price, he'll get witnesses on the spot to say she's sold, but leave me dreaming about the money. "Soon," he'll say, "come back tomorrow." I can even bear that as long as he does pay up, unfair as it is. I've got to face the facts of the situation. When you've entered this profession, you have to accept the misbehaviour of young men and grit your teeth. (*resignedly*) But nobody's going to pay me; I'm wasting my time trying to balance my books.

[13] Sannio was presumably intending to sell his girl for thirty minas or even forty, typical sums in comedy for the purchase of a girl from a pimp (see *Phormio* 557 and note there).

II. II: SYRUS. SANNIO.

SYR   tace! egomet conveniam iam ipsum. cupide accipiat faxo
       atque etiam

210   bene dicat secum esse actum. quid istuc Sanniost quod te
       audio

       nescioquid concertasse cum ero?

SAN   numquam vidi iniquius
       certationem comparatam quam haec hodie inter nos fuit.
       ego vapulando, ill' verberando, usque ambo defessi su-
       mus.

SYR   tua culpa.

SAN   quid facerem?

SYR   adulescenti morem gestum oportuit.

215 SAN qui potui melius qui hodie usque os praebui?

SYR   age, scis quid loquar:
       pecuniam in loco negligere maxumum interdumst lu-
       crum. hui!
       metuisti, si nunc de tuo iure concessisses paullulum
       atque
       adulescenti esses morigeratus, hominum homo stultis-
       sume,
       ne non tibi istuc feneraret.

SAN   ego spem pretio non emo.

220 SYR numquam rem facies. abi, nescis inescare homines,
       Sannio.

SAN   credo istuc melius esse, verum ego numquam adeo astu-
       tus fui
       quin quidquid possem mallem auferre potius in prae-
       sentia.

SYR   age, novi tuom animum. quasi iam usquam tibi sint
       viginti minae

THE BROTHERS

Enter SYRUS *from Micio's house.*

SYR   (*speaking back inside to Aeschines*) Say no more! I'll speak to him in person. I'll have him eager to accept our offer and even declare it was a good deal. (*to Sannio*) What's this I hear, Sannio? You've had some sort of confrontation with my master?

SAN   Confrontation? I've never seen a more one-sided one than what we had today. We're both totally exhausted, him with beating and me with being beaten.

SYR   It was your own fault.

SAN   What was I supposed to do?

SYR   You should have let the young man have his way.

SAN   How better than by offering him both cheeks?

SYR   Come on, you know what I mean. Sometimes, at the right moment, it pays best to forget about money. Hey! Were you afraid that, if you made the tiniest concession and let the young man have his way, you wouldn't be paid back with interest? How stupid can you get?

SAN   I don't put cash on hopes.

SYR   You'll never be a businessman. Come off it, Sannio, you just don't know how to bait a trap.

SAN   I suppose that is a better way. But I've never been smart enough not to prefer to pocket whatever I can on the spot.

SYR   Come on, I know what you're like. It's not as if twenty minas means anything to you as long as you keep on his

dum huic obsequare. praeterea autem te aiunt proficisci
    Cyprum.

SAN   hem!

225 SYR coemisse hinc quae illuc veheres multa, navem conduc-
    tam. hoc, scio,
    animus tibi pendet. ubi illinc, spero, redieris tamen, hoc
    ages.

SAN nusquam pedem! perii hercle! hac illi spe hoc incepe-
    runt.

SYR   timet.

    inieci scrupulum homini.

SAN   o scelera! illud vide
    ut in ipso articulo oppressit. emptae mulieres

230   complures et item hinc alia quae porto Cyprum.
    nisi eo ad mercatum venio, damnum maxumumst.
    nunc si hoc omitto ac tum agam ubi illinc rediero,
    nil est: refrixerit res. "nunc demum venis?
    quor passu's? ubi eras?" ut sit satius perdere

235   quam hic nunc manere tam diu aut tum persequi.

SYR iamne enumerasti quod ad te rediturum putes?

SAN hoccin illo dignumst? hoccin incipere Aeschinum,
    per oppressionem ut hanc mi eripere postulet!

SYR labascit. unum hoc habe. vide si satis placet.

240   potius quam venias in periclum, Sannio,
    servesne an perdas totum, dividuom face.

---

232 ac tum agam *Cp*, actum agam *cett*.

14 Cyprus was always an important trading centre in the east Medi-
terranean, and, being an island sacred to Venus, was particularly appro-
priate for the dealings of a pimp.

right side. (*playing his trump card*) Anyway, they tell me you're leaving for Cyprus.[14]

SAN   (*aside*) What!

SYR   They say you've bought a lot of goods here to take over there and chartered a ship. Your mind's on that at the moment, I know. But, when you get back from there, as I hope you will, you can deal with this.

SAN   I'm not moving an inch. (*aside*) God damn it! So that's what put them up to this!

SYR   (*aside*) He's worried. I've put a stone in his shoe.[15] (*he walks triumphantly away*)

SAN   (*to himself*) It's criminal! Look at that! Caught on my weak spot! I've bought several women and some other goods here which I'm taking to Cyprus. If I don't get there in time for the market, it's a considerable loss. But if I drop this case now and take it up again when I return, it's no good: it will have gone cold. "Here you are at last," they'll say. "Why the delay? Where've you been?" Better to take a loss now than stay around here any longer or pursue it later.

SYR   (*returning*) Have you calculated how much profit you stand to make?[16]

SAN   (*ignoring this*) Is this proper behaviour on Aeschinus' part? How could he bring himself to steal the girl from me by force?

SYR   (*aside*) He's wavering. (*aloud*) Here's my final offer: see if you're happy with it. Rather than taking the risk of getting all or nothing, Sannio, split it down the middle. He'll

---

[15] An idiomatic expression that is found also in *Phormio* (line 954).
[16] That is, at the market in Cyprus.

minas decem corradet alicunde.

SAN   ei mihi!

etiam de sorte nunc venio in dubium miser?
pudet nil? omnis dentis labefecit mihi,
245   praeterea colaphis tuber est totum caput.
etiam insuper defrudet? nusquam abeo.

SYR   ut lubet.

numquid vis quin abeam?

SAN   immo hercle hoc quaeso, Syre:

utut haec sunt acta, potius quam litis sequar,
meum mihi reddatur saltem quanti emptast, Syre.
250   scio te non usum antehac amicitia mea;
memorem me dices esse et gratum.

SYR   sedulo

faciam. sed Ctesiphonem video. laetus est
de amica.

SAN   quid quod te oro?

SYR   paullisper mane.

II. III: CTESIPHO. SANNIO. SYRUS.

CTE abs quivis homine, quomst opus, beneficium accipere
     gaudeas.
255   verum enimvero id demum iuvat si quem aequomst
     facere is bene facit.

o frater, frater, quid ego nunc te laudem? satis certo scio,
numquam ita magnifice quicquam dicam, id virtus quin
     superet tua.

itaque unam hanc rem me habere praeter alios praeci-
     puam arbitror,

fratrem homini nemini esse primarum artium magis
     principem.

260 SYR o Ctesipho!

scrape up ten minas from somewhere.

SAN   Oh no! Does a poor chap now risk losing his principal? Has Aeschinus no shame? He's loosened all my teeth, and beside that my whole head's swollen with blows: is he going to swindle me as well? (*defiantly*) I'm not going anywhere.

SYR   As you like. (*turning to go*) Anything else, or can I go?

SAN   Yes there is, by god, this one thing, please, Syrus. Whatever's happened here, rather than take you to court, let me at least get back the price I paid for her, Syrus. I know you haven't enjoyed my friendship in the past, but you'll find I don't forget a favour.

SYR   I'll do my best. (*looking down the street*) But here comes Ctesipho. He looks delighted about his girl.

SAN   What about my request?

SYR   Wait a minute. (*they stand aside as Ctesipho approaches*)

Enter CTESIPHO *left from the direction of the country.*

CTE   (*to himself*) It's a joy to receive a kindness from anybody when you're in need. But it doubles the pleasure if the person who does the kindness is the right person to do it. Oh brother, brother, how can I now praise you? I'm quite sure I can't say anything extravagant enough to do you justice. I reckon I'm uniquely blessed in the whole world: nobody else has a brother who is such a master of every noble quality.

SYR   (*approaching him*) Ctesipho!

CTE   o Syre, Aeschinus ubist?

SYR   ellum, te exspectat domi.

CTE   hem!

SYR   quid est?

CTE   quid sit? illius opera, Syre, nunc vivo. festivom caput!
quin omnia sibi post putarit esse prae meo commodo.
maledicta, famam, meum laborem et peccatum in se
    transtulit.
nil pote supra. quidnam foris crepuit?

SYR   mane, mane! ipse exit foras.

II. IV: AESCHINUS. CTESIPHO. SYRUS. SANNIO.

265   AES   ubist ille sacrilegus?

SAN   me quaerit. numquidnam effert? occidi:
nil video.

AES   ehem, opportune! te ipsum quaero. quid fit, Ctesipho?
in tutost omnis res. omitte vero tristitiem tuam.

CTE   ego illam hercle vero omitto quiquidem te habeam fra-
    trem. o mi Aeschine,
o mi germane! ah! vereor coram in os te laudare amplius,

270   ne id assentandi magis quam quo habeam gratum facere
    existumes.

AES   age, inepte, quasi nunc non norimus nos inter nos, Ctesi-
    pho.
hoc mihi dolet, nos paene sero scisse et paene in eum lo-
    cum
redisse ut, si omnes cuperent, nil tibi possent auxiliarier.

CTE   pudebat.

AES   ah! stultitiast istaec, non pudor. tam ob parvulam

280

CTE   Syrus! Where's Aeschinus?

SYR   (*pointing to Micio's house*) In there. He's waiting for you at home.

CTE   Oh!

SYR   What's the matter?

CTE   What's the matter? It's thanks to him, Syrus, that I'm alive. The wonderful fellow! He saw everything else as second to my interests. He took upon himself the insults, the gossip, my troubles, my misdeeds. He couldn't have done more. (*as the door of Micio's house opens*) Was that the door?

SYR   Wait! Wait! It's him coming out!

Enter AESCHINUS from Micio's house.

AES   Where's that blasphemer?

SAN   (*aside*) It's me he wants. Is he bringing any money? Damnation! I can't see any.

AES   (*catching sight of Ctesipho*) Oh! That's convenient: I was looking for you. How're you doing, Ctesipho? Everything's all right, so you can stop being so gloomy.

CTE   I most certainly can, god knows, with a brother like you. Oh Aeschinus! My own true brother! I'm afraid to praise you too much to your face in case you take it for flattery rather than gratitude.

AES   Come on, don't be silly. As if we don't know each other well enough, Ctesipho! My only regret is that it was almost too late when we found out. We'd almost got to the point where, even if the whole world wanted to help you, they wouldn't have been able to.

CTE   I was ashamed to tell you.

AES   Oh! That's stupidity, not shame. To think that you nearly fled the country for such a little thing! It doesn't bear

281

275 rem paene e patria! turpe dictu. deos quaeso ut istaec
prohibeant.

CTE peccavi.

AES   quid ait tandem nobis Sannio?

SYR   iam mitis est.

AES ego ad forum ibo ut hunc absolvam. tu intro ad illam,
Ctesipho.

SAN Syre, insta.

SYR   eamus. namque hic properat in Cyprum.

SAN   ne tam quidem
quam vis. etiam maneo otiosus hic.

SYR   reddetur. ne time.

280 SAN at ut omne reddat.

SYR   omne reddet. tace modo ac sequere hac.

SAN   sequor.

CTE heus, heus, Syre!

SYR   hem quid est!

CTE   obsecro hercle te, hominem istum impurissumum
quam primum absolvitote ne, si magis irritatus siet,
aliqua ad patrem hoc permanet atque ego tum perpetuo
perierim.

SYR non fiet. bono animo esto. tu cum illa intus te oblecta in-
terim

285 et lectulos iube sterni nobis et parari cetera.
ego iam transacta re convortam me domum cum opsonio.

CTE ita quaeso. quando hoc bene successit, hilare hunc suma-
mus diem.

287 hilare *Acron apud Don.*, hilarem *codd.*

282

talking about. May heaven preserve you from such behaviour!

CTE　I was wrong.

AES　(*turning to Syrus*) What does our Sannio have to say, then?

SYR　He's calmed down now.

AES　I'll go to the forum and pay him off. Ctesipho, you join your girl inside. (*Ctesipho exits into Micio's house*)

SAN　(*to Syrus*) Press him, Syrus.

SYR　(*to Aeschinus*) Let's go. (*indicating Sannio*) He's in a hurry to leave for Cyprus.

SAN　Not so much as you'd like. I've plenty of time and I'm staying here.

SYR　(*to Sannio*) You'll be paid. Don't worry!

SAN　(*to Syrus*) Make sure I'm paid in full.

SYR　(*to Sannio*) You'll be paid in full. Shut up and come along with us.

SAN　I'm coming. (*Aeschinus and Sannio exit right in the direction of the forum with Syrus following*)

CTE　(*reappearing from Micio's house*) Hey, Syrus!

SYR　(*turning back*) What! What is it?

CTE　I implore you, for god's sake, pay off that filthy soundrel as soon as you can. If he gets any angrier, news of this may leak to my father, and then I'm utterly ruined.

SYR　It won't happen. Cheer up! Have fun with your girl inside meanwhile, and make sure the couches are laid for us and everything else got ready. I'll proceed home with the food as soon as we've finished this business. (*he exits right in the direction of the forum*)

CTE　Suits me. Since this has gone so well, let's spend the day in celebration. (*he exits into Micio's house, leaving the stage empty*)

ACTUS III

III. I: SOSTRATA. CANTHARA.

SOS   obsecro, mea nutrix, quid nunc fiet?

CAN   quid fiat rogas?
    recte edepol, spero. modo dolores, mea tu, occipiunt pri-
      mulum.

290   iam nunc times, quasi numquam adfueris, numquam
      tute pepereris?

SOS   miseram me! neminem habeo—solae sumus, Geta au-
    tem hic non adest—
    nec quem ad obstetricem mittam, nec qui accersat
      Aeschinum.

CAN   pol is quidem iam hic aderit. nam numquam unum inter-
    mittit diem
    quin semper veniat.

SOS   solus mearum miseriarumst remedium.

295 CAN e re nata melius fieri haud potuit quam factumst, era,
    quando vitium oblatumst, quod ad illum attinet potissu-
      mum,
    talem, tali genere atque animo, natum ex tanta familia.

SOS   ita pol est ut dicis. salvos nobis deos quaeso ut siet.

III. II: GETA. SOSTRATA. CANTHARA.

GET   nunc illud est quom, si omnia omnes sua consilia con-
    ferant

300   atque huic malo salutem quaerant, auxili nil adferant,
    quod mihique eraeque filiaeque erilist. vae misero mihi!
    tot res repente circumvallant se unde emergi non potest,
    vis, egestas, iniustitia, solitudo, infamia.

ACT THREE

Enter SOSTRATA *from her house with the nurse* CANTHARA.

SOS   For goodness' sake, my dear nurse, what's going to happen now?

CAN   You ask what's going to happen? It's going to be all right, I'm sure. Her pains are only just beginning, my dear. Are you worried already, as if you'd never been present at a birth or had a child yourself?

SOS   Oh dear! We're alone. Geta isn't here, and there's nobody to send for the midwife or to fetch Aeschinus.

CAN   Well, *he*'ll be here soon, by heaven. He never lets a day pass without coming.

SOS   He's the only cure for my troubles.

CAN   In the circumstances, things couldn't have turned out better than they have, mistress. I mean, given she's been raped, that *he*'s the person involved, such a nice young man of such good birth and from such a fine family.

SOS   You're quite right. May the gods keep him safe for us!

Enter GETA *right from the direction of the forum in a state of great agitation.*

GET   (*to himself*) Now we're in a situation where, if everybody in the world put their heads together and tried to find a solution to the problem afflicting me and my mistress and my mistress's daughter, they wouldn't be able to help at all. Oh, it's awful! All of a sudden we're enclosed by so many things from which there's no escape: violence, poverty, injustice, loneliness, disgrace. What an age we live

6666666666

6666

		hoccin saeclum! o scelera, o genera sacrilega, o hominem impium!
305	SOS	me miseram! quidnamst quod sic video timidum et properantem Getam?
	GET	quem neque fides neque iusiurandum neque illum misericordia
		repressit neque reflexit neque quod partus instabat prope
		quoi miserae indigne per vim vitium obtulerat.
	SOS	non intellego
		satis quae loquatur.
	CAN	propius obsecro accedamus, Sostrata.
	GET	ah!
310		me miserum! vix sum compos animi, ita ardeo iracundia.
		nil est quod malim quam illam totam familiam dari mi obviam,
		ut ego iram hanc in eos evomam omnem, dum aegritudo haec est recens.
		satis mihi id habeam supplici dum illos ulciscar meo modo.
		seni animam primum exstinguerem ipsi qui illud produxit scelus.
315		tum autem Syrum impulsorem, vah, quibus illum lacerarem modis!
		sublimem medium primum arriperem et capite in terra statuerem,
		ut cerebro dispergat viam.
		adulescenti ipsi eriperem oculos, post haec praecipitem darem.
		ceteros ruerem, agerem, raperem, tunderem et prosternerem.
320		sed cesso eram hoc malo impertire propere?

286

in! What villainy, what wickedness, what a god-forsaken
fellow!

SOS (*aside*) There's Geta! Oh dear! Why on earth is he so up-
set and in such a hurry?

GET His sense of honour didn't hold him back or make him
think twice, nor his oath, nor pity, nor the the fact that the
poor girl he'd so shockingly violated was about to go into
labour.

SOS (*to Canthara*) I can't quite make out what he's saying.

CAN (*to Sostrata*) For goodness' sake, Sostrata, let's go up
closer.

GET Oh misery! I can scarcely control myself, I'm so on fire
with anger. There's nothing I'd like better than for the
whole household to be put in front of me, so that I could
disgorge all my fury on them while I'm still in this dis-
tressed state. I'd be happy with their punishment if I
could take revenge in my own way. First I'd choke out the
life of the old man who reared this monster. Then Syrus,
who put him up to this: oh, how I'd tear him to pieces! I'd
grab him round the waist, lift him off his feet and put him
down on his head,[17] so as to spatter the street with his
brains. As for the young man himself, I'd gouge out his
eyes and then fling him flat on his face. And the rest—I'd
hunt them down, round them up, strip them bare, beat
them, and throw them to the ground. But I must hurry up
and tell my mistress this dreadful news. (*he makes to run
on*)

[17] This description seems to be based on the throws of wrestling.

---

313 meo *addidit Bothe*.

SOS   revocemus. Geta!

GET   hem!

        quisquis es, sine me.

SOS   ego sum Sostrata.

GET   ubi east? te ipsam quaerito,

te exspecto. oppido opportune te obtulisti mi obviam.

era—

SOS   quid est? quid trepidas?

GET   ei mihi!

CAN   quid festinas, mi Geta?

animam recipe.

GET   prorsus—

SOS   quid istic "prorsus" ergost?

GET   periimus!

325   actumst!

SOS   eloquere, obsecro te, quid sit.

GET   iam—

SOS   quid "iam," Geta?

GET Aeschinus—

SOS   quid is ergo?

GET   alienus est ab nostra familia.

SOS   hem!

perii! quare?

GET   amare occepit aliam.

SOS   vae miserae mihi!

GET neque id occulte fert. ab lenone ipsus eripuit palam.

SOS   satin hoc certumst?

GET   certum. hisce oculis egomet vidi, Sostrata.

322 *Getae dant codd. edd., Sostratae Lindsay-Kauer*

323–324 quid . . . recipe *Cantharae dat Asper apud Don., Sostratae*
codd.

SOS   (*to Canthara*) Let's call him back. (*aloud*) Geta!

GET   (*stopping but not looking round*) What? Leave me alone, whoever you are.

SOS   It's Sostrata.

GET   Where? (*catching sight of her*) Just the person I've been looking for. I was trying to find you. It's an absolute stroke of luck I've met you here. (*with a deep breath*) Mistress—

SOS   What's the matter? Why are you trembling?

GET   It's terrible!

CAN   Why've you been running, Geta? Get your breath back.

GET   We've absolutely—(*he pauses for breath*)

SOS   Absolutely what?

GET   —had it! It's all over!

SOS   For goodness' sake, explain what's going on.

GET   As of now—(*he pauses again*)

SOS   What's "as of now," Geta?

GET   Aeschinus—(*and again*)

SOS   What about him?

GET   —doesn't want to know us.

SOS   What! It's the end of me! Why?

GET   He's fallen in love with someone else.

SOS   Oh, it's awful!

GET   And he's not keeping it secret. He stole the girl himself from the pimp in full view of everybody.

SOS   Are you quite sure of this?

GET   Quite sure. I saw it myself with my own eyes, Sostrata.

SOS ah!

330 me miseram! quid iam credas aut quoi credas? nos-
trumne Aeschinum,
nostram vitam omnium, in quo nostrae spes opesque om-
nes sitae
erant? qui sine hac iurabat se unum numquam victurum
diem?
qui se in sui gremio positurum puerum dicebat patris,
ita obsecraturum ut liceret hanc sibi uxorem ducere?

335 GET era, lacrumas mitte ac potius quod ad hanc rem opus est
porro prospice.
patiamurne an narremus quoipiam?

CAN au au, mi homo, sanun es?
an hoc proferendum tibi videtur esse?

GET miquidem non placet.
iam primum illum alieno animo a nobis esse res ipsa in-
dicat.
nunc, si hoc palam proferimus, ille infitias ibit, sat scio.

340 tua fama et gnatae vita in dubium veniet. tum si maxume
fateatur, quom amat aliam, non est utile hanc illi dari.
quapropter quoquo pacto tacitost opus.

SOS ah! minume gentium!
non faciam.

GET quid ages?

SOS proferam.

CAN hem! mi Sostrata, vide quam rem agis.

SOS peiore res loco non potis est esse quam in quo nunc sitast.

345 primum indotatast. tum praeterea, quae secunda ei dos
erat,
periit: pro virgini dari nuptum non potest. hoc reli-
cuomst:

SOS   (*in tears*) Oh dear, oh dear! What can you now believe? Who can you trust? Our Aeschinus, the life of us all, in whom lay all our hopes and strength! Who swore that he couldn't live a single day without her! Who said that he would put the baby in his father's lap and beg to be allowed to marry her!

GET   Stop crying, mistress, and think ahead. What do we need to do about all this? Should we put up with it or tell someone?

CAN   Heavens, man, are you out of your mind? Do you think we should make this public?

GET   No, I don't like the idea myself. In the first place, the facts make it clear that he's now estranged from us. If we make this public now, he's going to deny it, I'm quite sure. Your reputation and your daughter's future will be put at risk. Even if he makes a full confession, since he's in love with someone else, it's not in her interest to be married to him. So, whichever way you look at it, we must keep it quiet.

SOS   No! Not in all the world! I won't do it.

GET   What will you do?

SOS   I'll make it public.

CAN   What! Sostrata dear, watch what you're doing!

SOS   Matters couldn't be worse than they are now. First, she has no dowry. Then she's lost the next best thing: she can't be given in marriage as a virgin. There's one thing left: if he insists on denying it, I have in my possession as

---

336–337 au au . . . esse *Cantharae dant AG Don., Sostratae cett.*

si infitias ibit, testis mecumst anulus quem miserat.

postremo, quando ego conscia mihi sum a me culpam esse hanc procul

neque pretium neque rem ullam intercessisse illa aut me indignam, Geta,

350   experiar.

GET   quid istic? cedo ut melius dicas.

SOS   tu, quantum potest,

abi atque Hegioni cognato huius rem enarrato omnem ordine.

nam is nostro Simulo fuit summus et nos coluit maxume.

GET   nam hercle alius nemo respiciet nos.

SOS   propera tu, mea Canthara,

curre, obstetricem accerse, ut quom opus sit ne in mora nobis siet.

III. III: DEMEA. SYRUS. DROMO.

355 DEM   disperii! Ctesiphonem audivi filium

una fuisse in raptione cum Aeschino.

id misero restat mihi mali si illum potest,

qui aliquoi reist, etiam eum ad nequitiem adducere.

ubi ego illum quaeram? credo abductum in ganeum

360   aliquo. persuasit ille impurus, sat scio.

sed eccum Syrum ire video. hinc scibo iam ubi siet.

atque hercle hic de grege illost. si me senserit

eum quaeritare, numquam dicet carnufex.

non ostendam id me velle.

347 miserat *A*, amiserat Σ

350 cedo *edd.*, accedo *codd. Don.* dicas *codd. Don. Eugr.*, dicis *Prisc. Grant* (*sine* ut)

---

18 As a pledge of his good intentions; it was not a formally binding

evidence the ring that he sent.[18] In the end, since I know in my heart that no blame attaches to me in this and that no money or anything else has changed hands which would be unworthy of her or me, Geta, I shall go to court.

GET (*unwillingly*) Very well. I suppose you're right.

SOS Off you go as fast as you can and relate the whole story from beginning to end to my relative Hegio. He was my husband Simulus' best friend and he's always looked after our interests.

GET Well, by god, nobody else is going to give us a second thought. (*he exits left in the direction of the country*)

SOS Canthara dear, quickly, run and fetch the midwife, so she doesn't keep us waiting when we need her. (*Canthara exits right in the direction of the forum, while Sostrata returns to her house, leaving the stage empty*)

Enter DEMEA *left from the direction of the country.*

DEM (*to himself*) Damn it all! They tell me my son Ctesipho took part with Aeschinus in the abduction of the girl. That's all I need to complete my misery, if the son who is still good for something can be led into debauchery by the other. Where am I going to find him? I suppose he's been taken to some den of vice; that filthy scoundrel has led him astray, I'll be bound. (*looking down the street*) But look, there's Syrus coming. I'll find out from him where Ctesipho is. But, by heaven, he's one of the gang. If he realises I'm looking for Ctesipho, he won't tell me a thing, the gallows bird. I won't let him see that's what I want.

engagement ring, since parental consent was necessary for marriage and in this case Micio is still unaware of the relationship.

SYR		omnem rem modo seni
365	quo pacto haberet enarramus ordine.	
	nil quicquam vidi laetius.	
DEM		pro Iuppiter,
	hominis stultitiam!	
SYR		collaudavit filium.
	mihi, qui id dedissem consilium, egit gratias.	
DEM	dirrumpor.	
SYR		argentum annumeravit ilico.
370	dedit praeterea in sumptum dimidium minae.	
	id distributum sanest ex sententia.	
DEM		em,
	huic mandes si quid recte curatum velis.	
SYR	ehem, Demea! haud aspexeram te. quid agitur?	
DEM	quid agatur? vostram nequeo mirari satis	
375	rationem.	
SYR		est hercle inepta, ne dicam dolo, atque
	absurda. piscis ceteros purga, Dromo.	
	gongrum istum maxumum in aqua sinito ludere	
	tantisper. ubi ego venero, exossabitur;	
	prius nolo.	
DEM		haecin flagitia!
SYR		miquidem non placent
380	et clamo saepe. salsamenta haec, Stephanio,	
	fac macerentur pulchre.	

378 venero Σ, rediero A

---

19 That is, fifty drachmas, a generous amount; compare *The Woman*

Enter SYRUS *right from the direction of the forum with slaves carrying baskets of food.*

SYR   (*to himself*) We've just told the old man the whole story from start to finish. I've never seen anyone more delighted.

DEM   (*aside*) Jupiter! The stupidity of the fellow!

SYR   (*to himself*) He congratulated his son and thanked me for suggesting the whole idea.

DEM   (*aside*) I'll explode.

SYR   (*to himself*) He counted out the money on the spot, and gave us half a mina[19] on top to spend on the party, which I have disposed of entirely to my satisfaction.

DEM   (*aside*) Look at that! If you want a job well done, give it to him.

SYR   (*catching sight of Demea*) Oh hello, Demea! I didn't see you. How're you doing?

DEM   How am I doing? I never cease to be amazed at the way you people live.

SYR   Heaven knows, it's silly, to be perfectly honest; in fact, it's ridiculous. (*to one of the slaves*) Clean the rest of the fish, Dromo. Let the big eel play in the water for a while. I want it filleted when I come in, but not before. (*Dromo exits into the house*)

DEM   This is scandalous!

SYR   I don't like it either. I often protest. (*to another of the slaves*) Stephanio, see that this salted fish is nicely soaked. (*Stephanio exits into the house with another basket*)

of Andros 514, where ten drachmas is regarded as niggardly expenditure on a wedding feast.

DEM   di vostram fidem!
utrum studione id sibi habet an laudi putat
fore si perdiderit gnatum? vae misero mihi!
videre videor iam diem illum quom hinc egens
385   profugiet aliquo militatum.

SYR   o Demea,
istuc est sapere, non quod ante pedes modost
videre sed etiam illa quae futura sunt
prospicere.

DEM   quid? istaec iam penes vos psaltriast?

SYR ellam intus.

DEM   eho! an domist habiturus?

SYR   credo, ut est
390   dementia.

DEM   haecin fieri!

SYR   inepta lenitas
patris et facilitas prava.

DEM   fratris me quidem
pudet pigetque.

SYR   nimium inter vos, Demea, ac
(non quia ades praesens dico hoc) pernimium interest.
tu quantus quantus nil nisi sapientia's,
395   ill' somnium. sineres vero illum tu tuom
facere haec?

DEM   sinerem illum? aut non sex totis mensibus
prius olfecissem quam ille quicquam coeperet?

SYR vigilantiam tuam tu mihi narras?

DEM   sic siet
modo ut nunc est, quaeso.

SYR   ut quisque suom volt esse, itast.
400 DEM quid eum? vidistin hodie?

SYR   tuomne filium?

DEM   Heaven help us! Is he doing this on purpose? Does he think it'll be to his credit if he ruins the boy? It's terrible! I can see the day coming when he hasn't a penny and runs away to serve as a soldier somewhere.

SYR   That's real wisdom, Demea, not merely to see what lies under your feet but to foresee the future.

DEM   Well, what about the music girl? Is she still with you?

SYR   (*pointing to the house*) Take a look inside.

DEM   Oh! Is he going to keep her at home?

SYR   I'm sure he is. He's crazy enough.

DEM   Is this really happening?

SYR   It's his father's foolish indulgence and misguided permissiveness.

DEM   I'm ashamed of my brother, and annoyed.

SYR   There's a big difference between you two, Demea, in fact a very big one, and I don't say that just because you are present. You're nothing but wisdom from tip to toe, he's a dreamer. Would *you* allow *your* son to do this?

DEM   Allow him? Wouldn't I have got wind of it six whole months before he started anything?

SYR   You don't have to tell *me* about your vigilance.

DEM   I pray he will always be as he now is.

SYR   Sons turn out as their fathers wish them to.

DEM   But what about him? Have you seen him today?

SYR   Your son? (*aside*) I'll pack him off to the farm. (*aloud*) I

		abigam hunc rus. iamdudum aliquid ruri agere arbitror.
	DEM	satin scis ibi esse?
	SYR	oh! qui egomet produxi?
	DEM	optumest.
		metui ne haereret hic.
	SYR	atque iratum admodum.
	DEM	quid autem?
	SYR	adortust iurgio fratrem apud forum
405		de psaltria ista.
	DEM	ain vero?
	SYR	vah! nil reticuit.
		nam ut numerabatur forte argentum, intervenit
		homo de improviso. coepit clamare: "o Aeschine,
		haecin flagitia facere te! haec te admittere
		indigna genere nostro!"
	DEM	oh! lacrumo gaudio!
410	SYR	"non tu hoc argentum perdis sed vitam tuam."
	DEM	salvos sit! spero. est similis maiorum suom.
	SYR	hui!
	DEM	Syre, praeceptorum plenust istorum ille.
	SYR	phy!
		domi habuit unde disceret.
	DEM	fit sedulo,
		nil praetermitto, consuefacio. denique
415		inspicere tamquam in speculum in vitas omnium
		iubeo atque ex aliis sumere exemplum sibi.
		"hoc facito."
	SYR	recte sane.
	DEM	"hoc fugito."
	SYR	callide.
	DEM	"hoc laudist."

think he's been busy on the farm for a while.

DEM Are you quite sure he's there?

SYR Of course. I saw him off myself.

DEM That's excellent. I was afraid he was hanging about here.

SYR And he was pretty angry.

DEM What about?

SYR He had a quarrel with his brother in the forum about the music girl.

DEM Really?

SYR I'll say! And he didn't mince his words. Just as the money was being counted out, he came up out of the blue and started shouting: "Aeschinus! How can you behave so outrageously? How can you bring disgrace upon our family?"

DEM Oh! I weep for joy!

SYR "It's not the money that you're squandering, it's your life."

DEM Bless him! He gives me hope. He's a chip off the old block.[20]

SYR (*pretending to be impressed*) Wow!

DEM Syrus, he's full of these maxims.

SYR Phew! (*slyly*) He had someone to learn from at home.

DEM One does one's best. I never turn a blind eye. I teach him good habits. Above all I tell him to look into the lives of others as if into a mirror and to take from them an example for himself. "Do this," I say.

SYR Quite right.

DEM "Avoid that."

SYR Splendid.

DEM "This is praiseworthy."

---

20 Literally, "he's similar to his ancestors."

SYR   istaec res est.

DEM   "hoc vitio datur."

SYR   probissume.

DEM   porro autem—

SYR   non hercle otiumst

420   nunc mi auscultandi. piscis ex sententia
nactus sum. hi mihi ne corrumpantur cautiost.
nam id nobis tam flagitiumst quam illa, Demea,
non facere vobis quae modo dixti. et quod queo
conservis ad eundem istunc praecipio modum.

425   "hoc salsumst, hoc adustumst, hoc lautumst parum.
illud recte, iterum sic memento." sedulo
moneo quae possum pro mea sapientia.
postremo tamquam in speculum in patinas, Demea,
inspicere iubeo et moneo quid facto usu' sit.

430   inepta haec esse nos quae facimus sentio.
verum quid facias? ut homost, ita morem geras.
numquid vis?

DEM   mentem vobis meliorem dari.

SYR   tu rus hinc ibis?

DEM   recta.

SYR   nam quid tu hic agas,
ubi si quid bene praecipias nemo obtemperat?

435 DEM   ego vero hinc abeo, quando is quam ob rem huc veneram
rus abiit. illum curo unum, ille ad me attinet.
quando ita volt frater, de istoc ipse viderit.
sed quis illic est procul quem video? estne Hegio

---

21 The citizen body was divided into tribes both at Athens and at
Rome. But the tribes were much too large for everybody to know each
other. It is likely that in Menander the word was "fellow demesman,"
the deme being a smaller unit.

SYR Just the thing.

DEM "This is wrong."

SYR Excellent.

DEM Then again—

SYR I really don't have time to listen to you at the moment. I've got just the fish I wanted, and I must make sure they're not spoiled. That's as much a disgrace for us, Demea, as for you to neglect the things you were talking about just now. As far as I can, I instruct my fellow slaves on the same principles as yours. "Too salty," I say. "A bit burnt. Not clean enough. Just right: be sure to do the same next time." I do my best to advise them with such wisdom as I have. Above all I tell them to look into the saucepans as if into a mirror, Demea, and I advise them what lessons to learn. I realise that the goings-on in our house are silly. But what can you do? You have to take people as you find them. (*turning to go*) Is there anything else?

DEM Only that you people should have a change of attitude.

SYR Are you going to the farm?

DEM Right away.

SYR Well, you won't achieve much here. If you give any good advice, nobody takes any notice. (*he exits into Micio's house, leaving Demea onstage alone*).

DEM (*to himself*) Yes, I'm off, since the one I came here to see has gone to the farm. He's the one I care for, the one that concerns me. Since my brother wants it that way, he can see to the other one. (*looking down the street*) But who's that I see in the distance? Is it our fellow tribesman[21]

301

		tribulis noster? si satis cerno is herclest. vaha!
440		homo amicus nobis iam inde a puero. o di boni!
		ne illius modi iam magna nobis civium
		paenuriast. homo antiqua virtute ac fide.
		haud cito mali quid ortum ex hoc sit publice.
445		quam gaudeo, ubi etiam huius generis reliquias
		restare video! ah! vivere etiam nunc lubet.
		opperiar hominem hic ut salutem et colloquar.

III. IV: HEGIO. DEMEA. GETA. (PAMPHILA.)

	HEG	pro di immortales, facinus indignum, Geta!
		quid narras?
	GET	sic est factum.
	HEG	ex illan familia
		tam illiberale facinus esse ortum! o Aeschine,
450		pol haud paternum istuc dedisti.
	DEM	videlicet
		de psaltria hac audivit. id illi nunc dolet
		alieno, pater is nihili pendit. ei mihi!
		utinam hic prope adesset alicubi atque audiret haec!
	HEG	nisi facient quae illos aequomst, haud sic auferent.
455	GET	in te spes omnis, Hegio, nobis sitast.
		te solum habemus, tu's patronus, tu pater.
		ille tibi moriens nos commendavit senex.
		si deseris tu, periimus.
	HEG	cave dixeris!
		neque faciam neque me satis pie posse arbitror.
460	DEM	adibo. salvere Hegionem plurumum
		iubeo.

Hegio? By heaven it is, if my eyes don't deceive me. Splendid! A man who's been a friend of ours right from boyhood. Heaven knows, there's a great shortage of such citizens these days. A man of old-fashioned virtue and honour. It'll be a long time before *he's* the cause of any public scandal. How delighted I am, when I see that there are still people left of his type! Ah! Life still seems worth living. I'll wait here to pay my respects and have a word with him.

Enter HEGIO *left from the direction of the country, talking to* GETA.

HEG   Ye immortal gods! What a shocking business, Geta! What a story!

GET   It's the truth.

HEG   Such ungentlemanly conduct from that family! Oh Aeschinus! In this, by heaven, you're not your father's son.

DEM   (*aside*) He's evidently heard about the music girl. It distresses him as an outsider, whereas the boy's father doesn't care a damn. Oh dear! If only he were here somewhere and could hear all this!

HEG   They won't get away with it so easily, if they don't do the proper thing.

GET   All our hope lies in you, Hegio. You're the only person we have, our champion, our father. It was to you that the old man entrusted us on his deathbed. If you abandon us, we're lost.

HEG   Don't speak of it. I wouldn't do that. I deem it inconsistent with my sense of duty.

DEM   (*aside*) I'll go up to him. (*aloud*) My warmest greetings to Hegio.

303

	HEG	oh! te quaerebam ipsum. salve, Demea.
	DEM	quid autem?
	HEG	maior filius tuos Aeschinus,
		quem fratri adoptandum dedisti, neque boni
		neque liberalis functus officiumst viri.
465	DEM	quid istuc est?
	HEG	nostrum amicum noras Simulum atque
		aequalem?
	DEM	quidni?
	HEG	filiam eius virginem
		vitiavit.
	DEM	hem!
	HEG	mane. nondum audisti, Demea,
		quod est gravissumum.
	DEM	an quid est etiam amplius?
	HEG	vero amplius. nam hoc quidem ferundum aliquo modost.
470		persuasit nox, amor, vinum, adulescentia:
		humanumst. ubi scit factum, ad matrem virginis
		venit ipsus ultro lacrumans, orans, obsecrans,
		fidem dans, iurans se illam ducturum domum.
		ignotumst, tacitumst, creditumst. virgo ex eo
475		compressu gravida factast. mensis decimus est.
		ill' bonus vir nobis psaltriam, si dis placet,
		paravit quicum vivat; illam deserit.
	DEM	pro certo tu istaec dicis?
	HEG	mater virginis
		in mediost, ipsa virgo, res ipsa, hic Geta
480		praeterea, ut captust servolorum, non malus
		neque iners. alit illas, solus omnem familiam
		sustentat. hunc abduce, vinci, quaere rem.

HEG Oh! I was looking for you. Good day, Demea.

DEM What's the matter?

HEG Your elder son Aeschinus, whom you gave to your brother to adopt, has not behaved like an honest man or a gentleman.

DEM What do you mean?

HEG You knew our friend and comrade Simulus?

DEM Of course.

HEG Aeschinus has raped his daughter.

DEM What!

HEG Wait! You haven't heard the most serious thing yet.

DEM Is there anything worse?

HEG Yes, there is. That can be borne somehow. He was led astray by darkness, love, wine, youthful ardour: it's only human. When he realised what he had done, he went to the girl's mother of his own accord, weeping, begging, entreating, promising, swearing that he would marry the girl. He was forgiven, the matter was hushed up, his word was trusted. The girl became pregnant from that assault, and she's in her tenth month.[22] And now, please god, our fine fellow has acquired a music girl to live with, and abandoned the other one.

DEM Are you quite sure about this?

HEG The girl's mother will vouch for it, then there's the girl herself, and the sheer facts of the case. And besides there's Geta here, who's honest and resourceful, as slaves go; he keeps these women from starving; the whole family depends on him. Take him away, tie him up, interrogate him.

[22] The final month of pregnancy, calculated in antiquity as ten lunar months.

GET immo hercle extorque, nisi ita factumst, Demea.
postremo non negabit. coram ipsum cedo.
485 DEM pudet, nec quid agam nec quid huic respondeam
scio.
PAM   miseram me! differor doloribus.
Iuno Lucina, fer opem. serva me, obsecro.
HEG   hem!
numnam illa, quaeso, parturit?
GET   certe, Hegio.
HEG em, illaec fidem nunc vostram implorat, Demea.
490 quod vos vis cogit, id voluntate impetret.
haec primum ut fiant deos quaeso ut vobis decet.
sin aliter animus voster est, ego, Demea,
summa vi defendam hanc atque illum mortuom.
cognatus mihi erat; una a pueris parvolis
495 sumus educti; una semper militiae et domi
fuimus; paupertatem una pertulimus gravem.
quapropter nitar, faciam, experiar, denique
animam relinquam potius quam illas deseram.
quid mihi respondes?
DEM   fratrem conveniam, Hegio.
500 HEG sed, Demea, hoc tu facito cum animo cogites.
quam vos facillume agitis, quam estis maxume
potentes, dites, fortunati, nobiles,
tam maxume vos aequo animo aequa noscere
oportet, si vos voltis perhiberi probos.

489 em edd., hem codd.
499a is quod mi de hac re dederit consilium id sequar (= Ph. 461)
ΣA², omittunt A¹ edd.

GET   (*to Demea*) Yes, and torture me as well,[23] if it isn't true, Demea. At the end of the day he won't deny it. Let me have him face to face.

DEM   (*aside*) I'm ashamed, and I don't know what to do or how to answer him.

PAM   (*Pamphila cries from inside*) Oh! oh! I'm wracked with pain. Juno Lucina,[24] help me, save me, I beg you.

HEG   What! Is she in labour, if you please?

GET   Yes, she must be, Hegio.

HEG   (*to Demea*) There you are! She's now calling upon the honour of your family, Demea. Let her gain of your own free will what the force of the law demands. I pray heaven first of all that you people handle the matter in a way that does you credit. But, if your intentions are otherwise, Demea, I shall defend her and her dead father with all my might. He was a relative of mine; we were brought up together from early boyhood; we stood together always in war and peace; we endured the burdens of poverty together. So I will do my utmost, go to court, and indeed lay down my life before I abandon these women. What is your answer?

DEM   I'll speak to my brother, Hegio.

HEG   All right, Demea, but be sure to keep this in mind: the easier your life is, the more powerful, rich, and prosperous you are, the higher the status you enjoy, the more it is your duty to be fair-minded and to act justly, if you want to be regarded as honourable men.

[23] There is an allusion here to the torturing of slaves for evidence (compare *The Mother-in-Law* 773).

[24] Juno Lucina was the Roman goddess of childbirth. There is a similar offstage cry at *The Woman of Andros* 473.

505 DEM redito. fient quae fieri aequomst omnia.

HEG decet te facere. Geta, duc me intro ad Sostratam.

DEM non me indocente haec fiunt. utinam hic sit modo
defunctum! verum nimia illaec licentia
profecto evadit in aliquod magnum malum.

510 ibo ac requiram fratrem ut in eum haec evomam.

III.V: HEGIO.

HEG bono animo fac sis, Sostrata, et istam quod potes
fac consolere. ego Micionem, si apud forumst,
conveniam atque ut res gestast narrabo ordine.
si est facturus ut sit officium suom,

515 faciat. sin aliter de hac rest eius sententia,
respondeat mi, ut quid agam quam primum sciam.

ACTUS IV

IV. I: CTESPHO. SYRUS.

CTE ain patrem hinc abisse rus?

SYR   iamdudum.

CTE   dic, sodes.

SYR   apud villamst.
nunc quom maxume operis aliquid facere credo.

CTE   utinam quidem!
quod cum salute eius fiat, ita se defetigarit velim

520 ut triduo hoc perpetuo prorsum e lecto nequeat surgere.

DEM Come back later. Everything that should be done will be done.

HEG That's what I expect of you. (*to Geta*) Geta, take me in to Sostrata. (*Hegio and Geta exit into Sostrata's house, leaving Demea onstage alone*)

DEM (*to himself*) This is exactly what I said would happen. If only things could end here! But I'm sure that excessive licence will lead to some major disaster. I'll go and find my brother and discharge all this onto him. (*he exits right in the direction of the forum*)

Enter HEGIO from Sostrata's house.

HEG (*speaking back inside to Sostrata*) Don't worry, Sostrata, and comfort your daughter as best you can. I'll find Micio, if he's in the forum, and tell him the story from the beginning. If he's intending to do his duty, let him do it. But if he takes a different view of the matter, he must give me an answer, so that I can decide what to do without delay. (*he exits right in the direction of the forum*)

ACT FOUR

Enter CTESIPHO and SYRUS from Micio's house.

CTE You say my father's gone back to the farm?

SYR Some time ago.

CTE Please explain.

SYR He's at the farmhouse. I expect he's working on some job this very minute.

CTE I only hope he is. As long as he doesn't come to any harm, I'd like him to get himself so exhausted that for the next three days he can't get out of bed at all.

SYR	ita fiat, et istoc si qui potis est rectius.
CTE	ita. nam hunc diem

misere nimis cupio, ut coepi, perpetuom in laetitia de-
gere.

et illud rus nulla alia causa tam male odi nisi quia pro-
pest.

quod si abesset longius,

525   prius nox oppressisset illi quam huc revorti posset ite-
rum.

nunc ubi me illi non videbit, iam huc recurret, sat scio.

rogitabit me ubi fuerim: "ego hodie toto non vidi die."

quid dicam?

SYR	nilne in mentemst?
CTE	numquam quicquam.
SYR	tanto nequior.

cliens, amicus, hospes nemost vobis?

CTE	sunt. quid postea?
530 SYR	hisce opera ut data sit?
CTE	quae non data sit? non potest fieri.
SYR	potest.
CTE	interdius. sed si hic pernocto, causae quid dicam, Syre?
SYR	vah! quam vellem etiam noctu amicis operam mos esset

dari!

quin tu otiosus esto: ego illius sensum pulchre calleo.

quom fervit maxume, tam placidum quam ovem reddo.

CTE	quomodo?
535 SYR	laudarier te audit lubenter. facio te apud illum deum,

virtutes narro.

CTE	meas?

SYR   Yes indeed, and an even better fate than that if possible.

CTE   Yes. I'm desperately keen to spend the whole day in happiness, as I've begun. I hate that farm for no other reason than that it's near. If it were further away, darkness would overtake him before he could get back here a second time. As it is, when he doesn't find me there, he'll come running back here straightaway, I'm sure of it. He'll ask me where I've been. "I haven't seen you all day," he'll say. What shall I tell him?

SYR   Can't you think of anything?

CTE   Nothing at all.

SYR   So much the worse for you. Don't you people have clients, friends, guest-friends?[25]

CTE   Yes, we do. What of it?

SYR   So you can say you've been offering your services to them.

CTE   When I haven't? It can't be done.

SYR   Yes, it can.

CTE   (*weakening*) In the daytime. But, if I spend the night here, what excuse can I give, Syrus?

SYR   Oh! How I wish it was the custom to offer services to friends at night as well! But don't worry. I can read his mind pretty well. When he's boiling over, I can make him as gentle as a lamb.

CTE   How?

SYR   He likes to hear you praised. I make you out to be a god. I recount your virtues.

CTE   Mine?

[25] The term "guest-friend" (*hospes*) refers to the ties of duty and friendship which bound those who had been entertained in each other's houses.

SYR	tuas. homini ilico lacrumae cadunt
	quasi puero gaudio. em tibi autem!
CTE	quidnamst?
SYR	lupus in fabula.
CTE	pater est?
SYR	ipsust.
CTE	Syre, quid agimus?
SYR	fuge modo intro. ego videro.
CTE	si quid rogabit, nusquam tu me. audistin?
SYR	potin ut desinas?

IV. II: DEMEA. CTESIPHO. SYRUS

540	DEM	ne ego homo sum infelix! fratrem nusquam invenio gentium.
		praeterea autem, dum illum quaero, a villa mercennarium
		vidi. is filium negat esse ruri, nec quid agam scio.
	CTE	Syre!
	SYR	quid est?
	CTE	men quaerit?
	SYR	verum.
	CTE	perii!
	SYR	quin tu animo bono's.
	DEM	quid hoc, malum, infelicitatis? nequeo satis decernere,
545		nisi me credo huic esse natum rei, ferundis miseriis.
		primus sentio mala nostra, primus rescisco omnia,
		primus porro obnuntio, aegre solus si quid fit fero.

540 primum fratrem *codd.*, fratrem *edd.*

---

26 Literally, "the wolf in the fable"; the reference must be to a story in which a wolf suddenly appeared when it was being talked about (the phrase occurs also at Plautus, *Stichus* 577).

SYR   Yours. Tears of joy instantly fall from his eyes, like a small boy. (*looking down the street*). But look!

CTE   What is it?

SYR   Talk of the devil![26]

CTE   It's my father?

SYR   In person.

CTE   Syrus, what do we do?

SYR   Just run off inside. I'll see to him.

CTE   If he asks, you've not seen me anywhere. Do you understand?

SYR   Can't you stop it? (*he pushes Ctesipho towards Micio's house*)

Enter DEMEA *right from the direction of the forum.*

DEM   (*to himself*) I'm an ill-starred wretch, that's for sure! My brother's vanished from the face of the earth and, on top of that, while I was looking for him, I ran into a hired hand from the farm who told me my son wasn't there. Now I don't know what to do.

CTE   (*whispering from the doorstep*) Syrus!

SYR   What is it?

CTE   Is he looking for me?

SYR   Yes.

CTE   I'm ruined!

SYR   Just don't worry!

DEM   (*to himself*) What damned bad luck! I can't explain it, unless I'm to believe I was born to endure misery. I'm the first to be aware of our troubles, I'm the first to find them all out, I'm the first to bring the bad news as well, and I'm the only one who's upset at what's happening.

313

SYR	rideo hunc. primum ait se scire: is solus nescit omnia.
DEM	nunc redeo: si forte frater redierit viso.
CTE	Syre,
550	obsecro, vide ne ille huc prorsus se irruat.
SYR	etiam taces?
	ego cavebo.
CTE	numquam hercle ego hodie istuc committam tibi.
	nam me iam in cellam aliquam cum illa concludam. id tutissumumst.
SYR	age, tamen ego hunc amovebo.
DEM	sed eccum sceleratum Syrum.
SYR	non hercle hic quidem durare quisquam, si sic fit, potest.
555	scire equidem volo quot mihi sint domini. quae haec est miseria!
DEM	quid ille gannit? quid volt? quid ais, bone vir? est frater domi?
SYR	quid, malum, "bone vir" mihi narras? equidem perii.
DEM	quid tibist?
SYR	rogitas? Ctesipho me pugnis miserum et istam psaltriam usque occidit.
DEM	hem! quid narras?
SYR	em, vide ut discidit labrum!
560 DEM	quam ob rem?
SYR	me impulsore hanc emptam esse ait.
DEM	non tu eum rus hinc modo produxe aibas?

554 hic quidem *codd. Don.*, hic qui volt *Non.*

SYR (*aside*) He makes me laugh! He says he's the first to know, but he's the only one who's completely in the dark.

DEM (*to himself*) I've come back here now to see if maybe my brother has returned.

CTE (*whispering*) Syrus, for goodness' sake, make sure he doesn't rush straight in here.

SYR (*to Ctesipho*) Do be quiet. I won't let him.

CTE Well, I'm not going to leave this in your hands, for god's sake. I'll lock myself up in some back room with my girl. That's the safest course.

SYR Go on then. But I'll still get rid of this one. (*Ctesipho exits into the house and closes the door; Syrus comes forward as if just entering from the house*)

DEM (*to himself*) But there's that villain Syrus.

SYR (*as if to himself, rubbing some imaginary bruises*) For god's sake, nobody can stick it out here with this kind of treatment. I want to know how many masters I've got. What a miserable life!

DEM (*to himself*) What's he whining about? What does he want? (*aloud*) Answer me, my good man! Is my brother at home?

SYR Why the hell are you calling me a "good man"? I'm finished.

DEM What's the matter?

SYR A fine question! Ctesipho has pummelled poor me and that music girl practically to death.

DEM Oh! What are you saying?

SYR Look! (*pointing*) See how he's split my lip!

DEM What for?

SYR He says it was all my doing the girl was bought.

DEM (*suspiciously*) Didn't you say just now you'd seen him off to the farm?

315

SYR   factum. verum venit post insaniens.
        nil pepercit. non puduisse verberare hominem senem!
        quem ego modo puerum tantillum in manibus gestavi
           meis!

DEM   laudo. Ctesipho, patrissas. abi, virum te iudico.

565 SYR   laudas? ne ille continebit posthac, si sapiet, manus.

DEM   fortiter!

SYR   perquam, quia miseram mulierem et me servolum
        qui referire non audebam vicit. hui! perfortiter!

DEM   non potuit melius. idem quod ego sentit te esse huic rei
        caput.
        sed estne frater intus?

SYR   non est.

DEM   ubi illum inveniam cogito.

570 SYR   scio ubi sit, verum hodie numquam monstrabo.

DEM   hem! quid ais?

SYR   ita.

DEM   diminuetur tibi quidem iam cerebrum.

SYR   at nomen nescio
        illius hominis. sed locum novi ubi sit.

DEM   dic ergo locum.

SYR   nostin porticum apud macellum hanc deorsum?

DEM   quidni noverim?

SYR   praeterito hanc recta platea sursum. ubi eo veneris,

575   clivos deorsum vorsumst: hac te praecipitato. postea
        est ad hanc manum sacellum: ibi angiportum propter est.

DEM   quodnam?

SYR   illi ubi etiam caprificus magnast.

574 hanc *Gratwick*, hac *codd*.

SYR   Yes, I did. But he came back demented: no holds barred!
      Fancy not being ashamed to beat up an old man! The boy
      I cradled in my arms not so long ago when (*gesturing*) he
      was so big!

DEM   Good for him! Ctesipho, you take after your father. Go
      on! Now you're a man.

SYR   Good for him? He'll keep his hands to himself in the fu-
      ture, if he's got any sense.

DEM   Well done!

SYR   Extremely! A victory over a poor girl and a mere slave
      who didn't dare to strike back! Bravo! Very well done!

DEM   He couldn't have done better. He sees exactly what I do,
      that you're at the bottom of this whole thing. But is my
      brother at home?

SYR   (*sullenly*) No, he isn't.

DEM   I'm wondering where I can find him.

SYR   I know where he is, but I'm not going to tell you.

DEM   Oh! What are you saying?

SYR   You heard.

DEM   (*raising his stick*) I'll bash your brains out.

SYR   (*as if cowed by this*) Well, I don't know this fellow's name.
      But I know the place.

DEM   Tell me the place, then.

SYR   You know the portico down that way (*pointing*) by the
      market?

DEM   Of course I know it.

SYR   Go past it straight up the street. When you get to the top,
      there's a downhill slope in front of you; run down there.
      Then there's a shrine on this side (*pointing*) and not far
      away there's an alley.

DEM   Which one?

SYR   The one by the large fig tree.

317

	DEM	novi.
	SYR	hac pergito.
	DEM	id quidem angiportum non est pervium.
	SYR	verum hercle. vah!

censen hominem me esse? erravi. in porticum rursum
  redi.

580 sane hac multo propius ibis et minor est erratio.
  scin Cratini huius ditis aedis?

	DEM	scio.
	SYR	ubi eas praeterieris,

ad sinistram hac recta platea, ubi ad Dianae veneris,
ito ad dextram. prius quam ad portam venias, apud ipsum
  lacum
est pistrilla et exadvorsum fabrica: ibist.

	DEM	quid ibi facit?
585	SYR	lectulos in sole ilignis pedibus faciundos dedit.
	DEM	ubi potetis vos? bene sane! sed cesso ad eum pergere?
	SYR	i sane. ego te exercebo hodie, ut dignus es, silicernium!

Aeschinus odiose cessat, prandium corrumpitur.
Ctesipho autem in amorest totus. ego iam prospiciam
  mihi.
590 nam iam abibo atque unum quicquid, quod quidem erit
  bellissumum,
carpam et cyathos sorbilans paulatim hunc producam
  diem.

DEM I know it.

SYR Proceed down this.

DEM But there's no through way.

SYR Of course not. Blast! You must think I've lost my senses!
My mistake. Go back to the portico. In fact this is a much
shorter route and there's less chance of losing your way.
You know the house of that wealthy Cratinus?

DEM Yes.

SYR When you've passed this, turn left, go straight down the
street, and, when you get to the temple of Diana, go
right. Before you get to the city gate, right by the pond,[27]
there's a bakery, and facing that a workshop. That's where
he is.

DEM (*suspiciously*) What's he doing there?

SYR (*inventing furiously*) He's having some couches made,
outdoor ones, with oak feet.

DEM For your drinking parties? What a good idea! But I must
hurry up and find him. (*he exits right in the direction of
the forum, leaving Syrus onstage alone*)

SYR (*calling after him*) Very well, go. I'll give you some well
deserved exercise today, you old skeleton![28] (*to himself*)
Aeschinus is annoyingly late, and the meal's spoiling. And
Ctesipho's engrossed in his love affair. So I'll look after
myself now. I'll go off and sample all the nicest bits, take a
few sips of wine, and spin out the day at my leisure. (*he
exits into Micio's house, leaving the stage empty*)

[27] Donatus explains that it was customary to have a *lacus* (the Latin
word covers lake, pond, reservoir, trough) at the gate of the city to water
baggage animals and also to help extinguish fires lit by enemies.

[28] The word *silicernium* literally means "funeral feast," a striking
term of abuse for an old man with one foot in the grave.

IV. III: MICIO. HEGIO.

MIC ego in hac re nil reperio quam ob rem lauder tanto opere,
   Hegio.

   meum officium facio; quod peccatum a nobis ortumst
    corrigo.

   nisi si me in illo credidisti esse hominum numero qui ita
    putant,

595 sibi fieri iniuriam ultro si quam fecere ipsi expostules,

   et ultro accusant. id quia non est a me factum agis gra-
    tias?

HEG ah! minume. numquam te aliter atque es in animum in-
    duxi meum.

   sed quaeso ut una mecum ad matrem virginis eas, Micio,

   atque istaec eadem quae mihi dixti tute dicas mulieri:

600 suspicionem hanc propter fratrem eius esse et illam psal-
    triam.

MIC si ita aequom censes aut si ita opus est facto, eamus.

HEG   bene facis.

   nam et illic animum iam relevabis, quae dolore ac miseria

   tabescit, et tuo officio fueris functus. sed si aliter putas,

   egomet narrabo quae mihi dixti.

MIC   immo ego ibo.

HEG   bene facis.

605 omnes quibus res sunt minus secundae magis sunt nes-
    cioquo modo

   suspiciosi. ad contumeliam omnia accipiunt magis.

   propter suam impotentiam se semper credunt claudier.

   quapropter te ipsum purgare ipsi coram placabilius est.

MIC et recte et verum dicis.

HEG   sequere me ergo hac intro.

MIC   maxume.

THE BROTHERS

Enter MICIO *and* HEGIO *right from the direction of the forum.*

MIC I can't see any reason why you should praise me so much in this matter, Hegio. I'm doing my duty; I'm putting right a wrong for which we are responsible. Or did you suppose I was one of those who think themselves the injured party when you reproach them for injuring others and then proceed to accuse you in turn? Are you thanking me because I haven't behaved like them?

HEG No! Not at all. I've never entertained the thought that you are other than you are. But would you please come with me to the girl's mother, Micio, and tell her in person exactly what you've told me, that this is all a misunderstanding on account of his brother and the music girl?

MIC If you think that's right or if it's necessary, let's go.

HEG You're very kind. You'll put her mind at rest—she's pining away in pain and misery—and you'll have done your duty. But if you'd rather not, I'll tell her myself what you told me.

MIC No, I'll go.

HEG You're very kind. People who are less prosperous are more mistrustful somehow; they tend to take everything as an insult. Because of the weakness of their position, they always believe that they're being taken advantage of. So it's more likely to satisfy her if you explain the situation in person to her face.

MIC You're right. It's quite true.

HEG Come inside with me, then.

MIC By all means. (*they exit into Sostrata's house, leaving the stage empty again*)

IV. IV: AESCHINUS

610 AES discrucior animi!
610a hoccine de improviso mali mi obici tantum
ut neque quid me faciam nec quid agam certum siet!
membra metu debilia sunt; animus timore obstipuit.
pectore consistere nil consili quit. vah!
quo modo me ex hac expediam turba?
615 tanta nunc suspicio de me incidit neque ea immerito.
Sostrata credit mihi me psaltriam hanc emisse. id anus
mi indicium fecit.

nam ut hinc forte ad obstetricem erat missa, ubi vidi, ilico
accedo. rogito Pamphila quid agat, iam partus adsiet,
620 eon obstetricem accersat. illa exclamat: "abi, abi iam,
Aeschine,
satis diu dedisti verba, sat adhuc tua nos frustratast
fides."
"hem! quid istuc, obsecro" inquam "est?" "valeas, habeas
illam quae placet!"
sensi ilico id illas suspicari, sed me reprehendi tamen
ne quid de fratre garrulae illi dicerem ac fieret palam.

625 nunc quid faciam? dicam fratris esse hanc? quod minu-
mest opus
usquam efferri. ac mitto: fieri potis est ut ne qua exeat.
ipsum id metuo ut credant. tot concurrunt veri similia:
egomet rapui ipse, egomet solvi argentum, ad me abduc-
tast domum.

---

29 This is one of the three lyric passages in Terence, which would
have been sung in the original performance. The intention is to
heighten the emotional effect.

THE BROTHERS

Enter AESCHINUS *right from the direction of the forum.*

AES   (*to himself, singing*) This is sheer agony!
Faced with this problem out of the blue
I've no idea what to do with myself, what action to take.
My limbs are weak with fear, dread numbs my mind,
I can't think straight.
Blast! How can I get myself out of this mess?
I'm under suspicion brought on by myself.
Sostrata thinks the music girl was bought for me.
So the old nurse informs me.[29]

(*more calmly*) I happened to see her, when she was on
her way to the midwife. I went straight up to her and
asked how Pamphila was doing and whether the birth
was near and if that was why she was fetching the mid-
wife. "Go away, go away, Aeschinus," she shouted;
"You've deceived us long enough. We've had enough of
your broken promises." "What!" I said, "What's this all
about, for goodness' sake?" "Good riddance!" she said,
"Have the girl you prefer." I realised at once what they
suspected but I stopped myself saying anything about my
brother. A word to to that old gossip and the whole thing
would be public knowledge.

    Now what am I going to do? Say that the girl's my
brother's? That must never be revealed on any account.
I'll forget the idea: it's still possible that the truth may not
come out. I'm afraid they won't believe it anyway: so
many clues point in one direction. I was the one who car-
ried off the girl, I was the one who paid the money, it was
to my house that she was brought. And this situation here

323

haec adeo mea culpa fateor fieri. non me hanc rem patri,
630   utut erat gesta, indicasse! exorassem ut eam ducerem.
cessatum usque adhuc est: iam porro, Aeschine, exper-
    giscere.
nunc hoc primumst: ad illas ibo ut purgem me. accedam
    ad fores.
perii! horresco semper ubi pultare hasce occipio miser.
heus, heus, Aeschinus ego sum! aperite aliquis actutum
    ostium.
635   prodit nescioquis. concedam huc.

IV. V: MICIO. AESCHINUS.

MIC   ita uti dixi, Sostrata,
facite. ego Aeschinum conveniam, ut quo modo acta
    haec sunt sciat.
sed quis ostium hic pultavit?

AES   pater herclest! perii!

MIC   Aeschine!

AES   quid huic hic negotist?

MIC   tune has pepulisti fores?
tacet. quor non ludo hunc aliquantisper? melius est,
640   quandoquidem hoc numquam mihi ipse voluit credere.
nil mihi respondes?

AES   non equidem istas, quod sciam.

MIC   ita? nam mirabar quid hic negoti esset tibi.
erubuit. salva res est.

AES   dic, sodes, pater,
tibi vero quid istic est rei?

MIC   nil mihi quidem.
645   amicus quidam me a foro abduxit modo
huc advocatum sibi.

(*pointing to Sostrata's house*) is all my own fault, I admit.
Fancy not telling my father the whole story, bad as it was!
I should have persuaded him to let me marry her. You've
put things off long enough, Aeschinus: now you've got to
stir yourself! The first thing to do is to face the women
and clear myself. I'll go up to the door. (*he does so*) Damn
it! Oh dear, I shudder every time I'm about to knock
here. (*plucking up courage and knocking*) Hello there!
Hello! It's Aeschinus. Hurry up and open the door, some-
body! (*to himself*) There's someone coming out. I'll stand
aside here.

Enter MICIO *from Sostrata's house.*

MIC   (*speaking back inside to Sostrata*) You do as I say,
Sostrata. I'll go and find Aeschinus and let him know
what we've arranged. (*looking around*) But who knocked
on the door?

AES   (*aside*) By god, it's my father. I'm lost!

MIC   Aeschinus!

AES   (*aside*) What's he doing here?

MIC   Was it you who banged on the door? (*aside*) He's lost his
tongue. Why don't I tease him just for a while? Good idea,
seeing that he refused to trust me with his secret. (*aloud*)
Aren't you going to answer my question?

AES   It wasn't me, (*lamely*) so far as I know.

MIC   Really? I was wondering what you were doing here.
(*aside*) He's blushing! All's well!

AES   If I may ask, father, tell me, what business do *you* have
here?

MIC   Me? None. I was in the forum just now and a friend asked
me to come here to support him in a case.

AES		quid?
MIC		ego dicam tibi.

habitant hic quaedam mulieres pauperculae.
ut opinor, eas non nosse te, et certo scio.
neque enim diu huc migrarunt.

AES		quid tum postea?
650	MIC	virgost cum matre.
AES		perge.
MIC		haec virgo orbast patre.

hic meus amicus illi genere est proxumus.
huic leges cogunt nubere hanc.

AES		perii!
MIC		quid est?
AES	nil, recte. perge.	
MIC		is venit ut secum avehat.

nam habitat Mileti.

AES		hem! virginem ut secum avehat?
655	MIC	sic est.
AES		Miletum usque, obsecro?
MIC		ita.
AES		animo malest.

quid ipsae? quid aiunt?

MIC		quid illas censes? nil enim.

commenta mater est esse ex alio viro
nescioquo puerum natum, neque eum nominat;
priorem esse illum, non oportere huic dari.

660	AES	eho! nonne haec iusta tibi videntur postea?
MIC	non.	

---

30 For this law, which is Athenian rather than Roman, see *Phormio*
125–126.

AES   What case?

MIC   I'll tell you. In this house live some not very well-off women. I don't think you know them. In fact I'm sure you don't. They've only just come to live here.

AES   So?

MIC   There's a girl there with her mother.

AES   Go on.

MIC   The girl has lost her father. This friend of mine is her closest relative and the law requires her to marry him.[30]

AES   (*aside*) I'm lost!

MIC   What's the matter?

AES   Nothing, it's all right. Go on.

MIC   He's come to take her away with him. He lives at Miletus.[31]

AES   What! Take the girl away with him?

MIC   That's right.

AES   All the way to Miletus, for goodness' sake?

MIC   Yes.

AES   I feel sick. What about the women? What do they say?

MIC   What do you expect? There's nothing to say. The mother has made up a story that the girl has a child by some other man whom she doesn't name; she says that this other man has a prior claim and the girl shouldn't be given to my friend.

AES   (*indignantly*) Well, then! Doesn't this seem to you a fair objection, when all's said and done?

MIC   No.

[31] Miletus was a Greek city on the coast of what is now Turkey. The alleged relative must be an Athenian citizen living overseas and still liable to Athenian law.

327

AES   obsecro, non? an illam hinc abducet, pater?

MIC   quid illam ni abducat?

AES   factum a vobis duriter
immisericorditerque atque etiam, sist, pater,
dicendum magis aperte, illiberaliter.

665 MIC   quam ob rem?

AES   rogas me? quid illi tandem creditis
fore animi misero qui illa consuevit prior,
qui infelix haud scio an illam misere nunc amet,
quom hanc sibi videbit praesens praesenti eripi,
abduci ab oculis? facinus indignum, pater.

670 MIC   qua ratione istuc? quis despondit? quis dedit?
quoi quando nupsit? auctor his rebus quis est?
quor duxit alienam?

AES   an sedere oportuit
domi virginem tam grandem dum cognatus huc
illinc veniret exspectantem? haec, mi pater,

675   te dicere aequom fuit et id defendere.

MIC   ridiculum! advorsumne illum causam dicerem
quoi veneram advocatus? sed quid ista, Aeschine,
nostra? aut quid nobis cum illis? abeamus. quid est?

  quid lacrumas?

AES   pater, obsecro, ausculta.

MIC   Aeschine, audivi omnia

680   et scio. nam te amo, quo magis quae agis curae sunt mihi.

---

666 illa *A Don.*, illam *Don. in comm.*, cum illa Σ

---

32 Apparently a reference to the father of the bridegroom, whose
consent was in practice necessary in both Athens and Rome (compare
Phormio 232).

AES   No, for goodness' sake? Is he going to take her away, father?

MIC   Of course he is.

AES   You have acted cruelly, pitilessly, and, if I may speak even more frankly father, in a manner unworthy of a gentleman.

MIC   Why?

AES   A fine question! What do you suppose will be the feelings of the poor fellow who knew her first, who, for all I know, unhappy man, still loves her desperately, when he sees her snatched before his very eyes and taken away? It's outrageous behaviour, father.

MIC   How do you work that out? Who promised her in marriage? Who gave her away? Whom did she marry? When? Who gave his consent?[32] Why did this fellow marry a stranger?[33]

AES   Was a girl of her age to sit at home waiting for a relative to turn up here from Miletus? This is a point you should have made, father, and stuck to it.

MIC   Don't be absurd! Was I to argue the case against the man I'd come to support? But what's it got to do with us, Aeschinus? What business do we have with them? Let's go. (*changing his tone as Aeschinus begins to weep*) What's the matter? Why are you crying?

AES   Father, please, listen.

MIC   (*gently*) Aeschinus, I've heard everything. I know. I love you, and so I care all the more about what you do.

---

[33] The norm was for marriages to be arranged within family circles (compare *Phormio* 721).

AES ita velim me promerentem ames dum vivas, mi pater,
ut me hoc delictum admisisse in me, id mihi vehementer
    dolet
et me tui pudet.

MIC   credo hercle. nam ingenium novi tuom
liberale. sed vereor ne indiligens nimium sies.

685   in qua civitate tandem te arbitrare vivere?
virginem vitiasti quam te non ius fuerat tangere.
iam id peccatum primum sane magnum, at humanum
    tamen.
fecere alii saepe item boni. at postquam id evenit, cedo,
numquam circumspexti? aut numquid tute prospexti tibi

690   quid fieret, qua fieret? si te me ipsum puduit proloqui,
qua resc, iscerem? haec dum dubitas, menses abierunt
    decem.
prodidisti te et illam miseram et gnatum, quod quidem in
    te fuit.
quid? credebas dormienti haec tibi confecturos deos?
et illam sine tua opera in cubiculum iri deductum do-
    mum?

695   nolim ceterarum rerum te socordem eodem modo.
bono animo's. duces uxorem.

AES   hem!

MIC   bono animo's, inquam.

AES   pater,
obsecro, nunc ludis tu me?

MIC   ego te? quam ob rem?

AES   nescio.
quia tam misere hoc esse cupio verum, eo vereor magis.

---

687 sane *addit Kauer metri causa, alii alia*

AES   My dear father, I want to deserve your love until the day you die. I bitterly regret disgracing myself like this. I'm ashamed to look you in the face.

MIC   God knows, I don't doubt it. I know that your nature is honourable. But I'm afraid that you are being much too thoughtless. In what country, may I ask, do you think you're living? You raped a girl you had no right to touch. That was your first wrongdoing and serious enough, but it was human. Many good[34] men have done the same. But after the event, tell me, did you give the matter any thought? Did you think of the future: what needed to be done and how? If you were ashamed to tell me about this yourself, how was I to find out? While you sat around doing nothing, ten months[35] have passed. You've betrayed yourself and the poor girl and the child: you couldn't have behaved worse. Well, did you suppose the gods would take care of this for you while you were asleep? And she would be conducted to your home as your bride[36] without any effort on your part? I hope you won't be equally casual in the rest of your affairs. (*changing his tone again*) Cheer up! You shall marry her.

AES   What!

MIC   Cheer up, I said.

AES   Father, please, you're not making fun of me, are you?

MIC   Making fun of you? Why should I?

AES   I don't know. I so desperately want this to be true: it makes me all the more nervous.

---

[34] The word *bonus* (good) here has connotations of respectable, well bred.   [35] See note on line 475.

[36] Literally "to your bedroom"; the language ("conducted") is that of the marriage ceremony.

	MIC	abi domum ac deos comprecare ut uxorem accersas. abi!
700	AES	quid? iam uxorem?
	MIC	iam.
	AES	iam?
	MIC	iam, quantum potest.
	AES	di me, pater,

omnes oderint ni magis te quam oculos nunc amo meos.

	MIC	quid? quam illam?
	AES	aeque.
	MIC	perbenigne.
	AES	quid? ille ubist Milesius?
	MIC	periit, abiit, navem escendit. sed quor cessas?
	AES	abi, pater,

tu potius deos comprecare. nam tibi eos certo scio,
705 quo vir melior multo's quam ego, obtemperaturos magis.

MIC ego eo intro ut quae opus sunt parentur. tu fac ut dixi, si
sapis.

AES quid hoc est negoti? hoc est patrem esse aut hoc est
filium esse?
si frater aut sodalis esset, qui magis morem gereret?
hic non amandus, hicine non gestandus in sinust? hem!
710 itaque adeo magnam mi inicit sua commoditate curam
ne forte imprudens faciam quod nolit: sciens cavebo.
sed cesso ire intro, ne morae meis nuptiis egomet siem?

IV. VI: DEMEA.

DEM defessus sum ambulando. ut, Syre, te cum tua
monstratione magnus perdat Iuppiter!

---

[37] A proverbial expression (compare, for example, Catullus 3.4,
14.1).

MIC   Go inside and ask for the blessing of the gods, so that you can fetch your wife home. Off you go!

AES   What? My wife? Now?

MIC   Now.

AES   Now?

MIC   Now. As soon as you can.

AES   May all the gods hate me, father, if I don't love you more than my own eyes.[37]

MIC   What? More than her?

AES   Just as much.

MIC   (*laughing*) Very kind of you.

AES   But what about that man from Miletus?

MIC   (*shrugging his shoulders*) He's vanished, gone, taken ship. But what are you waiting for?

AES   You go, father, you ask the gods' blessing. They're more likely to take notice of you, I'm quite sure, seeing you're a much better man than I am.

MIC   I'm going inside to see to all the arrangements. You'll do as I say, if you've any sense. (*he exits into his house, leaving Aeschinus onstage alone*)

AES   (*to himself*) What about this? Is this what it means to be a father or a son? If he were a brother or a friend, how could he be more obliging? Isn't he a man to be loved and cherished? I should say so! He's been so considerate that I'm terribly afraid of doing something unwittingly he doesn't like. I won't do any such thing wittingly. But I'd better go in, or I'll be holding up my own wedding. (*he follows Micio into the house, leaving the stage empty*)

Enter DEMEA *right from the direction of the forum.*

DEM   (*to himself, wearily*) I'm worn out with walking. May almighty Jupiter destroy you, Syrus, you and your direc-

333

715   perreptavi usque omne oppidum: ad portum, ad lacum,
        quo non? neque illi fabrica ulla erat nec fratrem homo
        vidisse se aibat quisquam. nunc vero domi
        certum obsiderest usque donec redierit.

IV. VII: MICIO. DEMEA.

MIC   ibo. illis dicam nullam esse in nobis moram.
720 DEM   sed eccum ipsum. te iamdudum quaero, Micio.
MIC   quidnam?
DEM   fero alia flagitia ad te ingentia
        boni illius adulescentis.
MIC   ecce autem!
DEM   nova,
        capitalia.
MIC   ohe iam!
DEM   ah! nescis qui vir sit.
MIC   scio.
DEM   ah! stulte, tu de psaltria me somnias
725   agere. hoc peccatum in virginemst civem.
MIC   scio.
DEM   oho! scis et patere?
MIC   quidni patiar?
DEM   dic mihi,
        non clamas? non insanis?
MIC   non. malim quidem—
DEM   puer natust.
MIC   di bene vortant!
DEM   virgo nil habet—
MIC   audivi.
DEM   et ducenda indotatast.

tions! I've trudged all over the town, to the gate, to the pond, where not? There was no sign of a workshop and nobody said they'd seen my brother. I've decided to sit down outside the house now and wait until he returns.

Enter MICIO *from his house.*

MIC (*speaking back inside*) I'll go and tell them everything's ready on our side.

DEM (*aside*) There's the very man! (*to Micio*) I've been looking for you for a while, Micio.

MIC What for?

DEM I've further monstrous outrages to report on the part of that fine young man.

MIC (*aside*) Here we go again!

DEM Unheard of things, unforgivable things.

MIC Hold on now!

DEM Oh! You don't know what sort of man he is.

MIC Yes, I do.

DEM Oh! You fool, you imagine I'm talking about the music girl. This is a crime against a citizen girl.

MIC (*nonchalantly*) I know.

DEM Good god! You know and do nothing about it?

MIC Why should I?

DEM Tell me, doesn't it make you cry out? Doesn't it send you into a rage?

MIC No. It's true I'd prefer—

DEM A baby's been born.

MIC Good luck to it!

DEM The girl's penniless.

MIC So I've heard.

DEM She'll have to be married without a dowry.

	MIC	scilicet.
730	DEM	quid nunc futurumst?
	MIC	id enim quod res ipsa fert.
		illinc hinc transferetur virgo.
	DEM	o Iuppiter!
		istocin pacto oportet?
	MIC	quid faciam amplius?
	DEM	quid facias? si non ipsa re tibi istuc dolet,
		simulare certest hominis.
	MIC	quin iam virginem
735		despondi, res compositast, fiunt nuptiae,
		dempsi metum omnem. haec magis sunt hominis.
	DEM	ceterum
		placet tibi factum, Micio?
	MIC	non, si queam
		mutare. nunc quom non queo, animo aequo fero.
		ita vitast hominum quasi quom ludas tesseris.
740		si illud quod maxume opus est iactu non cadit,
		illud quod cecidit forte, id arte ut corrigas.
	DEM	corrector! nemp' tua arte viginti minae
		pro psaltria periere. quae quantum potest
		aliquo abiciundast, si non pretio, at gratiis.
745	MIC	nequest neque illam sane studeo vendere.
	DEM	quid igitur facies?
	MIC	domi erit.
	DEM	pro divom fidem!
		meretrix et materfamilias una in domo?
	MIC	quor non?

---

[38] Micio is referring not to games of mere chance but to those where
the skill lies in moving one's pieces according to the fall of the dice. The

MIC   Evidently.

DEM   What's going to happen now?

MIC   What the situation requires. The girl will be brought from that house (*pointing to Sostrata's house*) to this.

DEM   Jupiter! Is that the proper thing?

MIC   What more can I do?

DEM   What more? If you're not actually distressed by all this, it would at least be human to pretend to be.

MIC   Well, I've arranged the betrothal, everything is settled, the wedding is taking place, I've removed all their worries. That's being rather more human.

DEM   Even so, Micio, are you happy with the situation?

MIC   No, not if I could change it. As it is, since I can't, I accept it with good grace. Life is like a game of dice. If you don't get the exact throw you want, you have to use your skill and make the best of the one you do get.[38]

DEM   Make the best indeed! The fact is that, thanks to your skill, twenty minas have been wasted on the music girl. She must be got rid of somehow as soon as we can. If we can't sell her, we'll have to give her away.

MIC   No, we won't. And I'm certainly not keen to sell her.

DEM   What will you do, then?

MIC   She'll be kept at home.

DEM   Heaven help us! A wife[39] and a mistress under the same roof?

MIC   Why not?

Greeks and Romans both had a form of backgammon or draughts. The image of life as a game of dice is traditional also in Sophocles, Plato, and the Greek comic poet Alexis.

[39] The Latin *materfamilias* signifies not merely wife but the respected mistress of the household.

DEM   sanum te credis esse?

MIC   equidem arbitror.

DEM ita me di ament, ut video tuam ego ineptiam,

750   facturum credo ut habeas quicum cantites.

MIC quor non?

DEM   et nova nupta eadem haec discet?

MIC   scilicet.

DEM tu inter eas restim ductans saltabis?

MIC   probe.

DEM probe?

DEM   et tu nobiscum una, si opus sit.

DEM   ei mihi!

non te haec pudent?

MIC   iam vero omitte, Demea,

755   tuam istanc iracundiam atque ita ut decet

hilarum ac lubentem fac te gnati in nuptiis.

ego hos convenio, post huc redeo.

DEM   o Iuppiter!

hancin vitam! hoscin mores! hanc dementiam!

uxor sine dote veniet, intus psaltriast.

760   domus sumptuosa, adulescens luxu perditus,

senex delirans. ipsa si cupiat Salus,

servare prorsus non potest hanc familiam.

DEM Are you sure you're in your right mind?

MIC Well, I think so.

DEM Heaven help me, if I understand your stupidity, I believe you're setting up a singing partner for yourself.

MIC Why not?

DEM And the new bride will be taught to join in?

MIC Naturally.

DEM And you'll take the rope[40] and dance between them?

MIC Exactly.

DEM Exactly?

MIC And you can join us, if we need you.

DEM Oh dear! Do you have no shame?

MIC (*changing his tone*) The time has come, Demea, for you to control your temper and put on a happy smiling face for your son's wedding as the occasion demands. I'll go and fetch our neighbours and come back here. (*he exits into Sostrata's house, leaving Demea on stage alone*)

DEM (*to himself*) Jupiter! What a life! What a way to behave! What madness! There's a wife coming without a dowry, there's a music girl inside, the house is wallowing in extravagance, the young man's ruined by luxury, the old man's off his head. Salvation herself couldn't possibly save this house even if she wanted to.[41]

[40] The precise reference is unclear. It may be relevant that Livy (27.37.14) refers to a choir of maidens taking hold of a rope as they process towards the temple of Juno while singing a hymn.

[41] The paradox "Salvation couldn't save" is a recurrent one in comedy; compare Plautus, *The Captives* 529, *The Ghost* 351.

ACTUS V

V. I: SYRUS. DEMEA.

SYR   edepol, Syrisce, te curasti molliter
       lauteque munus administrasti tuom.
765   abi! sed postquam intus sum omnium rerum satur,
       prodeambulare huc lubitumst.
DEM   illud, sis, vide:
       exemplum disciplinae!
SYR   ecce autem hic adest
       senex noster. quid fit? quid tu's tristis?
DEM   o scelus!
SYR   ohe iam! tu verba fundis hic, Sapientia?
770 DEM   tu si meus esses—
SYR   dis quidem esses, Demea.
       ac tuam rem constabilisses.
DEM   —exemplo omnibus
       curarem ut esses.
SYR   quam ob rem? quid feci?
DEM   rogas?
       in ipsa turba atque in peccato maxumo,
       quod vix sedatum satis est, potatis, scelus,
775   quasi re bene gesta.
SYR   sane nollem huc exitum.

V. II: DROMO. SYRUS. DEMEA.

DRO   heus, Syre! rogat te Ctesipho ut redeas.
SYR   abi!
DEM   quid Ctesiphonem hic narrat?
SYR   nil.

---

771 exemplo *Bentley*, exempla A, exemplum Σ

THE BROTHERS

ACT FIVE

Enter SYRUS *from Micio's house, rather the worse for drink.*

SYR   (*to himself*) Well, Syrus my boy, you've looked after yourself in style and carried out your duties splendidly. Get away with you! But now I've had my fill of what's inside, I thought I'd take a stroll out here.

DEM   (*aside*) Look at that, if you please! What an example of discipline!

SYR   (*catching sight of Demea*) But look, here's our old man. (*to Demea*) How are things? Why are you so gloomy?

DEM   Oh, you villain!

SYR   Hold on now! Are you going to bandy words here, Mr Wisdom?

DEM   If you were my slave—

SYR   (*interrupting*) You'd be a rich man, Demea; you'd have secured your fortune.

DEM   —I'd make you an example for everyone.

SYR   (*innocently*) Why? What have I done?

DEM   You ask? Amidst all this mess and when this terrible wrongdoing has scarcely been put right, you go drinking, you villain, as if to celebrate some great achievement.

SYR   I'm sorry I came out.

DROMO opens the door of Micio's house and whispers to SYRUS.

DRO   Hey, Syrus! Ctesipho wants you to come back inside.

SYR   Go away! (*Dromo withdraws into Micio's house*)

DEM   What does he say about Ctesipho?

SYR   Nothing.

341

DEM	eho, carnufex!
	est Ctesipho intus?
SYR	non est.
DEM	quor hic nominat?
SYR	est alius quidam, parasitaster paullulus.
780	nostin?
DEM	iam scibo.
SYR	quid agis? quo abis?
DEM	mitte me.
SYR	noli, inquam.
DEM	non manum abstines, mastigia?
	an tibi iam mavis cerebrum dispergam hic?
SYR	abit.
	edepol comissatorem haud sane commodum,
	praesertim Ctesiphoni! quid ego nunc agam?
785	nisi, dum haec silescunt turbae, interea in angulum
	aliquo abeam atque edormiscam hoc villi. sic agam.

V. III: MICIO. DEMEA.

MIC	parata a nobis sunt, ita ut dixi, Sostrata.
	ubi vis—quisnam a me pepulit tam graviter fores?
DEM	ei mihi! quid faciam? quid agam? quid clamem aut querar?
790	o caelum, o terra, o maria Neptuni!

---

42 This is a translation of the Latin *parasitaster*, the diminutive form of *parasitus*.

43 The emergence of a character from a stage house in comedy is regularly preceded by a reference to the noise made by the door opening (compare *Phormio* 840 and note there). Even so, the word "pounding" here is strange; the Greek equivalent occurs at Menander, *Dyskolos* 188 and *Samia* 300.

DEM Look here, you gallows bird! Is Ctesipho in there?

SYR No, he isn't.

DEM Why was his name mentioned, then?

SYR It's somebody else, a young boy who hangs around here.[42] Do you know him?

DEM (*moving towards the door of Micio's house*) I'll soon find out.

SYR (*trying to hold him back*) What are you doing? Where are you going?

DEM Let me go.

SYR Stop, I say!

DEM Take your hands off me, you whipping post! (*brandishing his stick*) Or would you rather I knocked your brains out on the spot? (*he shakes himself free and marches into Micio's house, leaving Syrus onstage alone*)

SYR (*to himself*) He's gone! Well! Not exactly a welcome party guest, especially for Ctesipho! What shall I do now, other than retire to a corner somewhere and sleep off this drop of wine until the storm blows over. Yes, that's what I'll do. (*he exits warily into Micio's house, leaving the stage empty*)

Enter MICIO *from Sostrata's house.*

MIC (*speaking back inside to Sostrata.*) Everything's ready on our side, as I said, Sostrata. When you like—(*hearing a loud noise from his own house*) Who on earth was that pounding on my door?[43]

DEM (*bursting out from Micio's house*) Oh dear! What am I to do? How am I to act? What cry or lamentation can I utter? Oh heaven, oh earth, oh seas of Neptune's realm!

343

MIC   em tibi!
rescivit omnem rem. id nunc clamat. ilicet,
paratae lites, succurrendumst.

DEM   eccum adest
communis corruptela nostrum liberum.

MIC   tandem reprime iracundiam atque ad te redi.

795 DEM   repressi, redii. mitto maledicta omnia:
rem ipsam putemus. dictum hoc inter nos fuit
(ex te adeost ortum) ne tu curares meum
neve ego tuom? responde.

MIC   factumst. non nego.

DEM   quor nunc apud te potat? quor recipis meum?

800   quor emis amicam, Micio? numqui minus
mihi idem ius aequomst esse quod mecumst tibi?
quando ego tuom non curo, ne cura meum.

MIC   non aequom dicis.

DEM   non?

MIC   nam vetus verbum hoc quidemst,
communia esse amicorum inter se omnia.

805 DEM   facete! nunc demum istaec nata oratiost?

MIC   ausculta paucis nisi molestumst, Demea.
principio, si id te mordet, sumptum filii
quem faciunt, quaeso, hoc facito tecum cogites.
tu illos duo olim pro re tollebas tua,

810   quod satis putabas tua bona ambobus fore,
et me tum uxorem credidisti scilicet
ducturum. eandem illam rationem antiquam optine.

---

44 This is an old Greek proverb, ascribed by Donatus and others to

MIC (*aside*) Listen to that! He's discovered the whole story, hence the shouting. That's done it. The fight is on: I must go to the rescue.

DEM (*catching sight of Micio*) There he is, the ruination of both our children!

MIC Kindly control your temper and calm yourself.

DEM (*calming himself with an effort*) I *am* in control, I *am* calm. No more harsh words; let's consider the facts. Didn't we agree (and it was your suggestion) that you would not concern yourself with my son or I with yours? Answer me that.

MIC We did. I don't deny it.

DEM So why is my son drinking at your house? Why do you take him in? Why do you buy him a mistress, Micio? Isn't it fair that I should have the same rights with you as you with me? Since I'm not concerning myself with your son, don't concern yourself with mine.

MIC That's not a fair suggestion.

DEM No?

MIC There's an old saying that friends share everything in common.[44]

DEM Very clever! Isn't it a bit late to bring up that argument?

MIC Just listen to me a moment, if you don't mind, Demea. In the first place, if what's annoying you is the money our sons are spending, please think of it this way. You were once bringing up the two of them according to your means; you reckoned that your property would be sufficient for both and at that time you presumably believed that I would get married. Well, stick to your original plan.

the Pythagorean school of philosophy and quoted by both Plato (*Laws* 739c, *Phaedrus* 279c) and Aristotle (*Ethics* 8.9.1).

conserva, quaere, parce, fac quam plurumum
illis relinquas, gloriam tu istam optine.

815 mea, quae praeter spem evenere, utantur sine.
de summa nil decedet; quod hinc accesserit
id de lucro putato esse omne. haec si voles
in animo vere cogitare, Demea,
et mihi et tibi et illis dempseris molestiam.

820 DEM mitto rem: consuetudinem amborum—

MIC   mane.

scio, istuc ibam. multa in homine, Demea,
signa insunt ex quibus coniectura facile fit,
duo quom idem faciunt, saepe ut possis dicere
"hoc licet impune facere huic, illi non licet,"

825 non quo dissimilis res sit sed quo is qui facit.
quae ego inesse illis video, ut confidam fore
ita ut volumus. video sapere, intellegere, in loco
vereri, inter se amare. scire est liberum
ingenium atque animum. quovis illos tu die

830 redducas. at enim metuas ne ab re sint tamen
omissiores paullo. o noster Demea,
ad omnia alia aetate sapimus rectius.
solum unum hoc vitium affert senectus hominibus:
attentiores sumus ad rem omnes quam sat est,

835 quod illos sat aetas acuet.

DEM   ne nimium modo
bonae tuae istae nos rationes, Micio,
et tuos iste animus aequos subvortat.

MIC   tace!
non fiet. mitte iam istaec, da te hodie mihi,
exporge frontem.

DEM   scilicet ita tempu' fert.

Hoard, scrimp, save; endeavour to leave them as much as possible, and win yourself the credit for that. My wealth is an unexpected windfall: let them enjoy it. Your capital will be intact, and whatever I contribute you can count as pure gain. If you'll think this through properly, Demea, you'll spare me and yourself and them a lot of trouble.

DEM Never mind about the money. It's the way they both live—

MIC Hold on! I know. I was coming to that. There are many indications, Demea, by which you can readily assess the character of a person, so that, when two people do the same thing, you can say: "This person can safely be allowed to do this, that one can't," not because the deed is different but because the doer is. I can see indications in these boys that make me confident they'll turn out as we wish. I see in them good sense, intelligence, restraint where appropriate, and mutual affection. It's obvious that their natures and inclinations are fundamentally honourable, so you can bring them back into line any day you like. But I suppose you're afraid that they're a little careless in money matters. My dear Demea, in all other respects wisdom increases with advancing years. But there is one fault which old age brings to us. We all become far too worried about money, on which time will sharpen *their* attitudes soon enough.

DEM I only hope, Micio, that this fine philosophy of yours and your easygoing attitude don't prove our ruin.

MIC Hush! They won't. Forget all that. For today do me a favour and stop frowning.

DEM That's evidently what the occasion requires. I've no

840   faciundumst. ceterum ego rus cras cum filio
        cum primo luci ibo hinc.

MIC   de nocte censeo.
        hodie modo hilarum fac te.

DEM   et istam psaltriam
        una illuc mecum hinc abstraham.

MIC   pugnaveris.
        eo pacto prorsum illi alligaris filium.

845   modo facito ut illam serves.

DEM   ego istuc videro,
        atque ibi favillae plena, fumi ac pollinis
        coquendo sit faxo et molendo. praeter haec
        meridie ipso faciam ut stipulam colligat.
        tam excoctam reddam atque atram quam carbost.

MIC   placet.

850   nunc mihi videre sapere. atque equidem filium
        tum, etiam si nolit, cogam ut cum illa una cubet.

DEM   derides? fortunatu's qui isto animo sies.
        ego sentio—

MIC   ah! pergisne?

DEM   iam iam desino.

MIC   i ergo intro, et quoi reist ei rei hunc sumamus diem.

V. IV: DEMEA.

855 DEM   numquam ita quisquam bene subducta ratione ad vitam
             fuit
        quin res, aetas, usus semper aliquid apportet novi,
        aliquid moneat, ut illa quae te scisse credas nescias,
        et quae tibi putaris prima, in experiundo ut repudies.
        quod nunc mi evenit. nam ego vitam duram quam vixi
            usque adhuc

choice. But tomorrow I'm off to the farm with my son at the crack of dawn.

MIC Before dawn, if you want my advice. But just for today put on a happy face.

DEM And I'll drag that music girl off with me.

MIC (*approvingly*) That'll win the day. It should tie your son to the place for ever. Just make sure you keep her there.

DEM I'll see to that. I'll have her covered with soot, smoke, and flour from the cooking and grinding. And, what's more, I'll make her collect the straw in the midday sun until she's as burnt and black as charcoal.

MIC Quite right! Now you seem to be showing some sense. And, if I were you, I'd force your son to sleep with her even against his will.

DEM Are you mocking me? You're lucky to be in that frame of mind. I feel—

MIC Oh! Are you still going on?

DEM No, now I've finished.

MIC Come inside then, and let's spend the day as it ought to be spent. (*he exits into his house with Demea following*)

DEMEA pauses on Micio's doorstep and reflects.

DEM Nobody has ever had such a well worked-out plan of life that circumstances, age, and experience don't introduce some new factor, teach some new lesson, so that you no longer know what you thought you knew and you reject in practice what you had reckoned to be of prime importance. This is what has happened in my case. Now my course is almost run, I'm abandoning the hard life which I've lived right up to now. And why? I've discovered that

860 prope iam excurso spatio omitto. id quam ob rem? re ipsa
repperi
facilitate nil esse homini melius neque clementia.
id esse verum ex me atque ex fratre quoivis facilest nos-
cere.
ill' suam semper egit vitam in otio, in conviviis,
clemens, placidus; nulli laedere os, arridere omnibus;
865 sibi vixit, sibi sumptum fecit: omnes bene dicunt, amant.
ego ille agrestis, saevos, tristis, parcus, truculentus, tenax
duxi uxorem. quam ibi miseriam vidi! nati filii,
alia cura. heia autem, dum studeo illis ut quam pluru-
mum
facerem, contrivi in quaerundo vitam atque aetatem
meam.
870 nunc exacta aetate hoc fructi pro labore ab eis fero,
odium. ille alter sine labore patria potitur commoda.
illum amant, me fugitant. illi credunt consilia omnia,
illum diligunt, apud illum sunt ambo, ego desertu' sum.
illum ut vivant optant, meam autem mortem exspectant
scilicet.
875 ita eos meo labore eductos maxumo hic fecit suos
paullo sumptu. miseriam omnem ego capio, hic potitur
gaudia.
age age, nunciam experiamur contra ecquid ego possiem
blande dicere aut benigne facere, quando hoc provocat.
ego quoque a meis me amari et magni pendi postulo.
880 si id fit dando atque obsequendo, non posteriores feram.
deerit: id mea minime refert qui sum natu maxumus.

V. V: SYRUS. DEMEA.

SYR heus, Demea! orat frater ne abeas longius.

882 orat A, rogat Σ

350

in reality nothing is better for a man than to be generous and easygoing. Anyone can easily see the truth of this by comparing my brother and myself. He has always lived a life of leisure and conviviality; he's easygoing and even-tempered, he never gives offence, he smiles at everybody. He's lived for himself, he's spent for himself. Everyone speaks well of him, everyone loves him. I on the other hand am your typical rustic: aggressive, surly, stingy, ill-tempered, tight-fisted. I married a wife, and what misery that brought me! I had sons, another worry. Oh yes! In my eagerness to make as much as possible for them, I've worn out the best years of my life in money grubbing. And now at the end of my time the reward I get from them for my labours is hatred, while that brother of mine without lifting a finger gets all the benefits of fatherhood. They love him, they avoid me. They confide all their plans to him, they're fond of him, they both frequent his house; I'm left on my own. They wish him a long life; you can be sure they can't wait for me to die. I brought them up with a lot of labour; he has made them his with little expense. I get all the misery, he has all the joy. Very well then, let's see if I am capable on my side of winning words and kind deeds, since this is the challenge he throws down. I too have a right to be loved and valued by my family. If that's achieved by being generous and indulgent, I won't be left behind. The money will run out; but I couldn't care less, since I'm well on in years.

Enter SYRUS from Micio's house.

SYR   Hey, Demea, your brother asks you not to go too far away.

351

DEM quid homo? o Syre noster, salve. quid fit? quid agitur?
SYR recte.
DEM   optumest. iam nunc haec tria primum addidi
885 praeter naturam: "o noster," "quid fit?", "quid agitur?"
servom haud illiberalem praebes te et tibi
lubens bene faxim.
SYR   gratiam habeo.
DEM   atqui, Syre,
hoc verumst et ipsa re experiere propediem.

V. VI: GETA. DEMEA. (SYRUS.)

GET era, ego huc ad hos proviso quam mox virginem
890 accersant. sed eccum Demeam. salvos sies!
DEM o qui vocare?
GET   Geta.
DEM   Geta, hominem maxumi
preti te esse hodie iudicavi animo meo.
nam is mihi profectost servos spectatus satis
quoi dominus curaest, ita ut tibi sensi, Geta,
895 et tibi ob eam rem, si quid usus venerit,
lubens bene faxim. meditor esse affabilis,
et bene procedit.
GET   bonus es quom haec existumas.
DEM paullatim plebem primulum facio meam.

V. VII: AESCHINUS. DEMEA. SYRUS. GETA.

AES occidunt mequidem dum nimis sanctas nuptias

DEM   Who's that? Oh, Syrus my good fellow! Good day. How are things? How are you doing?

SYR   (*surprised by the warmth of this greeting*). All right.

DEM   Splendid! (*aside*) That's three things I've said already that don't come naturally: "my good fellow" and "how are things?" and "how are you doing?" (*to Syrus*) You've shown yourself quite a gentleman for a slave, and I'd be delighted to do you a good turn.

SYR   (*still puzzled*) Thank you very much.

DEM   Well, Syrus, I mean it, as you'll find out before too long. (*Syrus turns to leave but lingers as Sostrata's door opens*)

Enter GETA *from Sostrata's house.*

GET   (*speaking back inside to Sostrata.*) Mistress, I'm going next door to see how soon they're coming to fetch the bride. (*catching sight of Demea*) But there's Demea. A very good day to you!

DEM   Oh, what's your name?

GET   Geta.

DEM   Geta, I've formed the opinion today that you are a most admirable fellow. In my view, a slave has assuredly proved his worth who is concerned for his master's interests, as I see you are, Geta. For that reason, if the opportunity arises, I'd be delighted to do you a good turn. (*aside*) I'm practising being affable, and it's going well.

GET   (*puzzled but pleased*) It's good of you to think so.

DEM   (*aside*). I'm gradually winning over the lower classes as a start.

Enter AESCHINUS *from Micio's house.*

AES   (*to himself*) They're killing me with the fuss they're

900	student facere. in apparando consumunt diem.
DEM	quid agitur, Aeschine?
AES	ehem, pater mi! tu hic eras?
DEM	tuos hercle vero et animo et natura pater,
	qui te amat plus quam hosce oculos. sed quor non domum
	uxorem accersis?
AES	cupio. verum hoc mihi moraest,
905	tibicina et hymenaeum qui cantent.
DEM	eho!
	vin tu huic seni auscultare?
AES	quid?
DEM	missa haec face,
	hymenaeum, turbas, lampadas, tibicinas,
	atque hanc in horto maceriam iube dirui
	quantum potest. hac transfer, unam fac domum.
910	transduce et matrem et familiam omnem ad nos.
AES	placet,
	pater lepidissume.
DEM	euge! iam lepidus vocor.
	fratri aedes fient perviae, turbam domum
	adducet, sumptu amittet multa. quid mea?
	ego lepidus ineo gratiam. iube nunciam
915	dinumeret ille Babylo viginti minas.
	Syre, cessas ire ac facere?
SYR	quid ago?
DEM	dirue.
	tu illas abi et transduce.

making about the wedding ceremony. They're taking the whole day to prepare.

DEM (*approaching him*) How are you doing, Aeschinus?

AES Oh hello, my dear father! I didn't realise you were here.

DEM Your father indeed in heart and in nature, who loves you more than his own eyes.[45] But why don't you go and fetch your bride?

AES I want to. But we're waiting for the piper and the choir to sing the wedding hymn.[46]

DEM Say, are you willing to take advice from an old man?

AES What?

DEM Forget about all that, wedding hymns, congregations, torches, pipers. Get that garden wall knocked down as soon as you can. Fetch her across that way, unite the two families, bring the mother and the whole household over to us.

AES Good idea! Father, you're wonderful.

DEM (*aside*) Splendid! Now I'm called wonderful. My brother's house will become a thoroughfare, he'll have crowds of people in his home, it'll cost him a lot. Why should I care? I'm wonderful and I'm becoming popular. Now let that spendthrift[47] pay out his twenty minas! (*to Syrus*) Syrus, what are you waiting for? Go and do it!

SYR Do what?

DEM Knock the wall down. (*Syrus exits into Micio's house*) (*to Geta*) You go and bring the women over.

[45] See note 37.   [46] At both Athens and Rome the bride was conveyed to the bridegroom's house by a torchlight procession, accompanied by the singing of the marriage hymn.

[47] Literally, "that Babylonian": the Babylonians were proverbial for high spending.

GET   di tibi, Demea,
bene faciant, quom te video nostrae familiae
tam ex animo factum velle.

DEM   dignos arbitror.

920   quid tu ais?

AES   sic opinor.

DEM   multo rectiust
quam illam puerperam hac nunc duci per viam
aegrotam.

AES   nil enim melius vidi, mi pater.

DEM   sic soleo. sed eccum Micio egreditur foras.

V. VIII: MICIO. DEMEA. AESCHINUS.

MIC   iubet frater? ubi is est? tu iubes hoc, Demea?

925 DEM   ego vero iubeo et hac re et aliis omnibus
quam maxume unam facere nos hanc familiam,
colere, adiuvare, adiungere.

AES   ita quaeso, pater.

MIC   haud aliter censeo.

DEM   immo hercle ita nobis decet.
primum huius uxorist mater.

MIC   est. quid postea?

930 DEM   proba et modesta.

MIC   ita aiunt.

DEM   natu grandior.

MIC   scio.

DEM   parere iamdiu haec per annos non potest,
nec qui eam respiciat quisquamst. solast.

MIC   quam hic rem agit?

---

48 The point is twofold: she cannot bear any son to protect her, and
Micio is in no danger of gaining a son to share Aeschinus' inheritance.

GET   The gods bless you, Demea. I can see that you truly wish our household well.

DEM   I think they deserve it. (*Geta exits into Sostrata's house*) (*to Aeschinus*) What do you think?

AES   I agree.

DEM   This is much preferable than bringing a new mother here through the street in her condition.

AES   I've never heard a better suggestion, my dear father.

DEM   I'm like that. But look, there's Micio coming out.

Enter MICIO *from his house.*

MIC   (*speaking back inside to Syrus*) My brother told you to? Where is he? (*catching sight of Demea*) You told him to, Demea?

DEM   I did. In this and in every other way we should do our best to unite this household, cherish them, support them, and join them together with us.

AES   Yes, please, father.

MIC   (*without much enthusiasm*) I'm not opposed to that.

DEM   On the contrary, it's the only decent thing to do, for god's sake. First of all, (*indicating Aeschinus*) his wife has a mother.

MIC   She has. What of it?

DEM   She's a virtuous respectable lady.

MIC   So they say.

DEM   And she's getting on in years.

MIC   I know.

DEM   She's well past the age of childbearing,[48] and she's alone with nobody to look after her.

MIC   (*aside*) What's he getting at?

357

DEM   hanc te aequomst ducere, et te operam ut fiat dare.

MIC   me ducere autem?

DEM   te.

MIC   me?

DEM   te, inquam.

MIC   ineptis.

DEM   si tu sis homo,

935   hic faciat.

AES   mi pater!

MIC   quid tu autem huic, asine, auscultas?

DEM   nil agis.

fieri aliter non potest.

MIC   deliras.

AES   sine te exorem, mi pater.

MIC   insanis. aufer!

DEM   age, da veniam filio.

MIC   satin sanus es?

ego novos maritus anno demum quinto et sexagensumo

fiam atque anum decrepitam ducam? idne estis auctores

mihi?

940 AES   fac. promisi ego illis.

MIC   promisti autem? de te largitor, puer.

DEM   age, quid si quid te maius oret?

MIC   quasi non hoc sit maxumum.

DEM   da veniam.

AES   ne gravare.

DEM   fac, promitte.

MIC   non omittitis?

---

49 Presumably meaning "If you had the goodness to persuade him."
50 Donatus makes the interesting comment here that in Menander

THE BROTHERS

DEM It's only right that you should marry her, and (*to Aeschinus*) that you should see that he does.

MIC Me marry her, indeed?

DEM You.

MIC Me?

DEM You, I say.

MIC You're being absurd!

DEM (*to Aeschinus*) If you had any humanity,[49] he'd do it.

AES (*to Micio*) My dear father!

MIC (*to Aeschinus*) Why on earth do you pay any attention to him, you ass?

DEM You're wasting your time. You've no alternative.

MIC (*to Demea*) You're off your head.

AES Let me persuade you, father.

MIC (*to Aeschinus*) You're out of your mind. Forget it!

DEM Come on, do your son a favour.

MIC Have you gone crazy? Am I finally in my sixty-fifth year to become a bridegroom and marry a decrepit old hag? Is that what you're proposing for me?[50]

AES Do it. I promised them.

MIC You promised them, indeed? You be generous at your own expense, my boy.

DEM What if he asked you for a bigger favour?

MIC There couldn't be a bigger favour.

DEM Do it for him.

AES Don't be difficult.

DEM Do it, promise.

MIC Leave off, can't you?

the Micio character did not complain about the marriage, which suggests that Terence has made significant changes to the tone of the ending of the play.

AES non, nisi te exorem.

MIC   vis est haec quidem.

DEM   age prolixe, Micio.

MIC etsi hoc mihi pravom, ineptum, absurdum atque alienum
       a vita mea

945 videtur, si vos tanto opere istuc voltis, fiat.

AES   bene facis.

merito te amo.

DEM   verum quid ego dicam, hoc quom confit quod volo?

quid nunc quod restat? Hegio: est his cognatus proxu-
       mus,

affinis nobis, pauper. bene nos aliquid facere illi decet.

MIC quid facere?

DEM   agellist hic sub urbe paullum quod locitas foras.

950 huic demus qui fruatur.

MIC   paullum id autemst?

DEM   si multumst, tamen

faciundumst. pro patre huic est, bonus est, noster est.
       recte datur.

postremo non meum illud verbum facio quod tu, Micio,

bene et sapienter dixti dudum: "vitium commune omni-
       umst

quod nimium ad rem in senecta attenti sumus"? hanc
       maculam nos decet

955 effugere. et dictumst vere et re ipsa fieri oportet.

AES   mi pater!

MIC quid istic? dabitur quandoquidem hic volt.

---

946 confit *Don. ad And. 167*, fit *codd.*   955 *ad fin.* AE. mi pater
F Umpfenbach, MI. gaudeo *DLp, omittunt cett.*
       956 *ad fin.* DE. gaudeo *Umpfenbach*, AE. mi pater *codd., omittit F¹*

AES   No, not unless you agree.

MIC   You're twisting my arm.

DEM   Be generous, Micio.

MIC   Even though I think this perverse, silly, ridiculous, and foreign to my way of life, if you both want it so much, all right.

AES   You're very kind. No wonder I love you.

DEM   But—(*aside*) What shall I ask next, since this is going just as I wanted? (*aloud*) There still remains Hegio: what about him? He's their nearest relative, he's a family connection, and he's poor. We should do something for him.

MIC   Do what?

DEM   There's that small plot of land just outside town which you let out. Let's give him the enjoyment of that.

MIC   That's a little plot?

DEM   Even if it's a large one, we should do it. He's like a father to the girl, he's a good man, he's one of us. It's a gift well given. When all's said and done, can't I adopt for myself the remark which you made just now, Micio, so wisely and so well? "It's a common fault of all of us that in old age we are too worried about money." We should avoid that reproach. It's sound advice and we should carry it out in practice.

AES   Please, my dear father!

MIC   All right, then. He shall have it, since that's what Aeschinus wants.

DEM	gaudeo.

nunc tu germanu's pariter animo et corpore.
suo sibi gladio hunc iugulo.

V. IX: SYRUS. DEMEA. MICIO. AESCHINUS.

SYR	factumst quod iussisti, Demea.
DEM	frugi homo's. ergo edepol hodie mea quidem sententia

960   iudico Syrum fieri esse aequom liberum.

MIC	istunc liberum?

quodnam ob factum?

DEM	multa.
SYR	o noster Demea, edepol vir bonu's.

ego istos vobis usque a pueris curavi ambo sedulo.
docui, monui, bene praecepi semper quae potui omnia.

DEM	res apparet. et quidem porro haec: opsonare cum fide,

965   scortum adducere, apparare de die convivium.
non mediocris hominis haec sunt officia.

SYR	o lepidum caput!
DEM	postremo hodie in psaltria hac emunda hic adiutor fuit,

hic curavit. prodesse aequomst: alii meliores erunt.
denique hic volt fieri.

MIC	vin tu hoc fieri?
AES	cupio.
MIC	si quidem

970   tu vis, Syre, eho, accede huc ad me. liber esto.

SYR	bene facis.

omnibu' gratiam habeo et seorsum tibi praeterea, De-
mea.

DEM	gaudeo.

DEM I'm delighted. Now you are my true brother in heart as well as in body. (*aside*) I'm cutting his throat with his own sword.

Enter SYRUS *from Micio's house.*

SYR I've done as you told me, Demea.

DEM Good man. (*to Micio*) Well then, if you want my opinion, it's only right that Syrus should receive his freedom today.

MIC Freedom? Him? What on earth for?

DEM For many reasons.

SYR Demea, master, you really are kind. I did my best to care for both the boys right from childhood. I taught them, guided them, and always gave them the best training I could in everything.

DEM The facts speak for themselves. And there are other things besides: buying food on credit, hiring girls, arranging drinking parties in broad daylight. These are the services of no ordinary person.

SYR What a wonderful man!

DEM And to cap it all he assisted in the purchase of the music girl today; in fact he arranged it. It's only right to reward him; it will be an incentive for the others. Anyway, (*indicating Aeschinus*) he wants it.

MIC (*to Aeschinus*) You want it?

AES Very much.

MIC All right, if you want it. (*to Syrus*) Hey, Syrus, come over here. (*laying a hand on his head*) Accept your freedom.

SYR You're very kind. I'm grateful to all of you and especially to you, Demea.

DEM I'm delighted for you.

AES	et ego.
SYR	credo. utinam hoc perpetuom fiat gaudium, Phrygiam ut uxorem meam una mecum videam liberam!
DEM	optumam quidem mulierem.
SYR	et quidem tuo nepoti huius filio
975	hodie prima mammam dedit haec.
DEM	hercle vero serio, siquidem prima dedit, haud dubiumst quin emitti aequom siet.
MIC	ob eam rem?
DEM	ob eam. postremo a me argentum quantist sumito.
SYR	di tibi, Demea, omnes semper omnia optata offerant!
MIC	Syre, processisti hodie pulchre.
DEM	siquidem porro, Micio,
980	tu tuom officium facies atque huic aliquid paullum prae manu dederis unde utatur, reddet tibi cito.
MIC	istoc vilius.
DEM	frugi homost.
SYR	reddam hercle. da modo.
AES	age, pater.
MIC	post consulam.
DEM	faciet.
SYR	o vir optume!
AES	o pater mi festivissume!
MIC	quid istuc? quae res tam repente mores mutavit tuos?
985	quod prolubium? quae istaec subitast largitas?

---

51 Masters who freed their slaves were still expected to support them in their new status as freedmen.

AES   So am I.

SYR   I know you are. If only, so that my joy could be full, I could see my wife Phrygia freed with me!

DEM   An excellent woman.

SYR   Yes, and she was the first to breastfeed your grandson, (*indicating Aeschinus*) his son, today.

DEM   For god's sake, really and truly, if she was the first, there's no question. It's only right that she should be given her freedom.

MIC   For that?

DEM   For that. To settle the matter, I'll refund you whatever she's worth.

SYR   May all the gods always grant you all your desires, Demea!

MIC   (*to Syrus, wrily*) You've done pretty well for yourself today, Syrus.

DEM   Yes indeed, if you carry your duty further, Micio, and give him a little cash in hand to start him off.[51] He'll pay you back promptly.

MIC   (*snapping his fingers*) Not even that much.

DEM   He's a good man.

SYR   I'll pay you back, I swear. Just let me have it.

AES   Go on, father.

MIC   I'll think about it later.

DEM   He'll do it. (*Micio nods unwillingly*)

SYR   You're very kind.

AES   You're wonderful, father!

MIC   (*to Demea*) What is all this? What has changed your behaviour so suddenly? What is this whim? What is this unexpected extravagance?

DEM   dicam tibi:
    ut id ostenderem, quod te isti facilem et festivom putant,
    id non fieri ex vera vita neque adeo ex aequo et bono
    sed ex assentando, indulgendo et largiendo, Micio.
    nunc adeo si ob eam rem vobis mea vita invisa, Aeschine,
        est,

990   quia non iusta iniusta prorsus omnia omnino obsequor,
    missos facio. effundite, emite, facite quod vobis lubet.
    sed si voltis potius, quae vos propter adulescentiam
    minus videtis, magis impense cupitis, consulitis parum,

995   haec reprehendere et corrigere me et secundare in loco,
    ecce me qui id faciam vobis.

AES   tibi, pater, permittimus.
    plus scis quid opus factost. sed de fratre quid fiet?

DEM   sino:
    habeat, in istac finem faciat.

MIC   istuc recte.

Ω   plaudite.

991 missos *Grant*, missa *codd.*
997 istuc recte *Micioni dant codd. pl. Don. Eugr., Aeschino* γG

DEM I'll tell you. It was to show you that what they judge to be your good nature and generosity is not the product of sincerity or indeed of anything right or good but of weakness, indulgence, and extravagance, Micio. (*turning to Aeschinus*) Now, Aeschinus, if you two don't like my ways because I won't go along with everything you do indiscriminately right or wrong, I wash my hands of you. Spend, squander, do what you like. If on the other hand, where your youth makes you short-sighted, hot-headed or reckless, you need reproof and correction and support from time to time, here I am at your service.

AES We put ourselves in your hands, father. You know our needs better than we do. But what's to become of my brother?

DEM I permit him to keep the girl, but she must be his last.

MIC That's fair enough.[52]

ALL (*to the audience*) Give us your applause.[53]

---

[52] Some of the MSS give this line to Aeschinus, but others, supported by Donatus, assign it to Micio. In Micio's mouth, its interpretation is problematical, either grudging, "*That's* fair enough, but not your other arrangements" (as Donatus suggests), or simply, "All right, I acquiesce."

[53] See *Phormio* note 74.

METRICAL ANALYSIS

Phormio

1–152 iamb. sen.
153–63 mutatis modis canticum
    153 troch. oct.
    154 troch. sept.
    155 iamb. oct.
    156–157 troch. oct.
    158–159 troch. sept.
    160–162 iamb. oct.
    163 iamb. dim.
164–76 iamb. oct. (plus 177–178 iamb. sept.)
179–95 mutatis modis canticum
    179 troch. oct.
    180 troch. sept.
    181–182 iamb. oct.
    183 iamb. dim.
    184 iamb. oct.
    185 troch. sept.
    186 iamb. oct.
    187–188 troch. oct.
    189–190 troch. sept.
    191 troch. dim. cat.
    192–193 iamb. oct.

194 troch. dim.
195 iamb. sen.
196–215 troch. sept.
216–230 iamb. sen.
231–253 iamb. oct. (nisi 231–232, 252–253 troch. sept.)
254–314 iamb. sen.
315–347 troch. sept.
348–464 iamb. sen.
465–484 mutatis modis canticum
    465–468 troch. oct.
    469–470 troch. sept.
    471–478 iamb. oct.
    479–480 troch. oct.
    481–482 troch. sept.
    483 iamb. oct.
    484 troch. sept.
486–496 mutatis modis canticum
    486 iamb. oct.
    487–489 troch. sept.
    490 iamb. sen.
    491 iamb. sept.
    492 iamb. oct.
    493–495 troch. sept.
    496 iamb. oct.
497–566 troch. sept. (nisi 502–503, 515–516 iamb. oct.)
567–712 iamb. sen.
713–727 iamb. oct.
728–741 mutatis modis canticum
    728 troch. oct.
    729 troch. dim.
    730–731 troch. oct.
    732 troch. sept.

733–734 iamb. oct.
735–738 troch. oct.
739–741 troch. sept.
742–747 iamb. oct.
748–794 iamb. sept.
795–819 iamb. oct.
820–828 iamb. sept.
829–840 iamb. oct.
841–883 troch. sept.
884–1010 iamb. sen.
1011–1055 troch. sept.

Hecyra

1–197 iamb. sen.
198–216 iamb. oct. (nisi 201, 205–6, 216 iamb. sen.)
217–242 troch. sept.
243–273 iamb. sept.
274–280 troch. sept.
281–292 mutatis modis canticum
    281 troch. oct.
    282–283 troch. sept.
    284 troch. oct.
    285–288 troch. sept.
    289–291 troch. oct.
    292 troch. sept.
293–326 iamb. oct. (nisi 313, 325–6 iamb. sept.)
327–335 iamb. sen.
336–360 iamb. sept.
361–408 troch. sept.
409–450 iamb. sen.
451–484 troch. sept.

485–515 iamb. sen.
516–535 mutatis modis canticum
    516–517 troch. oct.
    518 troch. sept.
    519 troch. oct.
    520 troch. dim. cat.
    521 iamb. oct.
    522 troch. sept.
    523 iamb. oct.
    524 troch. oct.
    525 troch. sept.
    526–527 troch. oct.
    528 troch. sept.
    529 troch. oct.
    530–531 troch. sept.
    532–534 troch. oct.
    535 troch. sept.
536–565 troch. sept (nisi 544–6 iamb. oct.)
566–606 iamb. oct.
607–621 mutatis modis canticum (plus 622 iamb. sept.)
    607 iamb. sept.
    608 iamb. oct.
    609–611 troch. sept.
    612 iamb. sen.
    613 troch. oct.
    614 troch. sept.
    615 troch. oct.
    616–620 troch. sept.
    621 iamb. dim.
623–726 iamb. sen.
727–731 mutatis modis canticum
    727–730 iamb. oct.

731 iamb. dim. cat.
732–742 iamb. sept.
743–755 mutatis modis canticum
    743 troch. sept.
    744 iamb. oct.
    745 troch. sept.
    746–747 troch. oct.
    748–749 troch. sept.
    750 iamb. oct.
    751 troch. sept.
    752–754 iamb. oct.
    755 troch. sept.
756–767 troch. sept. (plus 768 troch. oct.)
769–797 iamb. sept. (plus 798 troch. oct.)
799–815 troch. sept.
816–840 iamb. sept.
841–853 mutatis modis canticum
    841 troch. oct.
    842–846 troch. sept.
    847 troch. oct.
    848–849 troch. sept.
    850 iamb. dim.
    851–852 troch. sept.
    853 iamb. oct.
854–858 iamb. sen.
859–868 iamb. oct.
869–880 troch. sept.

Adelphoe

1–154 iamb. sen.
155–169 mutatis modis canticum

155–157 troch. oct.
158 troch. dim. cat.
159 iamb. oct.
160 troch. oct.
161 troch. sept.
162 troch. oct.
163–164 troch. sept.
165 troch. oct.
166 iamb. oct.
167–169 troch. sept.
170–196 iamb. oct.
197–208 troch. sept.
209–227 iamb. oct. (nisi 209 troch. oct.)
228–253 iamb. sen.
254–287 iamb. oct.
288–298 mutatis modis canticum
    288 troch. sept.
    289–292 iamb. oct.
    293 iamb. sept.
    294 iamb. oct.
    295–298 troch. sept.
299–320 iamb. oct (nisi 303–304, 318–319 troch. sept., 317 iamb. dim.)
321–329 troch. sept.
330–354 iamb. oct.
355–516 iamb. sen.
517–527 mutatis modis canticum
    517 troch. oct.
    518 troch. sept.
    519–522 iamb. oct.
    523 troch. sept.
    524 troch. dim. cat.

525 troch. oct.
526 troch. sept.
527 iamb. oct.
528–539 iamb. oct.
540–591 troch. sept.
592–609 iamb. oct.
610–617 canticum lyricum
   611–612 chor. tetr.
   alia incerta
618–624 iamb. oct. (nisi 618 troch. sept.)
625–637 troch. sept.
638–678 iamb. sen.
679–706 troch. sept.
707–711 iamb. sept. (plus 712 iamb. oct.)
713–854 iamb. sen.
855–881 troch. sept.
882–933 iamb. sen.
934–955 iamb. oct. (plus 956–957 iamb. sen.)
958–997 troch. sept.

Composed in ZephGreek and ZephText by
Technologies 'N Typography, Merrimac, Massachusetts.
Printed in Great Britain by St Edmundsbury Press Ltd,
Bury St Edmunds, Suffolk, on acid-free paper.
Bound by Hunter & Foulis Ltd, Edinburgh, Scotland.